MATH ADVENTURES

A Key to Academic Math Advancement

GRADE 5

Author: Ace Academic Publishing

Ace Academic Publishing is a leading supplemental educational workbook publisher for grades K-12. At Ace Academic Publishing, we realize the importance of imparting analytical and critical thinking skills during the early ages of childhood and hence our books include materials that require multiple levels of analysis and encourage the students to think outside the box.

The materials for our books are written by award winning teachers with several years of teaching experience. All our books are aligned with the state standards and are widely used by many schools throughout the country.

Prepaze is a sister company of Ace Academic Publishing. Intrigued by the unending possibilities of the internet and its role in education, Prepaze was created to spread the knowledge and learning across all corners of the world through an online platform. We equip ourselves with state-of-the-art technologies so that knowledge reaches the students through the quickest and the most effective channels.

For inquiries and bulk orders, contact Ace Academic Publishing at the following address:
Ace Academic Publishing
3031 Village Market Place,
Morrisville, NC 27560, USA
www.aceacademicpublishing.com

ISBN: 978-1-962517-12-6

Introduction

About the Book

Welcome to "**Math Adventures - A Key to Academic Math Advancement**"! This workbook is specifically designed to align with the school curriculum and help students improve their analytical and logical thinking skills. With over **750 questions and several word problems**, this book aims to cover all the required syllabus for students in Grade 5.

Our workbook is an excellent resource for end-of-the-year state tests given by schools, as well as a great review book during the summer. Whether you are looking to improve your math skills or simply keep them sharp, "**Math Adventures**" provides a comprehensive and challenging set of problems to help you achieve your goals.

Our authors have extensive experience in teaching and developing math curricula for students at all levels. **They have carefully crafted each problem to challenge students and help them develop key problem-solving and critical thinking skills.** The book covers a wide range of topics, including arithmetic, algebra, geometry, and data analysis, providing students with a well-rounded education in math.

We believe that with practice, anyone can master math. "**Math Adventures**" is designed to help students build confidence in their abilities and develop a love for the subject. With clear explanations, helpful hints, and detailed solutions, this book is an excellent tool for anyone looking to improve their math skills.

Thank you for choosing "**Math Adventures - A Key to Academic Math Advancement**". We hope that you find it useful and enjoyable!

Common Core Math Workbooks

Common Core English Workbooks

The One Big Book Workbooks

Math Adventures Workbooks

 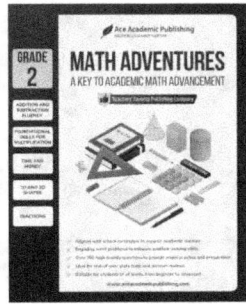  

 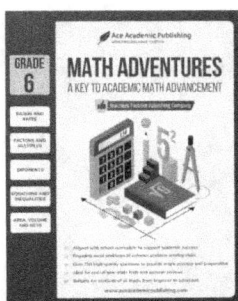 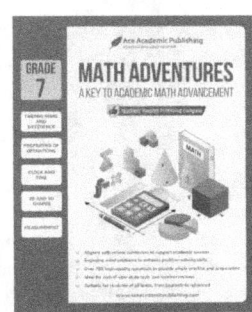 

Early Learning Workbooks

TABLE OF CONTENTS

TABLE OF CONTENTS

CHAPTER 1

NUMERICAL EXPRESSIONS

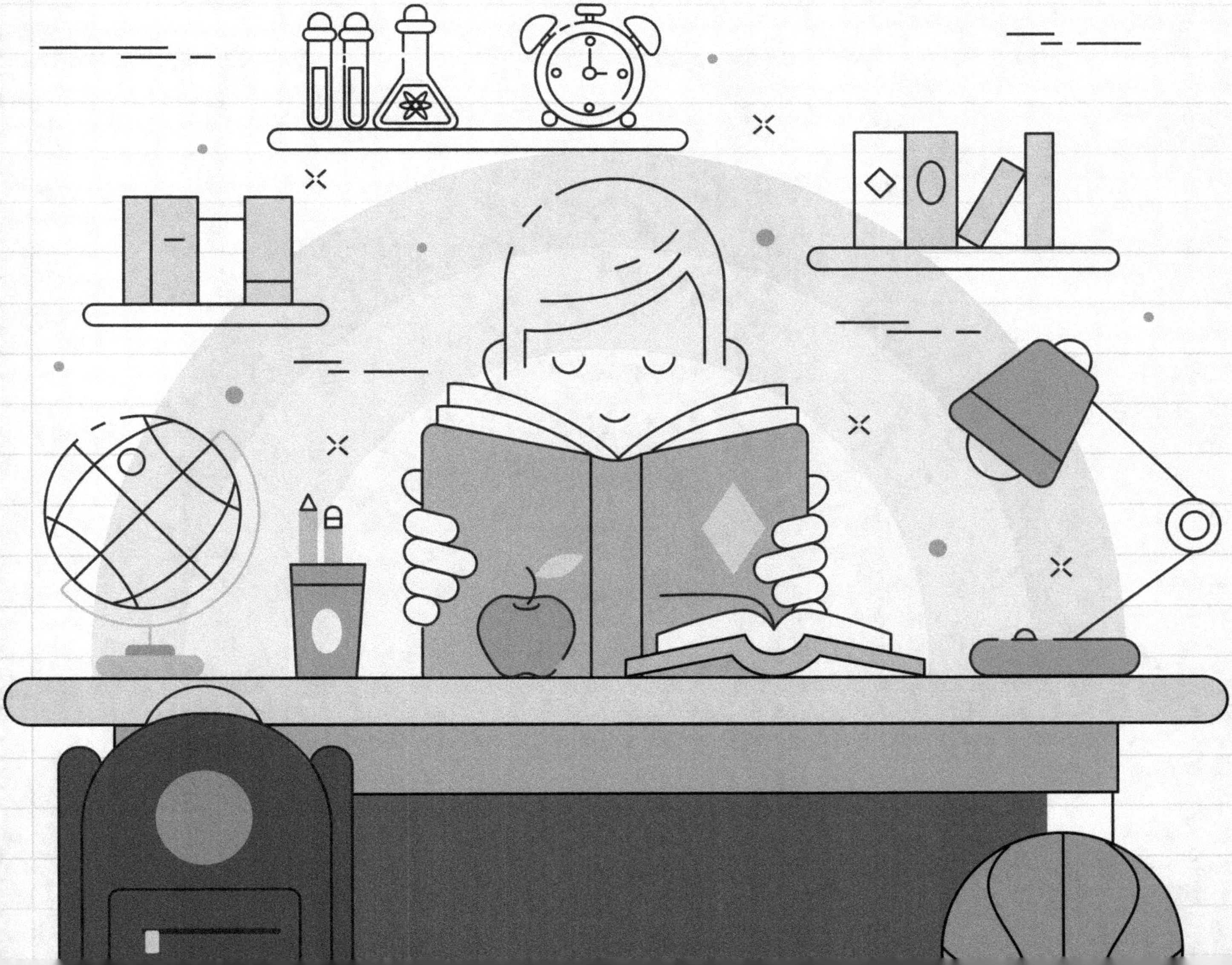

PARENTHESES IN MATH EXPRESSIONS

Parentheses are used to group parts of an expression together, indicating that these parts should be evaluated first. Parentheses can affect the order of operations and can change the value of the expression

You can simplify expressions by solving them within the parentheses first.

Example:

$$7 - (3 + 2)$$

Step 1: Start with the parentheses,

$$3 + 2 = 5$$

Step 2: Subtract the result from 7,

$$7 - 5 = 2$$

$$7 - (3 + 2)$$

$$7 - 5 = 2$$

NUMERICAL EXPRESSIONS

1.1 Parentheses In Math Expressions

1 On a recent science test, John scored 5 points for each of the 20 multiple-choice questions he answered correctly and 6 points for each of the 7 short-response questions he answered correctly.

Which expression can be used to solve the problem?

(A) (5×20) + (6×7)   (B) (5×7) + (6×20)

(C) (5+20) × (6-7)   (D) (5+20) × (6+7)

2 Mary is solving the problem 18 × 4 + (6 + 12). What should she do first? Explain your thinking.

_____

3 Which expression has a value of 60?

(A) 12 × 9 - 4   (B) 12 × (9-4)

(C) (12×9) - 4   (D) (12 × 9 - 4)

4 Simplify: 14 + [5 × (10 + 2)]

(A) 60   (B) 79   (C) 74   (D) 80

Parentheses In Math Expressions 1.1

5 Rocky writes an expression that has a value of 100. Where should he place the parentheses to make this expression have a value of 100?

$$20 \times 20 \div 20 - 16$$

(A) Around 20 times 20

(B) Around 20 divided by 20

(C) Around 20 minus 16

(D) Around 20 divided by 20 minus 16

6 Which symbol should be used to compare the two expressions?

$$15 + [25 \div (4 + 1)] _____ 7 + (4 \times 12) - 9$$

(A) >

(B) <

(C) =

(D) Not enough information

7 Tom is simplifying this expression:

$$8 + 64 \times 2$$

He says that he is going to add 8 and 64 first. What do you tell him?

_____

8 Olivia is simplifying this expression 5 - 13 + 7 × 8. What should she do first? Explain your reasoning.

_____

1.1 Parentheses In Math Expressions

9 Jenni is simplifying this expression: $90 \div [4 \times (15- 6)]$. She believes she should multiply 15 and 6 first. Do you agree or disagree? Why?

_____

10 Ellen writes an expression that has a value of 14. Which expression has the parentheses and bracket in the correct place?

(A) $2 \times [49 \div (2+ 5)]$

(B) $2 \times [49 \div 2 + 5]$

(C) $[2 \times (49 \div 2 + 5)]$

(D) $2 \times 49 \div 2 + 5$

11 Which expression follows this story?

"I have 12 boxes of colored pencils. Each box has 7 colored pencils in the first row and 7 colored pencils in the second row."

(A) $12 \times 7 + 7$

(B) $(12 \times 7) \times 7$

(C) $(12 \times 7) - 7$

(D) $12 \times (7 + 7)$

12 Which expression has a value of 75?

(A) $15 \times 9 - 4$

(B) $15 \times (9 - 4)$

(C) $(15 \times 9) - 4$

(D) $(15 \times 9 - 4)$

Parentheses In Math Expressions | 1.1

13 Emma scores 25 points fewer than Peter, who scores 45 points. Dane scores half as many points as Lisha. How many points does Dane score?

A) 10   B) 25   C) 20   D) 30

14 Mercy wants to buy a notebook for $4, a binder for $6, and a pack of pens for $4. She paid with $38. How much change will Mercy receive?

A) $30   B) $22   C) $20   D) $24

15 Fill in the missing operations to make the statement true.

$$(5 \text{\_\_\_} 3) \text{\_\_\_} 3 = 24.$$

A) (5+3) × 3   B) (5÷3) × 3

C) (5−3) × 3   D) (5×3) ÷ 3

16 The Sirsa family has 4 members. Three of the members have a motorcycle and a car each. The other member has only a car. How many vehicles do they have altogether?

A) 7   B) 6   C) 8   D) 5

1.1  **Parentheses In Math Expressions**

17 One dining table set includes 4 plates, 5 pieces of silverware, and a napkin. If there are 10 tables in the ballroom, how many total items are needed to set all 10tables?

(A) 77 (B) 96 (C) 110 (D) 100

18 Fill in the missing operations to make the statement true.

(8 ___ 2) ___ 9 = 36.

(A) (8+2) × 9 (B) (8÷2) × 9
(C) (8−2) × 9 (D) (8×2) ÷ 9

19 Mylan solved the problem below using the order of operations. Is his solution correct? Why or why not?

8 × (9 − 4) = 68.

(A) No, Mylan's solution is not correct

(B) Mylan's solution is correct

Parentheses In Math Expressions | 1.1

20 Tara goes to the book fair, where paperback books are $1.75 and hardback books are $5. Tara buys five paperbacks and two hardbacks. How much change will Tara receive from $30?

(A) $11.25   (B) $10.25   (C) $13.50   (D) $15.25

Next Section: Variables and Expressions »

VARIABLES AND EXPRESSIONS

An expression is a combination of both numbers and variables together with at least one arithmetic operation.

In the context of mathematics, variables are used to store values that can change or vary.

Example:

5x + 2 – x is a variable and + is the arithmetic operations.

Variables and Expressions 1.2

1 Carol bakes cookies every day. How many total cookies would she bake per week?

(A) 7 + z (B) 7 + 7z (C) 7 × z (D) 7z + 7

2 This expression is equivalent to 20. What is the value of x?
$$x \div (-25 + 20) + 13$$

(A) 80 (B) 240 (C) 160 (D) 320

3 This expression has a value of 90. What is the value of G?
$$G (70-40)$$

(A) 6 (B) 3 (C) 2 (D) 5

4 This expression has a value of 300. What is the value of k?
$$k + 5 \times 10$$

(A) 220 (B) 240 (C) 250 (D) 300

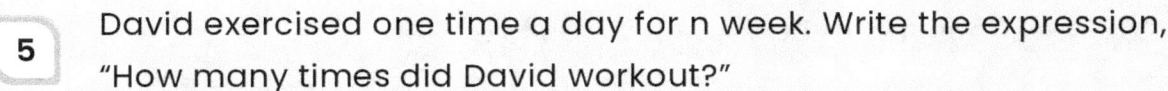

5 David exercised one time a day for n week. Write the expression, "How many times did David workout?"

(A) 7n (B) n+7 (C) 7n+1 (D) (7×n)+1

1.2 Variables and Expressions

6 Bella is writing an expression for three times as much as the difference between 655 and 346. She wrote (655 – 346) ÷ 3. Do you agree or disagree? Why?

_____

7 How can this expression be written in words?

$$(66 + 232) \times 8$$

_____

8 Does the expression 7 × 585 + 89 show seven times the sum of five hundred eighty-five and eighty-nine? Why or why not?

_____

9 The expression 5 × (4586 + 182) means:

(A) Five times 4586 and 182.

(B) Five times more than 4586 minus 182.

(C) Five more than 4586 and 182.

(D) Five times the sum of 4586 and 182.

10 Which expression matches this description?
Add 23 and 4, then multiply the sum by 5.

(A) $23 + 4 \times 5$

(B) $(23 + 4) \times 5$

(C) $23 + (4 \times 5)$

(D) $(23 + 4 \times 5)$

11 Which numerical expression represents this verbal expression?
Multiply 19 and 4, then add the difference of 8 and 2.

(A) $(19 \times 4) + (8 - 2)$

(B) $19 \times (4 + 8) - 2$

(C) $19 \times (4 + 8 - 2)$

(D) $19 \times 4 + 8 - 2$

12 Write an expression that shows 50 divided by the sum of 6 and 2.

_____

13 **True or False:** The expression $(1994 - 77) \div 2$ means the difference of 1,994 and 77 divided by 2.

_____

1.2   **Variables and Expressions**

14 **True or False:** 33 times the sum of 15 and 658 can be written as 33 × 15 + 658.

_____

15 Three ordered pairs in a sequence are (10, 2), (8, 5), (6, 8), (x, 11). What is the rule for finding the x-value.

(A) Add three   (B) Add two

(C) Subtract three   (D) Subtract two

16 Three ordered pairs in a sequence are (5, 6), (8, 10), (11, 14). What would the ordered pair just before (5,6) be?

(A) (1,1)   (B) (0,1)   (C) (2,2)   (D) (3, 2)

17 Which ordered pair is missing in the function table?

x	8	11	14	?
y	10	20	30	?

(A) (40,17)   (B) (17,40)

(C) (16, 40)   (D) (40, 16)

Variables and Expressions 1.2

18 **True or False:** A rule for this table could be x = y - 4.

x	14	28	42
y	18	32	46

_____

19 Mark plots a point on the graph at (8,40). He wants to plot another point according to this rule:

x-value: multiply by 2
y-value: divide by 8

Write an ordered pair to represent a point on Polo's graph

(A) (16, 5)　　(B) (10, 15)　　(C) (10, 30)　　(D) (16, 48)

20 The rule of a function is that "each y-value is 4 times each x-value". What is the value of x when y is 20?

(A) 4　　　　(B) 10　　　　(C) 6　　　　(D) 5

Next Section:
Multi-Step Expressions

MULTI-STEP EXPRESSIONS

Multi-step expressions can include a combination of addition, subtraction, multiplication, division, and parentheses.For example, a multi-step expression might look like this: 3 × 4 + 5 - 2 ÷ 2.

We can simplify expressions by starting with the grouping symbols first. Grouping symbols can include parentheses, brackets, or braces.

$$( ) [ ] \{ \}$$

Next, we will multiply or divide (depending on which operation comes first).Last, we will add or subtract (depending on which operation comes first).

Example:

$$[24 ÷ (12 - 6)] + (10 × 5)$$
$$[24 ÷ (6)] + (10 × 5)$$
$$[24 ÷ (6)] + (50)$$
$$[4] + (50)$$
$$54$$

Step 1: Subtract the values inside the first set of parentheses, 12 - 6 = 6
Step 2: Multiply the values inside the second set of parentheses, 10 × 5 = 50
Step 3: Divide 24 by the result from the first set of parentheses, 24 ÷ 6 = 4
Step 4: Add the result of the brackets to the product of the second set of parentheses, 4 + 50 = 54 .

Multi-Step Expressions | 1.3

1 John evaluates the expression (20-18) + (31+17) × 2 . What is his answer?

(A) 96   (B) 94   (C) 98   (D) 100

2 Simplify the expression. {100 ÷ [5 × (2+2+6)]} + 40.

(A) 46   (B) 44   (C) 48   (D) 42

3 Simplify the expression. 90-{(9×10) – [5+(5×5)]}.

(A) 66   (B) 30   (C) 58   (D) 70

4 Logan has 20 dollars. He buys 5 oranges for 85 cents each and 4 bananas for 38 cents each. Which expression can be used to find the amount of money he has spent on oranges and bananas?

(A) (5×85) + (4×38)   (B) (5+85) + (4+38)

(C) (5×85) × (4×38)   (D) (5+85) × (4+38)

1.3 Multi-Step Expressions

5 Mr. James has 64 yards of ribbon. He wants to use 6-yard ribbon pieces to wrap 3 boxes and 4-yard ribbon pieces to wrap 9 boxes. Which expression can be used to find the amount of ribbon Mr. James has left after wrapping his boxes?

A 64 – (6×3) + (4×9)   B 64 – (6×3) – (4×9)

C 64 + (6×3) – (4×9)   D 64 – (6+3) – (4+9)

6 What is the next step for simplifying this expression?
$$[40 - (14-7) - 4 \times 8]$$
Step 1 : Subtract 7 from 14

A Multiply 4 and 8   B Subtract 7 from 40

C Subtract 40 from 14   D None of the above

7 What is the next step for simplifying this expression?
$$42 - 23 + 6(18 - 9)$$
Step 1 : Subtract 9 from 18

A Subtract 23 from 42   B Subtract 6 from 23

C Multiply 6 by the difference from Step 1   D None of the above

Multi-Step Expressions | 1.3

8 Isabella is buying 6 hardback books and 12 paperback books. The hardback books cost $3 each. Each paperback book costs $2.50 each. Create an expression to represent the amount of money Isabella could spend on the books. Calculate the amount.

(A) $46   (B) $44   (C) $48   (D) $42

9 What operators should be added to this expression has a value of 1100 ?

$$\{9000 \_\_\_ 65(240 \_\_\_ 120) \_\_\_ 100\}$$

(A) {9000 – 65(240 – 120) + 100}   (B) {9000 + 65(240 – 120) + 100}

(C) {9000 – 65(240 + 120) + 100}   (D) {9000 – 65(240 – 120) + 100}

10 Olivia has $88. She buys 4 notebooks for $8 each, a backpack for $24 and a calculator for $35. Which expression shows how much money she spends?

(A) 88 – (4×8) + 24 + 35   (B) 88 – (4×8) – 24 + 35

(C) (4×8) + 24 + 35   (D) (4×8) + 24 + 35 – 88

1.3 Multi-Step Expressions

11 What operators should be added to this expression that has a value of 131?

$$[22 \_\_ 8 \_\_ (5 \_\_ 9)]$$

(A) [22 + 8 − (5 × 9)]　　　　(B) [22 × 8 + (5 × 9)]

(C) [22 × 8 − (5 + 9)]　　　　(D) [22 × 8 − (5 × 9)]

12 Noah walks 4 miles every day for 6 days each week. If he walks the same number of miles every week, write an expression to calculate the total number of miles Noah walks in half a year. (Hint: There are 52 weeks in 1 year.)

(A) 444 miles　(B) 624 miles　(C) 534 miles　(D) 664 miles

13 Do these expressions have the same value?

$$4 × [5 + (7−3)] \text{ and } 4 × [5 − (7−3)]$$

_____

14 A triangle has these 3 side lengths:

- Side A is 20 cm long.
- Side B is 8 cm shorter than Side A.
- Side C is 4 cm longer than Side B.

Does this expression represent the sum of the side lengths? Explain your thinking.

_____

15 Elijah is simplifying this expression:

$$[300 - (17 \times 7) + (9 - 7 \times 2)]$$

If his first step is to multiply 7 and 17, what could his next two steps be?

_____

16 Create an expression that has a value of 76. Use five numbers and at least two different operations.

_____

17 Ms. Mia invests $600 in stock. After one day, the amount of money she earns doubles. The next day, she loses half of what she earned. How much money does Ms. Mia have left?

(A) $1000   (B) $1200   (C) $1100   (D) $2000

1.3   Multi-Step Expressions

18 Amelia buys 8 pencils for 27 cents each, 6 erasers for a total of 88 cents and 5 notepads for 92 cents each. How much money does Amelia spend on pencils, erasers, and notepads?

(A) 1000 cents   (B) 200 cents   (C) 1100 cents   (D) 764 cents

19 Liam buys 6 shirts for $30 each, 12 pairs of socks for a total of $20, and 4 hats for a total of $32. He pays for these clothes using $300. How much money does Liam have left?

(A) $68   (B) $32   (C) $42   (D) $58

20 Emma buys 6 burgers for 15 dollars. She also buys 4 large fries for 3 dollars each, and 6 milkshakes for 4 dollars each. Which expression shows the amount of money Emma spends on burgers, fries, and milkshakes?

(A) $(6 \times 15) + (4 \times 3) + (6 \times 4)$ (B) $15 + (4 \times 3) + (6 \times 4)$

(C) $(6 + 15) + (4 \times 3) + (6 \times 4)$ (D) $15 + (4 \times 3) \times (6 \times 4)$

Next Section: Chapter Review

1 Does the expression (4365 - 225) ÷ 2 show half of the difference between 4365 and 225? Explain your reasoning.

_____

2 Write a numerical expression for each phrase.
The product of one-fifth and one-third minus the difference of five-ninths and one-half.

A $(\frac{1}{5} \times \frac{1}{3}) - (\frac{5}{9} - \frac{1}{2})$

B $(\frac{1}{5} \times \frac{1}{3}) + (\frac{5}{9} - \frac{1}{2})$

C $(\frac{1}{5} \times \frac{1}{3}) - (\frac{5}{9} + \frac{1}{2})$

D $(\frac{1}{5} \times \frac{1}{3}) - (\frac{1}{2} - 5)$

3 Add the missing symbol to create an expression that represents 32 times less than the sum of 677 and 876.

(677 _____ 876) ÷ 32

4 There are 348 markers in a bin. Five packages of 9 markers are added to the bin. Write an expression to show how many markers are in the bin altogether.

A 348 + (5×9)

B 348 + (5−9)

C 348 × (5×9)

D 348 − (5×9)

NUMERICAL EXPRESSIONS

5 Jack is graphing the ordered pairs for the rule $y = x + 3$. He plots the first point at (2,5). Where could the next 3 points be placed? Explain your reasoning.

_____

6 Write a numerical expression for the given phrase.

Four and fifty hundredths less the difference of sixteen and fifteen.

A) $4.50 - (16-15)$ B) $450 - (16-15)$

C) $450 + (16-15)$ D) $4.50 - (15-16)$

7 Amelia is graphing the ordered pairs for a sequence that starts at (2, 12). She will continue the sequence using this rule: $y = 10 + x$. Write one ordered pair that could belong in this sequence.

_____

8 Which symbol should be used to compare the two expressions?

$640,000 \div (799+1)$ _____ $640,000 \div (79+1)$.

A) >   B) <   C) =

9   What number is missing in the pattern? How do you know?

x	5	11	17	23
y	12	18	24	?

_____

10   Levi watches 8.15 hours of television in one week. Which expression can be used to determine how many seconds of television Levi watches?

(A) 8.15×60

(B) $8.15 \times 60 + 60$

(C) $8.15 \times 60 \times 60$

(D) $8.15 + (60 \times 60)$

11   The rule for the table is $y = x + 14$. What is the missing number?

x	1	2	3
y	?	16	17

(A) 14   (B) 15   (C) 10   (D) 13

1.4   **Chapter Review**

12 Lucy spends 2 hours completing her homework. She spends $\frac{1}{8}$ of the time on her science homework, $\frac{1}{4}$ of the time on her math homework, and the rest of the time on her reading homework. Write a numerical expression to represent the amount of time Lucy spends on her reading homework.

(A) $2 - (\frac{1}{8} + \frac{1}{4})$

(B) $2 + (\frac{1}{8} + \frac{1}{4})$

(C) $(\frac{1}{8} + \frac{1}{4}) - 2$

(D) $(\frac{1}{8} \times \frac{1}{4}) - 2$

13 The first ordered pair in a sequence is (4, 6). The rules for the sequence are x = ___ + 4 and y = ___ + 7. What will the third ordered pair in the sequence be?

(A) (11, 22)   (B) (11, 21)   (C) (12, 20)   (D) (12, 19)

14 There are thirty-six students in Mr. Asher's class. Mr. Asher has three hundred pencils and eighty pens. Write an expression to represent the number of pencils and pens that Mr. Asher will have left after giving each student an equal number of pencils and pens.

(A) $\frac{300-80}{36}$

(B) $(300+80) + 36$

(C) $300 + 80 - 36$

(D) $\frac{300+80}{36}$

15 The rule of a function is the y-value is 33 more than each x-value. What is the value of x when y is 55?

(A) 22   (B) 21   (C) 32   (D) 26

16 What is the next step for simplifying this expression? 92 – 87 + 6(14-7)

Step 1: Subtract 7 from 14

Step 2: _____.

17 There are 12 tables in the classroom, with 25 pencils and 12 pens on each table. Write an expression to represent the number of pencils and pens in the classroom. Explain your reasoning.

_____

18 An office building has 48 floors. Each floor has 30 offices, and one-fourth of the offices have windows. Write an expression to show the number of offices in the building that do not have windows.

(A) $48 \times (\frac{1}{4} + 30)$ (B) $48 + (\frac{3}{4} + 30)$

(C) $48 + (\frac{1}{4} + 34)$ (D) $48 \times (\frac{3}{4} \times 30)$

1.4   **Chapter Review**

19   Leo is simplifying this expression: 8 + (12 + 50) ÷ 3.
He believes that he needs to add 12 and 50 as a first step. Do you agree or disagree? Explain your reasoning.

_____

20   This expression has a value of 55. What is the value of n?

$$10 + (n \times 5)$$

(A) 10   (B) 15   (C) 8   (D) 9

Next Chapter: Place value

CHAPTER 2

PLACE VALUE

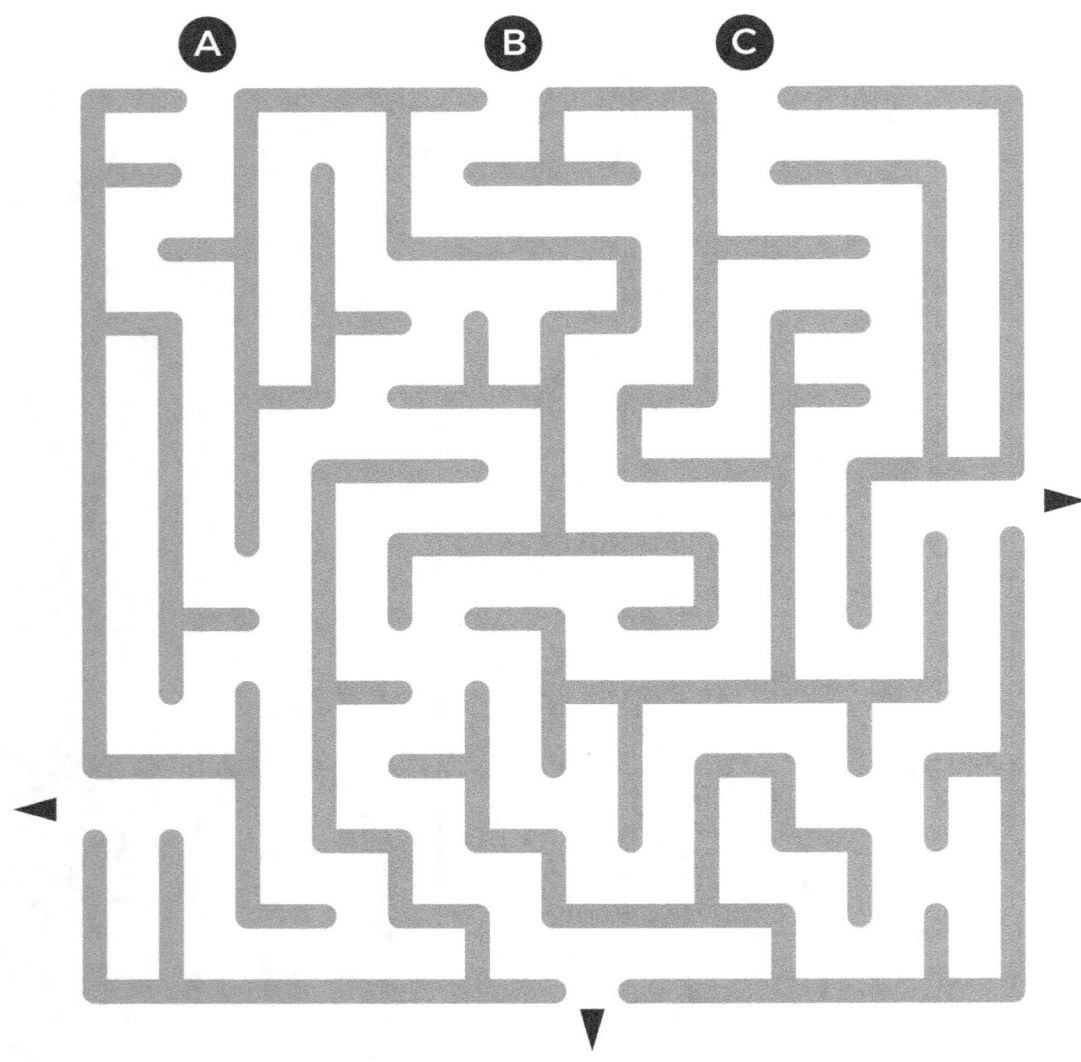

PATTERNS IN MULTIPLYING AND DIVIDING

Multiplication Patterns Other Than 10

Multiplication patterns in place value refer to the patterns that arise when multiplying numbers based on their place values. Multiplication by other numbers uses the same methods as multiplying by 10.

Example:

$$30 \times 6 = ?$$

Multiply the digits 3 x 6. This equal 18. Place a zero after the answer to account for the zero in the number 30.

$$30 \times 6 = 180.$$

Patterns in Division Not 10

Lesson Introduction:

Dividing by numbers with zeros other than 10 involves movement of the digit in place value.

Example:

$$80 \div 40 = ?$$

The 80 has one zero and the 40 has one zero. The zeros cancel out. The problem then becomes $8 \div 4 = 2$.

$$80 \div 40 = 2.$$

2.1   Patterns In Multiplying and Dividing

1 Evaluate: $40 \times 70 = ?$

(A) 2800   (B) 4400   (C) 3300   (D) 2100

2 Dividing the numbers with zero : $810 \div 90 = ?$

(A) 8   (B) 4   (C) 3   (D) 9

3 Maria has an album for her trading cards. Each page can hold 30 cards. There are 80 pages. How many cards are in the album?

(A) 2,400 cards   (B) 3,400 cards

(C) 1,400 cards   (D) 2,000 cards

4 Evaluate and choose the correct answer:
$1,800 \div 60 = ?$

(A) 80   (B) 30   (C) 40   (D) 60

5 How much larger is 360 than 6?

(A) 50 times   (B) 40 times   (C) 60 times   (D) 36 times

Patterns In Multiplying and Dividing 2.1

6 Complete the division sentence: 6,400 ÷ _____ = 8.

A) 800   B) 80   C) 8000   D) 8

7 Complete the multiplication sentence: 70 × _____ = 4,900.

A) 70   B) 17   C) 700   D) 7000

8 Find the missing value. _____ ÷ 440 = 20.

A) 220   B) 880   C) 800   D) 8800

9 Find the missing value. _____ × 40 = 3,600.

A) 90   B) 80   C) 60   D) 66

10 The high school band had 4,400 raffle tickets to sell. There are 2,200 band members. How many raffle tickets will each band member be required to sell?

A) 4   B) 3   C) 2   D) 6

2.1   **Patterns In Multiplying and Dividing**

11 Liam had 60 pieces of taffy. Henry had 20 times more taffy. How much taffy did Henry have?

Ⓐ 300   Ⓑ 1200   Ⓒ 80   Ⓓ 1000

12 John can allow 45,000 minutes for piano lessons this month. There are 900 children signed up for lessons. How many minutes will each child be allowed?

Ⓐ 50   Ⓑ 60   Ⓒ 80   Ⓓ 90

13 Tom had 40 pieces of cake. Jerry had 25 times more cakes. How many cakes did Jerry have?

_____

14 Robert trained athletes for 75 hours in week one, 85 hours in week two, and 200 hours in wek three. Each athlete trained for 20 hours. How many athletes did Robert train?

Ⓐ 22   Ⓑ 36   Ⓒ 20   Ⓓ 18

Patterns In Multiplying and Dividing   2.1

15 The pet shop has 30 times more pet supplies than the department store. The following totals are of pet supplies at the department store. How much of each would be at the pet shop?

- Bones: 300
- Toys: 260

_____

16 Marion baked 9 dozen cookies day 1. She increased her baking by 20 times on day 2. She increased the baking from day 2 by 40 times for day 3. How many dozen cookies did Marion bake over all three days?

_____

17 Jodie made batches of slime. She made 190 batches on Monday, 140 batches on Tuesday, and 270 batches on Wednesday. She packages them in boxes with 60 batches each. How many boxes does Jodie need?

_____

2.1 Patterns In Multiplying and Dividing

18 Alva was printing photos. She printed 60 photos in week 1. She increased the number of photos she printed by 20 times for the next week. Then she increased that amount 20 times again for week three. How many photos did she print week two and week three combined?

(A) 24,400   (B) 36,500   (C) 20,000   (D) 25,200

19 There are 30 students in the class. There are 1,000 dry erase markers available. Each student needs 30 markers. Will there be enough markers to make it through the year?

_____

20 David wanted to build a model plane. He uses 600 pieces of wood. Jase builds another model plane and uses 50 times more wood. How many more wood pieces does Jase use than David?

_____

Next Section: Multiplying And Dividing By 10 and 100

MULTIPLYING AND DIVIDING BY 10 AND 100

Multiplying and dividing by 10 and 100 are fundamental operations that involve changing the place value of a number.

Multiplication by 10 and 100

When multiplying a number by 10, each digit in the number moves one place to the left, and a zero is added to the right side. When multiplying by 100, each digit moves two places to the left, and two zeros are added to the right side.

Example:

$$15 \times 10 = ?$$

The 15 moves over one place value to the left and a zero is added to the number.

$$15 \times 10 = 150.$$

Dividing by 10 and 100

When we divide a number by 10, we are essentially dividing it by a single place value to the right, resulting in the original number being ten times smaller. Similarly, when we divide a number by 100, we are dividing it by two place values to the right, resulting in the original number being 100 times smaller.

Example:

$$80 \div 10 = ?$$

The 80 has one zero and the 10 as one zero. They cancel each other out.

$$80 \div 10 = 8.$$

2.2   **Multiplying and Dividing By 10 and 100**

1 Records by Ethan is a new shop. They plan to mark everything up 10 times over the original price. How much will the following markups be?

- Headphones – Original price: $13.46.
- Posters – Original price: $0.77.

_____

2 Jacob trained golfers for 40 hours in week one, 55 hours in week two, and 135 hours in week three. Each golfer trains for 10 hours. How many golfers did Jacob train?

(A) 20   (B) 23   (C) 21   (D) 25

3 Given the dividend of 640 and the quotient of 10, what is the divisor?

(A) 64   (B) 20   (C) 6.4   (D) 10

4 Given the dividend of 90 and the divisor of 10, what is the quotient?

(A) 0.9   (B) 9   (C) 9.9   (D) 900

Multiplying and Dividing By 10 and 100 | 2.2

5 If the divisor is 10, and the quotient is 55, what is the dividend?

(A) 65   (B) 5.5   (C) 550   (D) 45

6 Mr. Noah must buy glue sticks and scissors for the school. Each child must have one of each. The glue sticks are sold in boxes of 52 and the scissors in boxes of 32. He plans to buy 100 boxes of each. There are 5,000 students at the school. Will he have enough glue sticks? Explain?

_____

7 Given a dividend of 870 and a quotient of 10, what is the divisor?

_____

8 A charity collected $43,000, in equal amounts, from 100 donors. How much money did each donor give?

(A) $4,300   (B) $4.3   (C) $43   (D) $430

2.2 Multiplying and Dividing By 10 and 100

9 There are multiple questions on a game show. There are six 100-point questions and four 100-point questions. How many points are there in each episode?

(A) 1,000   (B) 400   (C) 200   (D) 100

10 Mila earns $100 for every hour she works. If she works 10 hours a day, six days a week, how much does she earn in a week?

(A) $60   (B) $600   (C) $1000   (D) $6000

11 Owen bought a pack of baseball cards for $26. He also bought a baseball jersey for 100 times that much. How much did Owen spend in all?

_____

12 There is 494.7 ounces of milk in total. The milk is in 100 containers. How much milk is in each container?

(A) 4.947   (B) 49.47   (C) 4   (D) 494.7

Multiplying and Dividing By 10 and 100   2.2

13 Ella and Daisy are training to run a marathon. Ella ran for 6.9 minutes. Daisy ran for 10 times as long, how long did the girls run in total?

(A) 75 minutes

(B) 79.5 minutes

(C) 75.9 minutes

(D) 69 minutes

14 The eighth-grade class went to the movies. How much money did 440 students and 12 teachers spend if each ticket costs $100?

_____

15 Students from 100 sixth-grade classrooms wrote letters to their local representatives supporting their school. If each class had 20 students, and each student wrote letters to 5 representatives, how many letters did they write?

_____

16 Creed had 3,300 Lays chips. Cruz had 33 lays chips. How many times more chips did Creed have?

(A) 100

(B) 10

(C) 1000

(D) 33

2.2 Multiplying and Dividing By 10 and 100

17 Garrett can allow 4,500 minutes for guitar lessons this month. There are 100 children signed up for lessons. How many minutes will each child be allowed?

(A) 10   (B) 100   (C) 45   (D) 450

18 Carson mows a lawn in his neighborhood in about 2 hours. How long will it take him to mow 56 lawns of the same size?

(A) 112   (B) 109   (C) 120   (D) 121

19 A delivery truck is driven at 100 miles per hour. It is driven 9 hours each day. How many miles will it have traveled in 2 days?

(A) 180   (B) 1800   (C) 100   (D) 44

20 Each child in a class has a box of 100 crayons. If there are 38 children in the class, how many crayons are there?

(A) 380 crayons   (B) 38 crayons

(C) 3,800 crayons   (D) 1,000 crayons

Next Section: Exponents »

EXPONENTS

Exponents are used to express repeated multiplication. The exponent tells how many times the base is multiplied by itself.

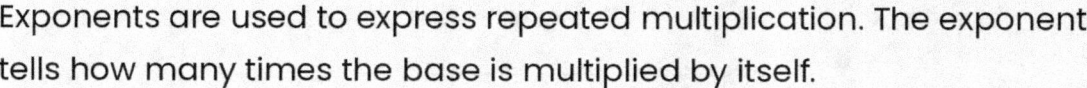

Base $\longrightarrow 2^3 \longleftarrow$ Exponent

$$2 \times 2 \times 2 = 8$$

Example:

$$3^2 = ?$$

The 3 is the base number. The 2 is the exponent. This tells us to multiply 3, 2 times.

$$3^2 = 3 \times 3 = 9.$$

2.3 Exponents

1 Rewrite the following as a base with an exponent:

$$4 \times 4 \times 4 \times 4 \times 4 = ?$$

(A) 4×5 (B) 5×4 (C) 5^4 (D) 4^5

2 Evaluate: $325 \times 10^3 =$ _____.

(A) 3,250,000   (B) 3,25,000   (C) 32,500   (D) 3,250,0000

3 Explain patterns in the number of zeros of the product: 8×10^6.

Place Value Chart						
Millions	Hundred Thousand	Ten Thousand	Thousands	Hundreds	Tens	Ones
10^6	10^5	10^4	10^3	10^2	10^1	10^0

_____

4 Evaluate: $645 \times 10^4 =$ _____.

(A) 6,450,000   (B) 6,45,000   (C) 64,500   (D) 6,450,0000

5 **True or False:** The equivalent form of 7.822 is $78.22 \div 10^2$.

(A) True   (B) False

6 **True or False:** The equivalent form of 9,360 is 93.6×10^4.

(A) True   (B) False

7 There are 440,750 gallons of water in an Olympic-size swimming pool. Which expression below correctly matches the amount of water in an Olympic size swimming pool?

(A) 440.75×10^2 gallons   (B) 44.075×10^4 gallons

(C) 4.4075×10^4 gallons   (D) 440.75×10^3 gallons

8 There are 10,000 ants living in a colony underground. If that amount doubles in the next year, there will be 20,000 ants living underground. Which equation below is correct?

(A) $2 \times 10^4 = 2,000$ (B) $2 \times 10^3 = 200$

(C) $2 \times 10^3 = 20,000$ (D) $2 \times 10^4 = 20,000$

2.3   **Exponents**

9   Find the missing value: $? \times 10^4 = 87.56$.

(A)   0.0008756

(B)   0.008756

(C)   0.08756

(D)   0.8756

10   Find the missing value: $7.56 \times ? = 756$.

(A) 10^2

(B) 10^3

(C) 10^4

(D)   10

11   Evaluate: $5.8 \times 10^4 =$ _____.

(A)   5,800

(B)   5,800,000

(C)   58,000

(D)   58,000,000

12   Evaluate: $455 \times 10^0 =$ _____.

(A)   455

(B)   4,550

(C)   0

(D)   1

13 Olivia is simplifying this: $300 \div [10^2 \times 3]$.
She got the answer: 1.
Do you agree or disagree? Why?

_____

14 Write the exponent from smallest to largest: 6^2, 7^4, 10^1, 99^0, 4^2, 5^2.

_____

15 Write the exponent from largest to smallest: 2^6, 3^4, 4^4, 6^2.

_____

16 The teacher gave one problem: Find the base of $(3456)^{234}$. Jane said 234 is the base, and Peter said 3456 is the base. Who is correct

(A) Jane   (B) Peter

17 Find the value of n.
$(54 \times 9) \div 10^4 = n$.

(A) 0.486   (B) 0.00486   (C) 0.0486   (D) 4.8600

2.3   **Exponents**

---

18   Find the missing exponent: $6^? = 216$.

(A) 3   (B) 4   (C) 12   (D) 11

---

19   Find the missing base: $?^2 = 81$.

(A) 8   (B) 7   (C) 9   (D) 11

---

20   Give one example to complete the table.

Exponential form	Expanded form	Standard form

Next Section: Comparing and Rounding Decimals >>

COMPARING AND ROUNDING DECIMALS

Comparing Decimals

Comparing decimals is the process of determining which decimal number is larger or smaller than another decimal number. Comparing decimals requires making the decimal places match. Adding zeros to the end of a decimal number does not affect the value. However, it makes it easier to compare the numbers.

Compare: 0.16 and 0.165

Add a zero to the first number so that it is easier to compare.

$$0.160 < 0.165 \text{ because } 160 < 165$$

When the whole numbers are the same, the decimal numbers must be compared.

Example:

Compare: 5.04 _____ 5.4

Add zeros where necessary so the decimal places match.

$$5.04 \text{ \_\_\_\_\_ } 5.4$$
$$5.04 < 5.4$$

Because 04 is less than 40,

5.04 is less than 5.4.

COMPARING AND ROUNDING DECIMALS

Rounding with decimals

Rounding with decimals is a mathematical process of approximating a given decimal number to the nearest specified place value. The rules for rounding decimals are similar to the rules for rounding whole numbers.

Students can use the estimation of decimals to check that their calculations are reasonable. When rounding decimals, we apply the same rules as when rounding whole numbers.

Rounding to the nearest whole:

4.628 – since the tenth digit 6 is 5 or greater, round up to 5 wholes, therefore 4.628 ≈ 5.

Rounding to the nearest tenth:

4.628 – since the hundredth digit 2 is less than 5, round down to 6 tenths, therefore 4.628 ≈ 4.6.

Rounding to the nearest hundredth:

4.628 – since the thousandth digit 8 is 5 or greater than 5, round up to 3 hundredths, therefore, 4.628 ≈ 4.63.

Example:

Estimate the sum 4.45 + 11.52 = ?

Solution:

First, round each decimal to the nearest whole number:

$$4.45 ≈ 4$$
$$11.52 ≈ 12$$

Therefore, 4.45 + 11.52 ≈ 4 + 12 = 16.

1 Round the following number to the nearest thousandth.

0.4532689.

(A) 0.453268   (B) 0.45327   (C) 0.4532   (D) 0.45326

2 Round the numbers to the nearest hundredth, then write them in order from least to greatest.

0.867, 0.857, 0.876, 0.852

_____

3 True or False:

The number 66.6 is 10 times larger than 6.66.

(A) True   (B) False

4 True or False:

The number 43.8 is 100 times larger than 4.38.

(A) True   (B) False

2.4 **Comparing and Rounding Decimals**

---

5 Evaluate: 78.69 ÷ 10 = _____.

(A) 78.69   (B) 7,869   (C) 7.869   (D) 786.9

---

6 Round the following number to the nearest ten-thousandth.

389.223542.

(A) 389.2236   (B) 389.2242   (C) 389.2235   (D) 389.223

---

7 Round the following number to the nearest tenth.

65.482.

(A) 65.5   (B) 65.4   (C) 65.48   (D) 65.49

---

8 Choose the correct comparison for the decimals.

0.889 _____ 0.998.

(A) >   (B) <   (C) =

---

9 There was a competition at school to determine who ran the most in one month. Who ran the most miles?

(A) Grace - 54.12 miles   (B) Noah - 54.126 miles

(C) James - 54.13 miles   (D) Jack - 54.125 miles

10 Elvis made 25.58 pounds of fudge. His mom asked him to round that to the nearest tenth. What would Elvis's correct response be?

(A) 25   (B) 25.58   (C) 25.59   (D) 25.6

11 Compare the two decimals by filling in the box using the >, <, or = symbol.

20.033		20.303

12 When rounding to the nearest hundredth, what place should you review?

(A) Tenths   (B) Hundredths

(C) Thousandths   (D) Ten-thousandths

13 The desks were to be lined up at least 9.5 feet apart. Which measurement would not be considered far enough?

(A) 9.88   (B) 9.55   (C) 9.45   (D) 9.59

2.4 **Comparing and Rounding Decimals**

14 Mr. Enzo weighed two chickens on the farm. One of them weighed 7.56 lbs. The other weighed less. What is the possible weight of the second chicken?

(A) 7.88   (B) 7.64   (C) 7.59   (D) 7.49

15 Cooper measured the boards of wood and placed them in order from least to greatest. If the lengths were listed as 87.65 ft., 87.75 ft., 87.79 ft. what could the longest of the lengths possibly be?

(A) 87.89   (B) 87.98   (C) 87.88   (D) 87.99

16 Emma measured pieces of 67.45 inches of twine to tie up the tomato plants. One of the pieces she measured was too short. What could the length of the shorter piece possibly be?

(A) 67.3   (B) 67.4   (C) 67.42   (D) 67.5

17 Solve and round the answer to the nearest thousandth.

$$1,304.0256 + 4,450.0122 = \ ?$$

Comparing and Rounding Decimals 2.4

18 Cyrus painted 6.56 yards of fencing on day one and 13.88 yards of fencing on day two. Round the total to the nearest tenth?

(A) 20.5   (B) 20.44   (C) 20.55   (D) 20.45

19 What could the value of X be?

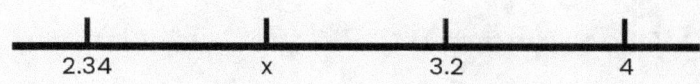

2.34   x   3.2   4

(A) 2.14   (B) 2.36   (C) 3.25   (D) 3.3

20 Mrs. Ethan wrote four numbers on the board. Which one is the largest?

(A) 67.4   (B) 67.678   (C) 67.920   (D) 67.288

Next Section: Chapter Review

2.5   Chapter Review

1 Peter and John are training to run a marathon. They ran a combined total of 4,200 minutes. If they both ran the same number of minutes over 30 days, how many minutes did each of them run each day?

(A) 60 minutes

(B) 65 minutes

(C) 70 minutes

(D) 75 minutes

2 A field is 20,000 feet long and 2,000 feet wide. If there are fence posts every 40 feet along the edge of the field, all the way around the field, how many fence posts are there?

_____

3 In a long jump, Alan jumped 48.37 feet. Devin jumped 48.372 feet. Jase jumped forty-eight and thirty-six hundredths' feet. Kyler jumped forty-eight and thirty-eight hundredths' feet. Who jumped the farthest?

(A) Alan

(B) Devin

(C) Jase

(D) Kyler

4 Brady scored a 86.3% on his test. Erick scored a 86.03% on his test. Gael scored a 86.33% on his test. Iker scored a 86.31% on his test. Who had the lowest test score?

(A) Brady

(B) Erick

(C) Gael

(D) Iker

5 Cesar needs 78 barrels of water. Each barrel holds 100 gallons. How many gallons of water will Cesar have?

A) 7.8   B) 780   C) 78,000   D) 7,800

6 Bryce bought lunch meat at the deli. He bought 7.076 lbs of pepperoni, 5.4 lbs of salami, and 3.779 lbs of ham. How many pounds of lunch meat, rounded to the nearest tenth, did Bryce buy?

A) 16.25   B) 16.24   C) 16.3   D) 16.2

7 There are 187 children coming to camp this summer. If one counselor is required per 8 campers, how many counselors should be hired?

A) 24   B) 14   C) 23   D) 25

8 Which number has an odd hundredth digit but, when rounded to the nearest tenth, the tenths digit is even?

A) 4.12   B) 7.59   C) 3.44   D) 4.49

9 Joseph has 9 ten-dollar bills. He is purchasing 2 shirts that are $ 29 and $ 16. How many bills should he give the clerk?

A) 3 bills   B) 4 bills   C) 5 bills   D) 6 bills

2.5 Chapter Review

10 A Ferris wheel completes a rotation in 78 seconds. How many seconds will it take to complete 17 rotations?

(A) 1,007 seconds

(B) 1,876 seconds

(C) 1,583 seconds

(D) 1,326 seconds

11 The garden had an equal amount of each vegetable. There are 50 different types of vegetables. Last year we planted 700 vegetable plants, but this year we planted double that amount. How many of each vegetable are there in the garden this year?

(A) 56 vegetables

(B) 18 vegetables

(C) 28 vegetables

(D) 31 vegetables

12 Henry made 2,200 toy keychains. He sold 400 of those toy keychains. He decided to give away the remaining toy keychains to 10 of his friends. How many toy keychains did each friend receive?

(A) 180 toy keychains

(B) 224 toy keychains

(C) 200 toy keychains

(D) 330 toy keychains

13 Alice bought a dress for $24 at a discount store. Emma bought the same dress for 100 times more. How much did both dresses cost altogether?

(A) $2,424

(B) $2,422

(C) $4,244

(D) $2,244

14 Clara practices the banjo every week for 2. 5 hours. To prepare for an audition, Clara practices for 30 times more than that per week. How many hours does Clara practice to prepare for the audition?

A) 75 hours   B) 56 hours   C) 45 hours   D) 67 hours

15 Jacob was making cheeseburgers. Each cheeseburger uses 10 ounces of meat. How many cheeseburgers can Jacob make if he has 700 ounces of meat?

A) 710   B) 70   C) 690   D) 7000

16 An orange juice machine makes 12 glasses of juice from one bag of oranges. How many glasses of juice does the machine make from 24 bags?

A) 124   B) 342   C) 288   D) 222

17 A team of football players spends 44 minutes of weight training every week. If their season is 22 weeks, how many minutes do they spend in the weight room during the entire season?

A) 888   B) 848   C) 898   D) 968

2.5 | **Chapter Review**

18 Helen wrote and published a book about her teacher. The book has 15 pages. There are a total of 75 pictures in the book. If each page has the same number of pictures, how many pictures did she put on each page?

(A) 8   (B) 5   (C) 7   (D) 15

19 Which expression is equivalent to $8500 \div 50$?

(A) $4500 \div 5$ (B) $850 \div 5$ (C) $8000 \div 50$ (D) $8050 \div 50$

20 A store sells soccer balls for $9.8. If they sell 5,311 soccer balls in a season, how much money do they make from soccer ball sales? Round the answer to the nearest 100

_____

Next Chapter: Decimals ≫

CHAPTER 3

DECIMALS

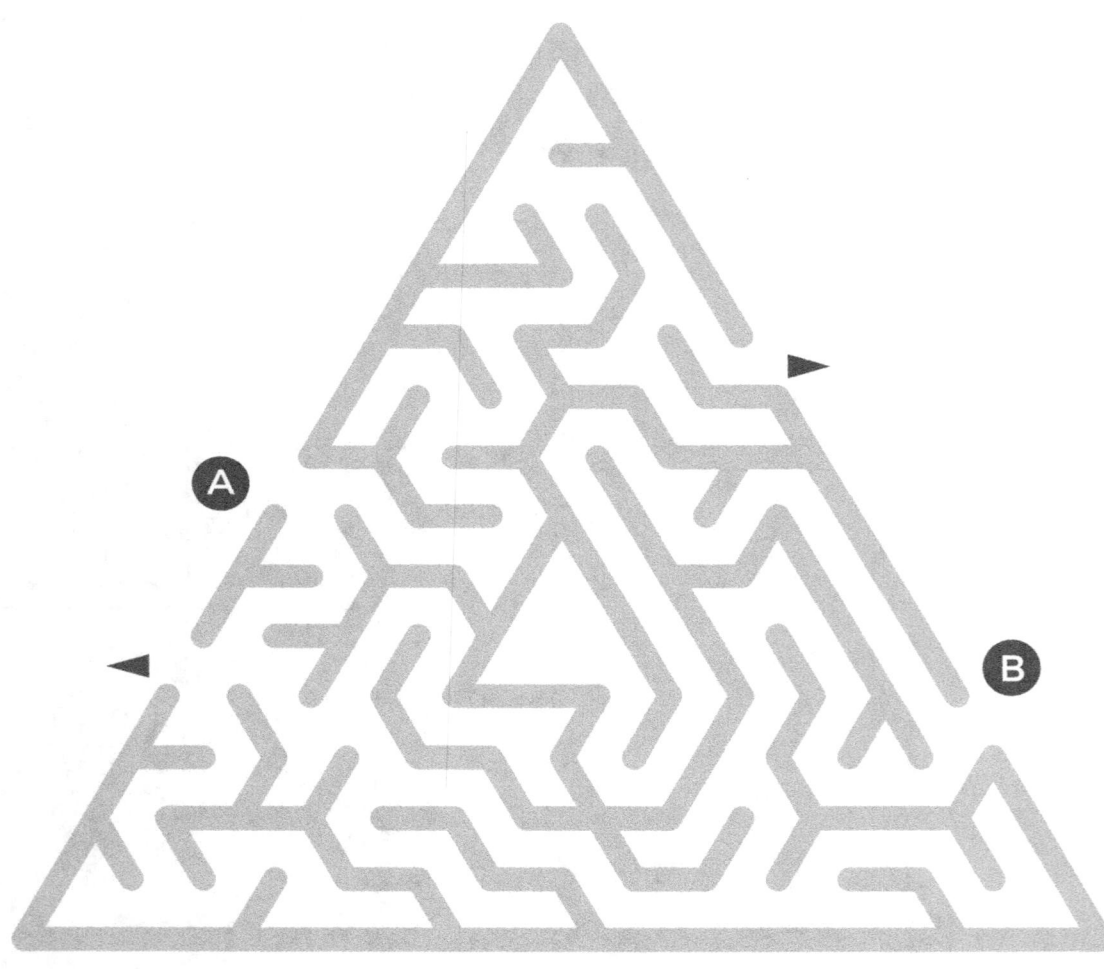

ADDITION AND SUBTRACTION FOR DECIMALS

Addition and subtraction for decimals is the process of adding or subtracting decimal numbers. The decimal points must be aligned before the operation is performed.

Add and subtract decimals using models and place values.

Area model: When we add and subtract decimals using an area model, we represent

Wholes as   Tenths as   Hundredths as

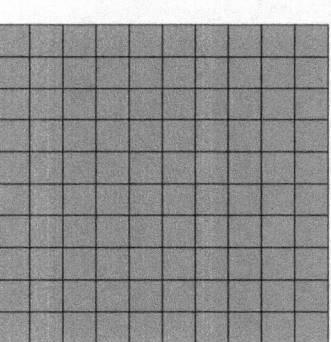 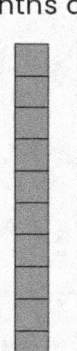

and combine them.

Example: Calculate $2.25 + 1.04$

Mental strategy:

We divide the total into whole numbers and decimals.

We then re-arrange the problem, adding the wholes and decimals separately;

We combine the two answers.

Example: Calculate $2.25 + 1.04$ using the area model.

Solution: $2.25 + 1.04 = (2+1) + (0.25+0.04) = 3 + 0.29 = 3.29$.

DECIMALS

3.1 **Addition and Subtraction For Decimals**

1 Represent the number 13.35 as a sum of two decimals if:

The digits in the one place are different;

The digits in the tenth position are the same;

The difference between two digits on the hundredth place is 1.

How many different solutions can you find?

(A) 4.18 + 9.17   (B) 4.12 + 9.22

(C) 6.18 + 7.17   (D) 5.22 + 7.17

2 Place the same digit in the gaps to get the smallest sum:

_____ 92 + 20 _____

3 Find the mistake in the number sentence below.

60.19 + 4.02 = (60+40) + (0.19+0.2)

_____

4 Find the numbers that are missing in the chain of calculations.

5.92 $\xrightarrow{-5.00}$ [ ] $\longrightarrow$ 3.65 $\longrightarrow$ 1.67

Addition and Subtraction For Decimals   **3.1**

5 Write two decimals that use the digits 5,6,7,8 exactly once. What is the greatest possible difference between these two decimals?

(A) 2.16   (B) 3.16   (C) 4.23   (D) 3.22

6 Find the missing number in the pattern below:
5.98, 6.64, 7.30, _____ , 8.62

(A) 7.96   (B) 8.01   (C) 7.86   (D) 7.99

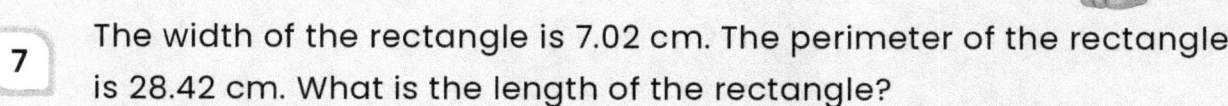

7 The width of the rectangle is 7.02 cm. The perimeter of the rectangle is 28.42 cm. What is the length of the rectangle?

(A) 6.99 cm   (B) 6.89 cm   (C) 7.19 cm   (D) 7.29 cm

8 What is the perimeter of a trapezoid whose three sides measure 3.49 ft, 4.28 ft, 4.44 ft, and whose longest side is 2.55 ft longer than the shortest side?

(A) 18.15 ft   (B) 18.25 ft   (C) 18.35 ft   (D) 18.45 ft

DECIMALS

3.1   Addition and Subtraction For Decimals

9 Which two decimals have a sum of 8.6 and a difference of 0.9?
(Use the length model for the calculation)

_____

10 Asher swims four days a week. Each Monday, he swims 4.14 miles. Each Tuesday, he swims 0.86 miles more than he does each Monday. Each Thursday, he swims 0.55 miles more than he does each Tuesday. Each Friday, he swims 0.45 miles more than he does each Thursday. How many miles does Asher swim each Friday?

(A) 5 miles   (B) 6 miles   (C) 7 miles   (D) 8 miles

11 Eddie has $78.80. He spent $18.45 on food, $52.50 on clothes. What amount of money is Eddie left with?

(A) $7.22   (B) $7   (C) $7.85   (D) $7.35

12 The width of the rectangle is 15.65 cm. The length of the rectangle is 3.66 cm longer than its width. What is the perimeter of the rectangle?

(A) 16 cm   (B) 16.88 cm   (C) 16.2 cm   (D) 69.92 cm

Addition and Subtraction For Decimals 3.1

13 Cora bought a toy that cost $76.32. If she paid the cashier $82.86 at the register, how much was the sales tax?

(A) $6.54   (B) $6.4   (C) $6.67   (D) $6.98

14 If Logan's family gave the cashier $60 for breakfast that cost $49.65, how much change did they receive?

(A) $9.4   (B) $10.35   (C) $9.35   (D) $11.35

15 During two days, you bike 11.76 miles and 22.55 miles. How many miles do you bike during these two days altogether?

(A) 34.31   (B) 35.33   (C) 34.7   (D) 32.1

16 This year a farmer harvested 45.86 big crates of tomatoes and 87.99 big crates of cucumbers. How many more crates of cucumbers did the farmer harvest?

(A) 42.22   (B) 42.53   (C) 42.33   (D) 42.13

17 Yesterday Otis ran 7.7 miles. Today, Otis ran 2.9 miles more than yesterday. How many miles did Otis run today?

(A) 10.6   (B) 11.88   (C) 6.89   (D) 5.02

DECIMALS

3.1   Addition and Subtraction For Decimals

18 Billie weighed two tubes with liquids during a chemistry class. The first tube weighed 0.24 pounds, and the second tube weighed 0.48 pounds. How much heavier is the second tube?

- (A) 0.2 pounds
- (B) 0.24 pounds
- (C) 0.4 pounds
- (D) 0.22 pounds

19 For the fruit salad, Milan bought 0.34 kg of avocado, 0.43 kg of mango, and 0.48 kg of melon. How much will the fruit salad weigh?

- (A) 2.35 g
- (B) 1.35 kg
- (C) 2.25 kg
- (D) 1.25 kg

20 Felix usually spent $333.65 a week on lunches. This week he spent $328.44. Which of the following statements is true?

- (A) This week Felix spent $5.21 less
- (B) This week Felix spent $6.90 less
- (C) This week Felix spent $7.10 more
- (D) This week Felix spent $5.21 more

Next Section: Multiplication and Division For Decimals

MULTIPLICATION AND DIVISION FOR DECIMALS

Multiplication of decimals involves multiplying the numbers as usual, but paying attention to the placement of the decimal point. Division of decimals involves dividing the numbers as usual, but again paying attention to the placement of the decimal point.

Multiplication of a decimal by a whole number.

<u>Area model:</u> When we multiply and divide decimals by whole numbers using an area model, we represent as

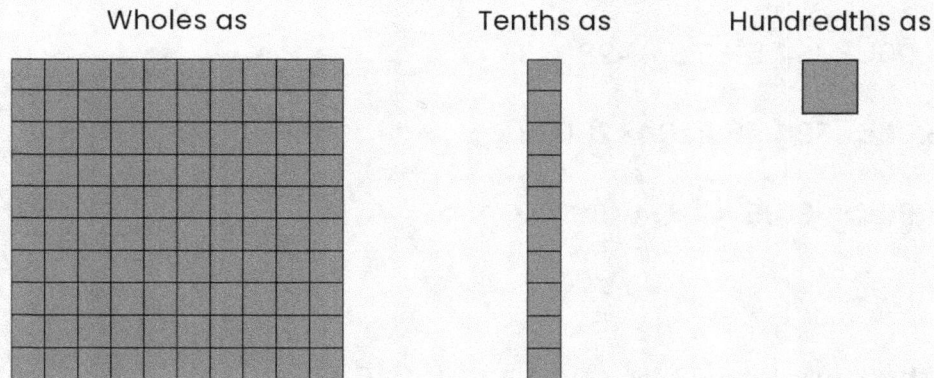

Wholes as   Tenths as   Hundredths as

and use repeating addition and subtraction.

Example: Divide 2.1 by 0.3.
Solution: Represent 2.1 as 2 wholes and 1 tenth.

Circle groups of 0.3 (three-tenths blocks) There are 7 equal groups of three-tenths. Therefore, 2.1 ÷ 0.3 = 7.

3.2 Multiplication and Division For Decimals

1 What is the value of u if u 0.7 = 4.9?

(A) 0.7   (B) 7   (C) 0.07   (D) 0.007

2 Compare the products without multiplying:
6.005 × 334.5 and 11.04 × 280.13.

(A) 6.005×334.5 > 11.04×280.13

(B) 6.005×334.5 < 11.04×280.13

(C) 6.005×334.5 = 11.04×280.13

3 Solve the equation: (1.8x − 0.4) ÷ 0.6 = 36.4.

(A) 12.35   (B) 12.6   (C) 12   (D) 12.4445

4 Kelvin went to school for 28 days in November. If he paid $3.80 for lunch each days, how much did he pay for lunch in November?

(A) $199   (B) $332   (C) $112   (D) $222

Multiplication and Division For Decimals 3.2

5 What is the value of m if 12 × m= 1.44?

_____

6 A rectangle's width is between 6 and 7 cm with one non-zero digit after the decimal point. Its length is represented by a decimal between 7.1 and 8.7 cm with two non-zero digits after the decimal point. What could be the smallest possible area of the rectangle?

(A) 43.371 cm²   (B) 43.33 cm²   (C) 44.371 cm²   (D) 44.44 cm²

7 Find the mistake in the calculation: 3.08 ÷ 0.9 = 308 ÷ 9 = 34.2.

_____

8 Kylo converts £8 into dollars. How much (in dollars) does Kylo receive if £1 is worth $1.37?

(A) $9.96   (B) $11.96   (C) $10.96   (D) $13

3.2 Multiplication and Division For Decimals

9 Rowan drinks 15.5 ounces of water a day. How many days will it take Rowan to finish 124 ounces of water?

A) 8 days   B) 9 days   C) 11 days   D) 7 days

10 Three friends went out to lunch. Each of them paid $18.60. How much money did they pay in total?

A) $59.96   B) $55.8   C) $60.6   D) $53.8

11 On average, it takes Steny 1.5 minutes to solve one math question. If Steny spent 12 minutes on a math test, how many questions did the test consist of?

A) 11 questions   B) 9 questions
C) 8 questions   D) 7 questions

12 Sofia bought a box of chocolates for $5.40. The box has 60 chocolates in it. What is the price of one chocolate in the box?

A) $ 0.06   B) $ 0.07   C) $ 0.08   D) $ 0.09

13 What is the area of the rectangle with the length of 0.79 m and the width of 0.5 m?

(A) 0.395 m²   (B) 0.35 m²   (C) 0.43 m²   (D) 0.45 m²

14 Iris spent $23.85 to fill up her car's gas tank. If the price of gas was $2.65 per gallon, how many gallons of gas did she buy?

(A) 7   (B) 8   (C) 9   (D) 10

15 Tia wants to convert her weight from kilograms to pounds. She weighs 58 kg and 1kg = 2.2 pounds. What is Tia's weight in pounds?

(A) 227.6 pounds   (B) 127.6 pounds

(C) 137.6 pounds   (D) 118.6 pounds

16 Mrs. Noah has 8.6 kg of raisins and 7.4 kg of candied fruit. She wants to share them among 18 bags so that each bag contains the same amount of raisins and the same amount of candied fruit. How much will one of these bags weigh?

(A) 1.1 kg   (B) 0.8 kg   (C) 1 kg   (D) 0.9 kg

3.2   **Multiplication and Division For Decimals**

17 A spool of thread has a thread measuring 69.6 m. 42.6 m of thread were cut off and the rest divided into 9 equal pieces. What is the length of one such piece of thread?

(A) 3 m   (B) 3.5 m   (C) 2 m   (D) 2.5 m

18 Fill in the missing decimal.

$14.3 \times (0.22+0.08) = 10 -$ _____.

19 Crew requires seven 0.15 m long pieces of rope. He has a rope that is 1.4 m long. Which of the following statements is true?

(A) Crew will need an additional 0.35 m of rope

(B) Crew has 0.35 m of extra rope

(C) Crew will need an additional 0.45 m of rope

(D) Crew has 0.45 m of extra rope

20 A game shop gives gamers toy snakes as the equivalent of a prize. Toy snakes cost $0.40 each. How many toy snakes can Taris exchange $3.2 for if he won a prize?

_____

Next Section: Divide Decimals Using Repeated Subtraction

DIVIDE DECIMALS USING REPEATED SUBTRACTION

Division of a whole number by a decimal using repeated subtraction:
To divide a whole number by a decimal, we subtract the decimal so many times that we get 0 as a remainder.

Example:

Divide 1.5 by 0.5.

Solution: Subtract 0.5 from 1, then subtract 0.5 from the difference and so on until you get zero.

	1	.5
−	0	.5
	1	.0

1st time

	1	0
−	0	.5
	1	.5

2nd time

	0	.5
−	0	.5
	0	.0

3rd time

Therefore, 1.5 ÷ 0.5 = 3.

Divide Decimals Using Repeated Subtraction

1 By how much do you need to multiply 2.5 to get a number equal to 0.32 divided by 0.02 ?

(A) 6.6   (B) 6.4   (C) 6   (D) 6.5

2 The area of one room is 1.5 times smaller than the area of another room. If the area of the larger room is 54 square meters and the smaller room is square, what is the perimeter of the smaller room?

(A) 36 m   (B) 64 m   (C) 54 m   (D) 16 m

3 Find the two missing digits. 12. _____ ÷ _____.2 = 3. How many solutions can you find?

_____

4 Which calculation has the result of 5?

(A) $3.5 \div 0.7$ (B) $3.5 \div 0.5$ (C) $3.5 \div 0.07$ (D) $3.5 \div 7$

5 Using repeated subtraction, divide $2.5 \div 0.5$.

(A) 6   (B) 4   (C) 5   (D) 3

3.3 Divide Decimals Using Repeated Subtraction

6 Which division does the repeated subtraction below represent?

	2.	8
-	0.	7
	2.	1

1st time

	2.	1
-	0.	7
	1.	4

2nd time

	1.	4
-	0.	7
	0.	7

3rd time

	0.	7
-	0.	7
	0.	0

4th time

(A) $2.8 \div 0.4$ (B) $2.8 \div 7$ (C) $2.8 \div 0.07$ (D) $2.8 \div 0.7$

7 Which division does the number line below represent?

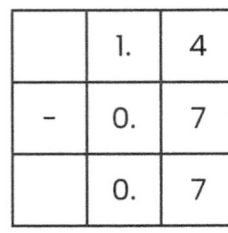

-0.5 -0.5 -0.5 -0.5

0   0.5   1   1.5   2

(A) $2 \div 0.04$ (B) $2 \div 0.4$ (C) $2 \div 0.5$ (D) $2 \div 0.05$

8 Using a number line, divide $4 \div 0.8 = ?$

(A) 6 (B) 4 (C) 5 (D) 3

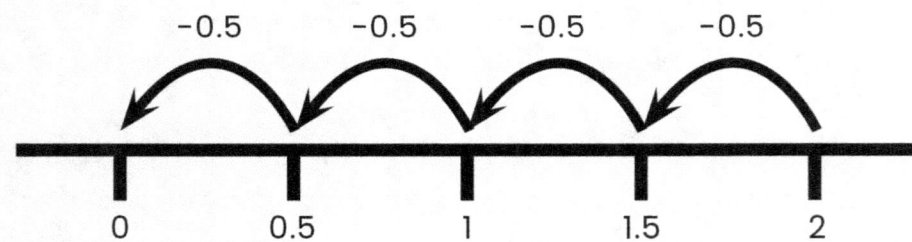

Divide Decimals Using Repeated Subtraction

9 Grace charges $8.50 per hour to babysit toddlers. If Grace earns $34, how many hours does she spend babysitting?

(A) 6 hours   (B) 4 hours   (C) 5 hours   (D) 3 hours

10 Kate pours 10.48 L of paint into containers. How many containers does she use, if each container holds 2.62 L of paint?

(A) 6   (B) 4   (C) 5   (D) 3

11 A chef used 60.66 grams of powder to bake some batches of cookies. If one batch of cookies requires 20.22 g of powder, how many batches of cookies did the chef bake?

(A) 6   (B) 4   (C) 5   (D) 3

12 The multi-floor building is 19.2 meters high. If the height of one floor is 3.2 meters, how many floors are in the building?

(A) 6 floors   (B) 4 floors   (C) 5 floors   (D) 3 floors

13 There are some balls in the bag. One ball weighs 0.25 kg. If the weight of all balls is 1.5 kg, how many balls are in the bag?

(A) 3 balls   (B) 4 balls   (C) 5 balls   (D) 6 balls

DECIMALS

3.3 Divide Decimals Using Repeated Subtraction

---

14 The distance between the two islands is 639.8km. Two ships with rates of 47.9 km/h and 43.5 km/h sail towards each other from these islands. In how many hours will they meet?

(A) 6 hours (B) 7 hours (C) 8 hours (D) 9 hours

---

15 Find two numbers a and b, if a - b = 10.36 and b = 0.26a.

a = _____ .

b = _____ .

---

16 Mia has 4.9L of juice. She pours out 0.9L of juice and the rest into 0.5 L jars. How many jars does she fill with juice?

(A) 6 jars (B) 7 jars (C) 8 jars (D) 9 jars

---

17 A table and some chairs weigh 12.9 kg. If the table weighs 4.5 kg and one chair weighs 1.2 kg, how many chairs were weighed?

(A) 7 chairs (B) 8 chairs (C) 9 chairs (D) 10 chairs

---

18 If 1.8 of a is 0.72 of 4 ,what is the value of a ?

(A) 1 (B) 1.2 (C) 1.4 (D) 1.6

Divide Decimals Using Repeated Subtraction   3.3

19 Calculate: $(12.8 - 6.8 \times 1.6) \div (1.4 - 0.6)$.

_____

20 **True or False?**

$$(17.6 + 6.8) \div 0.4 = (176 + 68) \div 4$$

(A) True   (B) False

Next Section: Writing Decimals Using Numerals

WRITING DECIMALS USING NUMERALS

Naming decimal place values depends on the placement after the decimal point. There are two ways to think of the decimal place.

1. The decimal point could be looked at as a number 1. Everything after the decimal point would be a zero.

$$0.124$$
$$\uparrow\uparrow\uparrow\ \uparrow$$
$$1\ 0\ 0\ \ 0$$

Since the 1 is in the place with " 10" under it, it is read as 1 tenth or $\frac{1}{10}$

Since the 2 is in the place with " 100" under it, it is read as 12 hundredths or $\frac{12}{100}$

Since the 4 is in the place with " 1,000 " under it, it is read as 124 thousandths or $\frac{124}{1000}$

2. Another way to think of it is that for each place after the decimal point, there is one zero. As you move to the right, another zero is added to the place value.

Decimal	1	2	3
	Tenths 10th	Hundredths 100th	Thousandths 1,000th

Example:

Name the following number in both numeral and word form. 0.43.
zero and forty-three hundredths or $\frac{43}{100}$

Note: The whole number is named, and the decimal point uses the word "and."

Writing Decimals Using Numerals 3.4

1 **Write the decimal using base-ten numerals.**
Four hundred fifteen and one hundred fifty-two thousandths

_____

2 **Write the decimal using base-ten numerals.**
Sixty-nine and six hundred twelve thousandths

_____

3 Compare by filling in the box using the >, <, or = symbol.

Twenty-six and seven hundred thirteen thousandths		Twenty-five and seven hundred fifteen thousandths

4 Compare by filling in the box using the >, <, or = symbol.

Eight hundred sixteen and one hundred sixty-two thousandths		Eight hundred sixteen and one hundred seventy-one thousandths

3.4 **Writing Decimals Using Numerals**

5 Compare by filling in the box using the >, <, or = symbol.

39.916		Thirty-nine and nine hundred sixteen thousandths

6 A teacher wrote 65.06 on the board. Four students named the number in different ways. Who is incorrect?

(A) Isaac – Sixty-five and six-hundredths

(B) Nicki – $65\frac{6}{100}$

(C) Ava – sixty-five and six-tenths

(D) Jackie – $60 + 5 + \frac{6}{100}$

7 Our family drove 44.89 miles to get to the zoo. How would this be written in expanded form?

(A) $40 + 4 + 8 + 9$

(B) $40 + 4 + \frac{89}{10}$

(C) $40 + 4 + \frac{8}{10} + \frac{9}{10}$

(D) $40 + 4 + \frac{8}{10} + \frac{9}{100}$

8   The lake is 7.095 miles long. What is the value of the 5?

(A) Five-thousandths   (B) Five-hundredths

(C) Five-tenths   (D) Five ones

9   Miya is a horse who weighs 906.87 lbs. What is the value of the 8?

(A) 80   (B) $\dfrac{8}{10}$ (C) $\dfrac{8}{100}$ (D) $\dfrac{8}{1000}$

10   Jenny worked 50.57 hours last week. How is this written in word form?

(A) Fifty, and fifty-seven

(B) Fifty, and fifty-seven tenths

(C) Fifty, and fifty-seven hundredths

(D) Fifty, fifty-seven

11   Which number is fifty-two hundredths?

(A) 67.052   (B) 9.52   (C) 5,200   (D) 13.252

3.4   Writing Decimals Using Numerals

12 The number 54.19 was written on the board. Joseph said this is fifty-four and nineteen tenths. Helen said this is fifty-four nineteen. Nancy said this is fifty-four and nineteen hundredths. Benita said this is fifty-four points nineteen. Which student is correct?

(A) Jospin   (B) Haran   (C) Nancy   (D) Benita

13 There are $5000 + 400 + 3 + \frac{2}{100}$ pounds of cement. How much is this in standard form?

(A) 5430.2   (B) 5403.2   (C) 5403.02   (D) 5430.02

14 The Kelley family traveled 42.12 miles Monday, 32.44 miles Tuesday, and 12.5 miles Wednesday. Write the total in word form.

_____

15 There are 6,403,023.89 gallons of water in the lake. How is this written in word form?

(A) Six million, four hundred three thousand, twenty-three, and eighty-nine thousandths

(B) Six million, four hundred three thousand, twenty-three, and eighty-nine hundredths

(C) Six billion, four hundred three thousand, twenty-three, and eighty-nine hundredths

(D) Six million, four hundred three thousand, twenty-three, and eighty-nine

16 Alex drank 52.84 ounces of water. He then drank ten times that much water during his basketball game. How much water did Alex drink during his game, written in word form?

_____

17 Stewart painted 6.16 yards of fencing on day one and 15.43 yards of fencing on day two. How would the total be written in expanded form?

_____

18 The number 9.186 was written on the board. The students were asked what the place value of the number eight is. Who was correct?

(A) Emma – eighth

(B) Brainy - ones

(C) David – tenths

(D) Crew – hundredths

3.4 Writing Decimals Using Numerals

19 Zackery wrote the number 8,467.029. Which of the following is not a correct way to name the nine?

(A) $\frac{9}{100}$

(B) Nine-thousandths

(C) Eight- thousandths

(D) $\frac{9}{1000}$

20 Four students stated that 23. 85 could be expressed in different ways. Which student is incorrect?

(A) Allen– twenty-three and eighty-five hundredths

(B) Chris – $20 + 3 + \frac{8}{10} + \frac{5}{100}$

(C) Robert– $(2×10)+(3×1)+8 \times \frac{1}{10} + 5 \times \frac{1}{100}$

(D) Peter– twenty-three and eighty- five tenths

Next Section: Chapter Review ≫

1 A city weatherman is calculating the total rainfall for the three summer months. In July, it rained 2.76 inches. In August, it rained 1.92 inches. In September, it rained 18.54 inches. What is the total rainfall, in inches?

_____

2 Mercy bought 7.6 pounds of gooseberries and blueberries at the store. If 5.94 pounds were gooseberries, how many pounds were blueberries?

_____

3 James went on a road trip. On the first day, he drove 400.76 miles, on the second day he drove 305.65 miles, and on the third day he drove 776.66 miles.

True or False: On the first and second day combined, James drove 10 times the distance that he drove on the third day.

(A) True   (B) False

3.5 **Chapter Review**

4 A new shipment of fabric arrived at the fabric store. The shipment contained 10 rolls of white cotton fabric, and each roll held 72.3 yards of fabric. The shipment also included 4 rolls of black cotton fabric, and each roll held 112.3 yards of fabric

True or False: In all, there was 10 times as much white cotton fabric as there was black cotton fabric.

(A) True   (B) False

5 Using the digits in 6.789, fill in the blanks below:

A. Ones digit: _____.

B. Tenths digit: _____.

C. Hundredths digit: _____.

D. Thousandths digit: _____.

6 A building has 100 windows. If it takes 5.43 minutes to wash each window, it will take _____ hours to wash all 100 windows.

7 Kolton wants to buy some T-shirts for $6.85 each. If Kolton has $61.65 to spend on T-shirts, how many T-shirts can he buy?

(A) 9   (B) 8   (C) 7   (D) 6

8 For his tourism club, Deon is making a container of nutrient mixture with 2.9 kg of nuts, and 2.25 kg of raisins. The rest of the 6 kg container will be candied fruit. How many kilograms of fruit does he need?

(A) 0.55 kg   (B) 0.65 kg   (C) 0.75 kg   (D) 0.85 kg

9 If a = 12.54, b = 2.4, c = 25, which of the following statements is true?

(A) $a \div (b \div c) = 0.209$

(B) $a \div b \div c = 0.209$

(C) $(b \div a) \div c = 0.209$

(D) $c \div (a \div b) = 0.209$

10 Sam is training for a marathon. On the first day, he ran 1.3 miles. He ran 0.55 miles more per day. In how many days will Sam run 6.25 miles?

(A) 9   (B) 8   (C) 10   (D) 11

11 Rebel and his brother weighed the candies they collected for Halloween and found that together they had 2.5 kg of candies, and Rebel's candies weighed 0.5 kg more than his brother's candies. How many candies did each brother collect?

_____

DECIMALS

12 Estimate the product 3.84×2.33 by rounding to the nearest whole number.

    (A) 9   (B) 8   (C) 10   (D) 11

13 Laken takes a measurement of a rectangular machine part. Its length is 9.24 centimeters, and its width is 6.75 centimeters. What is the area of the machine part?

    (A) 60.87 cm²   (B) 66.99 cm²

    (C) 63.86 cm²   (D) 62.37 cm²

14 A garbage dump was 160.6 feet long, 50.5 feet wide, and 50.5 feet deep. The volume of the inside of the garbage dump is _____ cubic feet.

    (A) 409,789.56   (B) 409,570.15

    (C) 409,239.88   (D) 409,855,87

15 Cleo needs to fill a water cooler. He has a container with 6.85 liters of water in it, and a bottle with 3.6 liters of water in it. How much water will Cleo pour into the cooler?

    (A) 10.45 L   (B) 10.5 L   (C) 10.65 L   (D) 10.25 L

16 Kerry planted a rose garden. She measured how much the flowers grew each day. Below are her measurements in inches. Rewrite the decimals in order from least to greatest.

0.333	0.303	0.330	0.033	0.336

17 Dr. Dana poured partial liters of water into five beakers. Below are the amounts of water he poured into each beaker. Rewrite the decimals in order from greatest to least.

0.707	0.727	0.071	0.077	0.772

18 Aaron has five $20 bills. He purchases two video games; one for $19.44 and the other for $42.5. How many bills should he give the clerk?

3.5 Chapter Review

19 A question on Kasey's test requires her to round 4.24759 to the ten thousandth place. Her answer was 4.2476. She is incorrect. What should her answer have been?

_____

20 Jaden put the cubes in a big box. One large cube weighs 0.25 kg, and one small cube weighs 0.06 kg. If there are 14 small and 6 large cubes in the box, what is the total weight of the box?

Ⓐ 3.54 kg   Ⓑ 2.64 kg   Ⓒ 2.74 kg   Ⓓ 2.34 kg

Next Chapter: Fractions ≫

CHAPTER 4

FRACTIONS

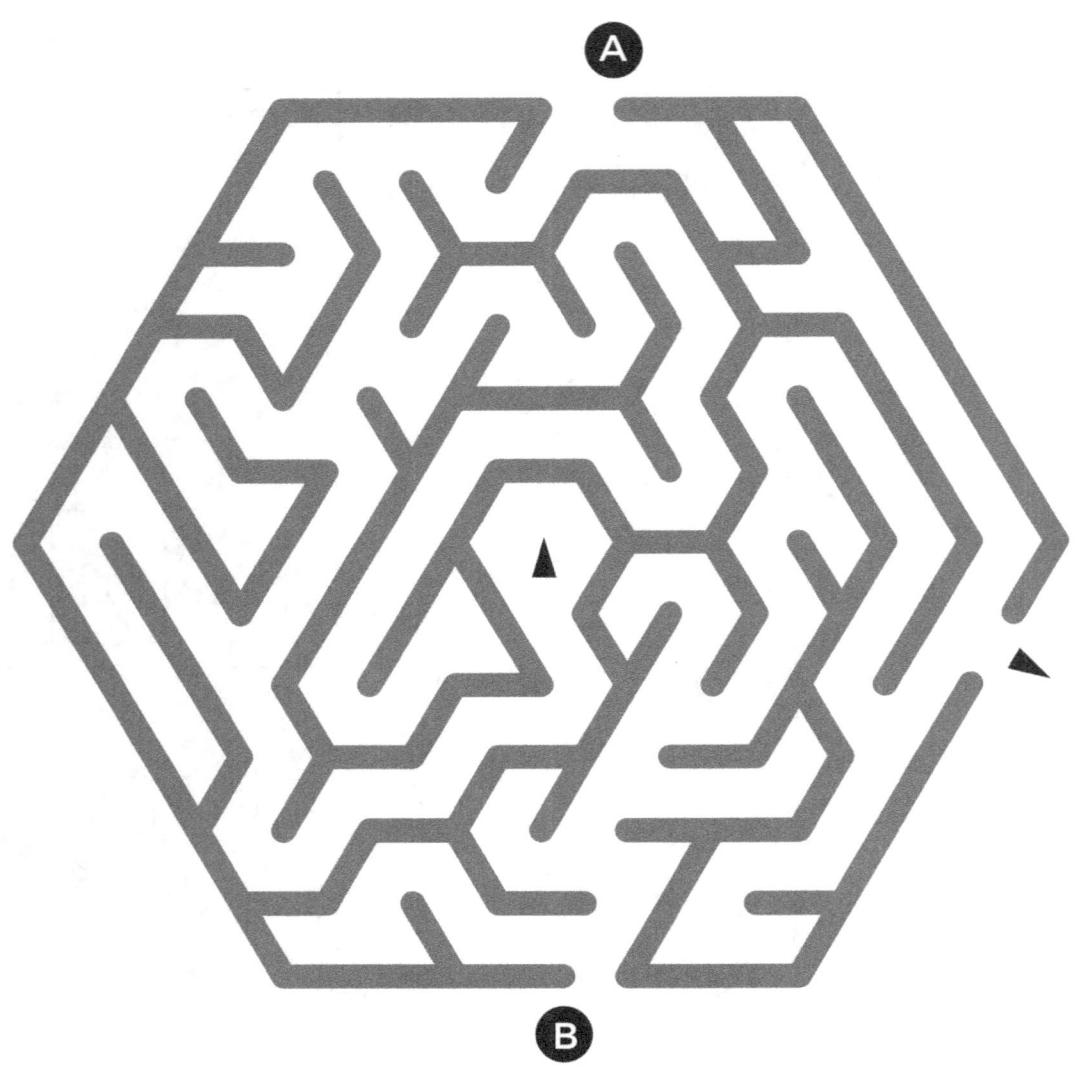

ADDITION AND SUBTRACTION – PROPER AND IMPROPER FRACTION

A proper fraction is a fraction where the numerator is less than the denominator, while an improper fraction is a fraction where the numerator is greater than or equal to the denominator.

Add and subtract fractions with unlike denominators

We can use the following three steps for adding and subtracting fractions with unlike denominators:

- get a common denominator using equivalent fractions;
- add and subtract the numerators;
- simplify the result if needed.

Add and subtract fractions with unlike denominators – mixed numbers

When adding or subtracting mixed numbers, complete the following steps:

- Break the mixed number into wholes and parts;
- Add or subtract the wholes;
- Add or subtract the parts;
- Combine the wholes and parts into a resulting mixed number.

Remark: Sometimes, when subtracting two mixed numbers, if the part of the second mixed number is greater than the part of the first mixed number, we need to borrow one whole from the first number's whole.

ADDITION AND SUBTRACTION – PROPER AND IMPROPER FRACTION

Example:

Calculate: $1\frac{4}{2} + 3\frac{2}{4}$

1st number: 1 whole and $\frac{4}{2}$

2nd number: 3 wholes and $\frac{2}{4}$

Add whole numbers:

$1 + 3 = 4$

Add parts:

$\frac{4}{2} + \frac{2}{4} = \frac{8}{4} + \frac{2}{4} = \frac{10}{4} = 2\frac{2}{4}$

Therefore, the answer is $6\frac{2}{4}$.

1 What missing value makes these fractions equivalent? Solve for x.

$$\frac{4}{7} = \frac{X}{21}$$

(A) 8   (B) 12   (C) 14   (D) 16

2 There are five digits 5,6,7,8. What could be the smallest possible value of the expression - + - if each digit can be used only once?

_____

3 What missing value makes these fractions equivalent? Solve for x.

$$\frac{5}{9} = \frac{45}{X}$$

(A) 78   (B) 25   (C) 18   (D) 81

4 Find the missing numbers.

$$\frac{5}{12} + \frac{?}{4} = \frac{1}{2} + \frac{1}{6}$$

4.1 Addition and Subtraction – Proper and Improper Fraction

5 Which response shows $6\frac{3}{5}$ as an improper fraction.

(A) $\frac{33}{5}$ (B) $\frac{31}{5}$ (C) $\frac{27}{5}$ (D) $\frac{34}{5}$

6 Which response shows $\frac{21}{6}$ as a mixed number?

(A) $3\frac{1}{6}$ (B) $2\frac{3}{6}$ (C) $3\frac{3}{6}$ (D) $4\frac{3}{6}$

7 Solve for x. $\frac{5}{12} + x = \frac{3}{4}$.

(A) $\frac{3}{4}$ (B) $\frac{1}{3}$ (C) $\frac{2}{3}$ (D) $\frac{3}{4}$

8 During the movie, Marion ate $\frac{1}{5}$ of the caramel popcorn and Olivia ate $\frac{2}{3}$ of all caramel popcorn. What fraction of all caramel popcorn did they eat together?

(A) $\frac{13}{15}$ (B) $\frac{11}{15}$ (C) $\frac{12}{15}$ (D) $\frac{13}{15}$

9 **True or False:** $2\frac{1}{3} + 1 = \frac{2}{3}$.

(A) True (B) False

Addition and Subtraction –
Proper and Improper Fraction

4.1

10 True or False: $4\frac{3}{5} + 1 > 1\frac{6}{5}$

(A) True

(B) False

11 Three sides of the triangle are fractions with three consecutive integers in the numerators and three consecutive integers in the denominators. If the smallest numerator is 1 and the greatest denominator is 4, what is the perimeter of the triangle?

(A) $\frac{23}{12}$

(B) $\frac{11}{12}$

(C) $\frac{13}{12}$

(D) $\frac{9}{12}$

12 At a dinner party, ricotta was equally shared among the dinner guests. If there were 16 people at the party, what fraction of the ricotta did each person get to eat?

(A) $\frac{1}{16}$

(B) $\frac{2}{16}$

(C) $\frac{3}{16}$

(D) $\frac{5}{16}$

13 Marson bought two bags of dog food. The first bag weighs $2\frac{4}{8}$ kg, the second weighs $2\frac{1}{3}$ kg more. How much do two bags weigh together?

(A) $6\frac{5}{6}$

(B) $2\frac{2}{6}$

(C) $6\frac{3}{6}$

(D) $4\frac{5}{6}$

FRACTIONS

4.1 Addition and Subtraction –
Proper and Improper Fraction

14 Three friends ate an extra-large pizza. Angel ate 5 slices, Rosy ate 6, and Cleo ate 4. If the pizza was equally cut into 18 slices, what fraction of the pizza was left over?

(A) $\frac{1}{18}$ (B) $\frac{2}{18}$ (C) $\frac{3}{18}$ (D) $\frac{5}{18}$

15 Patricia spent $2\frac{6}{14}$ hours in the meeting, which is $1\frac{1}{2}$ hours longer than she had planned. How long was the meeting scheduled?

(A) $1\frac{15}{14}$ hours   (B) $1\frac{11}{14}$ hours   (C) $2\frac{13}{14}$ hours   (D) $1\frac{13}{14}$ hours

16 Kerry makes a tray of brownies. Her mom eats $\frac{1}{11}$ of the tray. Her dad eats $\frac{1}{13}$ of the tray.

True or False: Together, her parents ate $\frac{1}{24}$ of the tray of brownies

(A) True   (B) False

17 Jessie went snowboarding. He went $\frac{1}{4}$ of the way down the hill. He stopped to catch his breath. Dustin then went another $\frac{2}{3}$ down the hill.

True or False: Dustin snowboarded down $\frac{3}{7}$ of the hill.

(A) True   (B) False

Addition and Subtraction –
Proper and Improper Fraction

4.1

18 The green strip on a flag has an area of $\frac{7}{12}$ square yards. The yellow strip on the flag has an area of $\frac{5}{9}$ square yards. What is the difference between the area of the green strip and the area of the yellow strip? What is the combined area of the flag?

_____

19 Diana makes a nut mixture for sale. She mixes $1\frac{1}{3}$ kg of walnuts, $\frac{1}{2}$ kg of hazelnuts and $\frac{3}{2}$ kg of almonds. What is the total weight of Diana's nut mixture?

Ⓐ $3\frac{1}{3}$　　Ⓑ $3\frac{2}{3}$　　Ⓒ $3\frac{4}{3}$　　Ⓓ $3\frac{5}{3}$

20 Max bakes 1 kg pie. $\frac{3}{5}$ kg is pie dough, and the rest is fruit. If $\frac{1}{3}$ is pumpkin and the rest are apples, how many apples are in the pie?

Ⓐ $\frac{2}{15}$　　Ⓑ $\frac{1}{5}$　　Ⓒ $\frac{1}{15}$　　Ⓓ $\frac{2}{3}$

Next Section: Multiplication and Division – Proper and Improper Fraction

MULTIPLICATION AND DIVISION – PROPER AND IMPROPER FRACTION

Multiplication and division of fractions involve multiplying or dividing the numerators and denominators of the fractions. A proper fraction is a fraction where the numerator is smaller than the denominator, while an improper fraction is a fraction where the numerator is equal to or larger than the denominator.

Multiplication

To multiply two mixed numbers:

- convert each mixed number to an improper fraction;
- write a multiplication sentence of improper fractions;
- multiply the first improper fraction by the second fraction;
- simplify the result.

Division with mixed numbers

To divide two mixed numbers:

- convert each mixed number to an improper fraction;
- write a division sentence of improper fractions;
- multiply the first improper fraction by the reciprocal of the second fraction;
- simplify the result.

Example:

Divide: $1\frac{4}{6}$ by $\frac{1}{2}$

Solution: First, convert $1\frac{4}{6}$ to an improper fraction: $\frac{10}{6}$
Now, divide $\frac{10}{6}$ by $\frac{1}{2}$

We get $\frac{10}{6} \times \frac{2}{1} = \frac{10}{3}$.

Multiplication and Division –
Proper and Improper Fraction

4.2

---

1 Rewrite the fraction $\frac{5}{7}$ as a division problem.

(A) 5÷7   (B) 5×7   (C) 7×5   (D) 7÷5

---

2 Simplify: $\frac{5}{3} \times \frac{4}{7}$

(A) $\frac{35}{12}$ (B) $\frac{20}{21}$ (C) $\frac{15}{28}$ (D) $\frac{9}{10}$

---

3 There are 3 boys at the movie theater. If each boy eats $\frac{7}{9}$ of a bucket of popcorn, how many buckets of popcorn should be ordered at the very least?

(A) 4 buckets (B) 5 buckets (C) 6 buckets (D) 7 buckets

---

4 **True or False:** $6\frac{1}{3} \times \frac{1}{3} = 6\frac{1}{3}$

(A) True   (B) False

---

5 Is $6 \times \frac{3}{7}$ greater or less than 6? Explain your answer below.

_____

4.2 **Multiplication and Division – Proper and Improper Fraction**

6 Shine collected 42 shells on the beach. If $\frac{1}{6}$ of the shells were white, how many of the shells were white?

(A) 6 shells   (B) 5 shells   (C) 8 shells   (D) 7 shells

7 Merlin mixed $2\frac{3}{5}$ teaspoons of spices into a batch of cookies. If she made 35 batches, how many teaspoons of spices did Merlin use in all?

(A) 91 teaspoons   (B) 66 teaspoons

(C) 35 teaspoons   (D) 103 teaspoons

8 The dentist used $4\frac{1}{4}$ tubes of toothpaste a day. How many total tubes of toothpaste did the dentist use in a period of 24 days?

(A) 100 tubes of toothpaste   (B) 101 tubes of toothpaste

(C) 102 tubes of oothpaste   (D) 103 tubes of toothpaste

9 Simplify: $\frac{3}{5} \div 4 =$ _____.

10 There was $\frac{1}{7}$ of an apple pie left over from the dinner party. If the pie was divided equally among 8 people, what fraction of the pie will each person get to eat?

(A) $\frac{1}{64}$ of the apple pie

(B) $\frac{1}{56}$ of the apple pie

(C) $\frac{1}{49}$ of the apple pie

(D) $\frac{1}{48}$ of the apple pie

11 There was $\frac{3}{4}$ of a pitcher of lemonade in the refrigerator. If the lemonade is shared equally among 6 friends, what fraction of the pitcher would each friend have to drink?

(A) $\frac{1}{4}$ of the pitcher

(B) $\frac{1}{6}$ of the pitcher

(C) $\frac{1}{9}$ of the pitcher

(D) $\frac{1}{8}$ of the pitcher

12 Julie wants to make 2 Halloween costumes from a piece of fabric that is a $\frac{1}{6}$ yard long.
True or False: She will have to use a $\frac{1}{12}$ yard of fabric for each costume.

(A) True

(B) False

4.2   **Multiplication and Division – Proper and Improper Fraction**

---

13   Eight friends go to a movie and share 4 buckets of Popcorn. They share $\frac{1}{4}$ of a bucket of popcorn equally.
True or False: Each person gets $\frac{1}{8}$ a bucket of popcorn.

   (A) True   (B) False

---

14   Oliver went on a 10-mile hike. If Oliver stopped to take a picture at every $\frac{1}{5}$ mile, how many pictures did Oliver take?

   (A) 50 pictures   (B) 5 pictures

   (C) $\frac{1}{50}$ pictures   (D) $\frac{1}{15}$ pictures

---

15   Last week, Kim spent $2\frac{1}{3}$ hours playing online games. Cruz spent three-fourth of this time playing online games. How many more hours did Kim spend than Cruz playing online games?

_____

---

16   A landscape designer can decorate $3\frac{1}{3}$ flowerbeds in $1\frac{1}{3}$ hours. In how many hours can the landscape designer decorate 6 flowerbeds?

   (A) 50 hours   (B) 15 hours

   (C) $\frac{1}{15}$ hours   (D) $\frac{1}{5}$ hours

Multiplication and Division –
Proper and Improper Fraction

4.2

17 A chocolate cookie recipe calls for $1\frac{1}{4}$ cups of milk. How much milk would you use to make $2\frac{1}{2}$ batches of cookies?

_____

18 If $a = \frac{3}{5} \div \frac{2}{b}$, what is b in terms of a?

(A) $b = \frac{10a}{3}$ (B) $b = \frac{3a}{10}$ (C) $b = \frac{a}{3}$ (D) $b = 10a$

19 Rosay's dog eats $2\frac{1}{4}$ cups of dog food each day. How much dog food will Rosay's dog in $3\frac{1}{2}$ days?

(A) $7\frac{6}{8}$ (B) $7\frac{7}{8}$ (C) $6\frac{7}{8}$ (D) $6\frac{6}{8}$

20 Ava cut a $2\frac{3}{6}$ -meter piece of wood into $5\frac{5}{12}$ -meter pieces. She used 4 such pieces. How many pieces of wood did Ava have left?

_____

Next Section: Multiplying Two Fractions
– Area Model and Length Model

MULTIPLYING TWO FRACTIONS – AREA MODEL AND LENGTH MODEL

Multiplying two fractions involves finding the product of two fractions. To multiply two fractions using the area model, multiply the numerators and denominators of the two fractions separately and then write the result as a new fraction.

The length model involves representing each fraction as a segment on a number line and then finding the product of the lengths of the two segments.

Multiply two fractions using an area model and length model – Halves, Thirds, Fourths

<u>Area model and Length model:</u> To multiply two fractions, we consider the multiplication as a fraction of the fraction.

<u>Multiplication rule:</u> To multiply two fractions, complete the following steps:

- multiply the numerators;
- multiply the denominators;
- simplify the fraction.

Example:

Multiply: $\dfrac{1}{2} \times \dfrac{3}{5}$

Solution: $\dfrac{1}{2} \times \dfrac{3}{5} = \dfrac{1 \times 3}{2 \times 5} = \dfrac{3}{10}$.

Multiplying Two Fractions – Area
Model and Length Model

4.3

1 Compare the fractions using >,<,= without multiplying:

$\frac{5}{14} \times \frac{2}{3}$ and $\frac{2}{3} \times \frac{3}{7}$

_____

2 **True or False:**

This is the associative property of multiplication:

$$\frac{1}{6} \times \left(\frac{1}{7} \times \frac{1}{8} \right) = \left(\frac{1}{6} \times \frac{1}{7} \right) \times \frac{1}{8}$$

(A) True   (B) False

3 Ryan said that $\frac{2}{9} \times \frac{4}{5}$ is the same as $\frac{2}{4} \times \frac{9}{5}$. Is he correct? Explain.

_____

4 Emily cleaned windows for $\frac{15}{16}$ hour. While cleaning, she listened to music for $\frac{4}{5}$ of the time and half of the time she was listening to music, she used headphones. How long did Emily use headphones?

(A) $\frac{3}{5}$ hour   (B) $\frac{3}{7}$ hour

(C) $\frac{3}{8}$ hour   (D) $\frac{3}{10}$ hour

119

4.3 **Multiplying Two Fractions – Area Model and Length Model**

5 Harry has a recipe for a fruit salad that calls for a pound of kiwi $\frac{5}{6}$ and $\frac{1}{6}$ of this amount of mangoes. He wants to make $\frac{2}{3}$ of the amount of the recipe. How many kiwis and mangoes will Harry need in total?

(A) $\frac{35}{54}$ pound (B) $\frac{25}{54}$ pound (C) $\frac{15}{54}$ pound (D) $\frac{15}{54}$ pound

6 Mia walked $\frac{7}{10}$ of a mile. Liam walked $\frac{6}{7}$ of the way with Mia. Jenny walked $\frac{5}{7}$ of the way with Mia. Who walked the furthest and by how much?

_____

7 A square has a side $\frac{3}{10}$ meter long. From the left upper corner, a small square with a side length of $\frac{1}{3}$ from the side length of a large square was cut. What is the area of the remaining region?

(A) $\frac{8}{25}$ m² (B) $\frac{4}{25}$ m² (C) $\frac{1}{25}$ m² (D) $\frac{2}{25}$ m²

8 Multiply two fractions using the multiplication rule. $\frac{5}{9} \times \frac{11}{45}$.

_____

Multiplying Two Fractions - Area Model and Length Model 4.3

9 Victor gave $\frac{1}{6}$ of his collection of football cards to his cousin. He presented half of the remaining cards to his brother. What fraction of his football cards did Victor leave for himself?

(A) $\frac{5}{12}$ (B) $\frac{6}{11}$ (C) $\frac{7}{12}$ (D) $\frac{7}{11}$

10 On a snowy day, $\frac{1}{8}$ of the students miss school. Half of these students call the teacher to report about their absence. What fraction of students call the teacher to report about their absence?

(A) $\frac{3}{16}$ (B) 16   (C) $\frac{1}{16}$ (D) $\frac{6}{16}$

11 Zelda picked $\frac{9}{10}$ of a pound of grapes. She gave $\frac{1}{4}$ of them to her mother for the grape pie. How many pounds of grapes did Zelda give her mother?

(A) $\frac{3}{10}$ (B) $\frac{9}{40}$ (C) $\frac{11}{40}$ (D) $\frac{1}{4}$

12 Aaron spent $\frac{9}{20}$ of a minute solving a one-question quiz. Peter says he can spend only two-thirds of this time on the same question. How much faster can Omar solve a one-question quiz than Amir?

(A) $\frac{3}{20}$ minute   (B) $\frac{3}{10}$ minute

(C) $\frac{9}{20}$ minute   (D) $\frac{9}{10}$ minute

4.3 **Multiplying Two Fractions – Area Model and Length Model**

13 Three friends went to the farm. Linda found $\frac{6}{7}$ pound of corn. Lisa found $\frac{1}{2}$ of what Linda found, and Sam found $\frac{1}{2}$ of what Liam found. How much corn did Sam find?

(A) $\frac{3}{5}$ pound   (B) $\frac{3}{14}$ pound   (C) $\frac{5}{4}$ pound   (D) $\frac{5}{14}$ pound

14 After a tennis practice, Jacob collected $\frac{3}{5}$ of a basket of tennis balls. Noah collected $\frac{2}{3}$ of what Jacob collected. What fraction of a basket of tennis balls did they collect in total?

(A) $\frac{1}{1}$ basket   (B) $\frac{3}{4}$ basket   (C) $\frac{5}{3}$ basket   (D) $\frac{5}{7}$ basket

15 Ethan walked $\frac{12}{15}$ km from the school to church and half of this distance from the church to home. What distance did he walk in total?

_____

16 $\frac{1}{8}$ of the boys in the school joined the basketball team. One-third of them have blue eyes. Which fraction of the boys are on the basketball team and have blue eyes?

_____

Multiplying Two Fractions – Area Model and Length Model 4.3

17 Multiply two fractions using the area models. $\frac{1}{2} \times \frac{1}{3}$.

18 There was $\frac{5}{4}$ kg of jam left in the fridge. David ate $\frac{1}{4}$ of the leftover jam. How much jam did he eat?

_____

19 Which calculation is represented by the area model below?

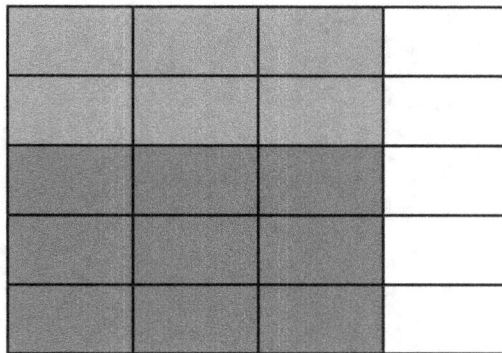

(A) $\frac{3}{5} \times \frac{2}{4}$ (B) $\frac{3}{5} \times \frac{1}{4}$

(C) $\frac{2}{5} \times \frac{2}{4}$ (D) $\frac{3}{10} \times \frac{2}{4}$

4.3 Multiplying Two Fractions - Area Model and Length Model

20 Emma babysits $\frac{1}{5}$ of a day with her younger brother. Oliver babysits with his younger sister $\frac{1}{3}$ of the amount of time that Emma babysits. What fraction of a day does Oliver babysit with her sister?

Next Section: Divide a Unit Fraction - Area Model and Length Model

DIVIDE A UNIT FRACTION – AREA MODEL AND LENGTH MODEL

Dividing a unit fraction means dividing a whole into equal parts and taking one of those parts. A unit fraction is a fraction with a numerator of 1, such as $\frac{1}{2}$, $\frac{1}{3}$, $\frac{1}{4}$, and so on.

Division of unit fractions by whole numbers:

<u>Area model:</u>

<u>Example:</u> Divide $\frac{1}{3}$ by 2

<u>Solution:</u> Divide one whole square into three equal parts, one of these parts represents $\frac{1}{3}$.

Divide the whole into two parts and shade one-third of it.

There are 6 equal parts, and one of them is shaded. Therefore, $\frac{1}{3} \div 2 = \frac{1}{6}$.

<u>Length model:</u>

<u>Example:</u> Divide $\frac{1}{3}$ by 2

<u>Solution:</u> Divide the unit segment into three equal parts

Now, divide each of these parts into two equal parts. Therefore, $\frac{1}{3} \div 2 = \frac{1}{6}$.

FRACTIONS

4.4 **Divide a Unit Fraction –**
Area Model and Length Model

1 Using an area model, calculate. $2 \div \frac{1}{4} =$ _____.

(A) 8   (B) $\frac{1}{2}$ (C) $\frac{1}{4}$ (D) 2

2 Ava is running a 3-mile race. There are distance marks every $\frac{1}{4}$ mile, including at the finish line. How many distance marks are there? (Use an area model for the calculation)

(A) $\frac{3}{4}$ (B) $\frac{1}{12}$ (C) 12   (D) 7

3 Fill in the missing digits. $\frac{1}{\rule{0.5cm}{0.4pt}} \div 12 = \frac{1}{72}$

(A) 8   (B) 7   (C) 4   (D) 6

4 Compare the given area model:

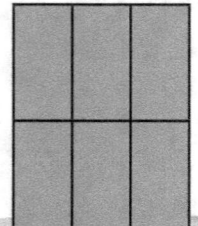 and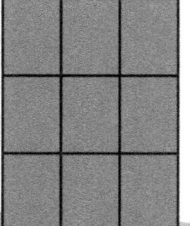

_____

**Divide a Unit Fraction –
Area Model and Length Model**

5   Using a length model, calculate: $4 \div \frac{1}{3}$ = _____.

6   **True or False**

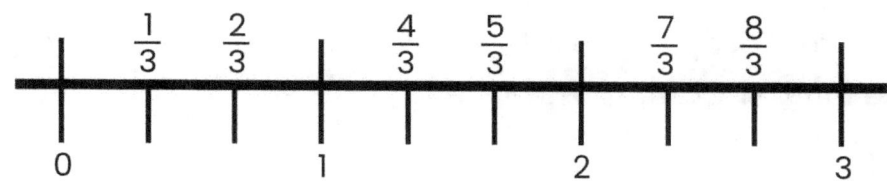

Equal to

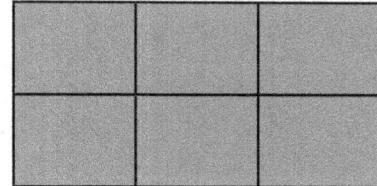

   Ⓐ   True   Ⓑ   False

7   How much of a chocolate bar will each child receive if 5 children share $\frac{1}{4}$ of the chocolate bar equally?

   Ⓐ   9   Ⓑ $\frac{1}{9}$ Ⓒ $\frac{1}{20}$ Ⓓ   20

4.4 **Divide a Unit Fraction – Area Model and Length Model**

8 Fill in the missing digits. How many solutions can you find?

$$\frac{1}{} \div \frac{1}{1} = \frac{1}{16}.$$

_____

9 Find the smallest positive integer which, when divided by $\frac{1}{3}$ gives a positive integer greater than 25.

_____

10 Select the calculation represented by the area model below.

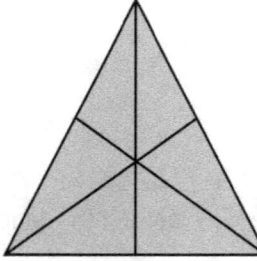
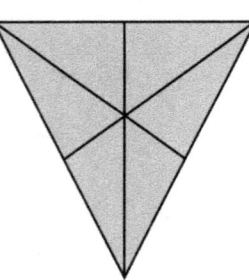
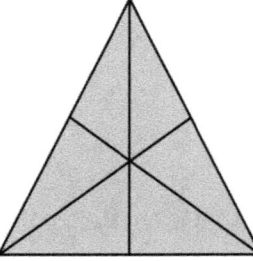

(A) $3 \div \frac{1}{6}$ (B) $3 \div \frac{1}{3}$ (C) $3 \div 6$ (D) $6 \div 3$

11 Find the smallest positive integer which, when divided by $\frac{1}{2}$ and $\frac{1}{3}$ gives a positive integer greater than 35.

_____

12 For the New Year's party, Mr. Mason cut four cakes into eight equal pieces each. How many pieces of cake did Mr. Mason get?

(A) $\frac{1}{2}$ piece   (B) 32 piece   (C) 12 piece   (D) $\frac{1}{12}$ piece

13 At the exam, the lecturer divided two-third of the stack of paper among thirty students. What part of the stack of paper did each student get?

(A) $\frac{1}{25}$ stack   (B) $\frac{1}{30}$ stack   (C) $\frac{1}{35}$ stack   (D) $\frac{1}{45}$ stack

14 Mia uses 4 packs of powder for one batch of cookies. How many batches of cookies can Mia bake having $\frac{1}{12}$ of a pack of powder?

(A) $\frac{1}{35}$ batch   (B) $\frac{1}{20}$ batch   (C) $\frac{1}{48}$ batch   (D) $\frac{1}{16}$ batch

4.4 Divide a Unit Fraction – Area Model and Length Model

15 The cyclist covered 6 km in $\frac{1}{4}$ of an hour. What was the average cyclist's rate?

(A) 24 km/h   (B) $\frac{1}{24}$ km/h   (C) 10 km/h   (D) $\frac{1}{10}$ km/h

16 Jack has $\frac{1}{2}$ kg of candy to treat 14 classmates on the occasion of his birthday. How much candy will each of his classmates get?

(A) 7 kg   (B) $\frac{1}{14}$ kg   (C) $\frac{1}{28}$ kg   (D) $\frac{1}{7}$ kg

17 Mr. Travis picked $\frac{1}{3}$ of a pound of blueberries. Before freezing, he wants to separate them equally into 6 containers. How many blueberries will each container hold?

(A) 2 pounds   (B) $\frac{1}{18}$ pound   (C) $\frac{1}{2}$ pound   (D) $\frac{1}{3}$ pound

18 A computer needs an average of $\frac{1}{8}$ of a minute to answer one math question. On average, how many questions can the computer answer in 4 minutes?

(A) $\frac{1}{32}$ (B) 32   (C) $\frac{1}{12}$ (D) 12

19 Samuel has 6 moving boxes, each of which is divided into 3 identical divider cells. How many divider cells will be in all of the moving boxes?

(A) $\frac{1}{18}$　　　(B) 18　　　(C) $\frac{1}{9}$　　　(D) 9

20 Taylen has a photo album with 10 empty pages. Each photo requires $\frac{1}{5}$ of a page. How many additional photos can Taylen put into the album?

(A) $\frac{1}{50}$ Photo　　　(B) 50 Photos

(C) $\frac{1}{2}$ Photo　　　(D) 2 Photos

Next Section: Chapter Review ≫

4.5 | **Chapter Review**

1 | Solve for x: $\frac{2}{7} - x = \frac{1}{14}$

(A) $\frac{1}{14}$ (B) $\frac{2}{14}$ (C) $\frac{3}{14}$ (D) $\frac{4}{14}$

2 | Solve for x: $2\frac{1}{5} - x = 2\frac{4}{5}$

(A) $\frac{1}{5}$ (B) $\frac{3}{5}$ (C) $\frac{2}{5}$ (D) $\frac{4}{5}$

3 | James and Jack walked $\frac{2}{3}$ of a mile to the grocery store. They then walked another $\frac{4}{9}$ of a mile to the movie theater. How many miles did both James and Jack walk in total?

(A) $\frac{7}{9}$ (B) $\frac{8}{9}$ (C) 1   (D) $\frac{10}{9}$

4 | Mathew has written $\frac{3}{5}$ of the essay in the morning and $\frac{1}{9}$ of this amount in the evening. What fraction of the essay has Mato written in the evening?

(A) $\frac{1}{15}$ (B) $\frac{1}{5}$ (C) $\frac{2}{15}$ (D) $\frac{1}{9}$

5 Twenty-four cake pieces were equally shared among 8 friends. How many cake pieces did each friend receive?

Write the division problem: _____.

Now write the division problem in the form of a fraction:

_____

6 There were 22 cups of sugar split equally into 12 pies. How many cups of sugar did each pie get?

Write the division problem: _____.

Now write the division problem in the form of a fraction:

_____

7 How many $\frac{1}{3}$ meter pieces of string can you cut from a 8 meter long string?

(A) $\frac{1}{24}$ (B) 24   (C) $\frac{8}{3}$ (D) $\frac{3}{8}$

8 After a busy day at the ice cream shop, there were only 8 scoops of ice cream left. If the scoops were split equally among the last 6 customers, each customer received _____scoops of ice cream.

4.5   **Chapter Review**

9 Mr. Jason has $\frac{5}{9}$ gallon of milk. He used $\frac{3}{7}$ of his milk for breakfast. How much milk does Mr. Jason has left?

(A) $\frac{60}{189}$ gallon   (B) $\frac{60}{199}$ gallon   (C) $\frac{50}{189}$ gallon   (D) $\frac{50}{199}$ gallon

10 Mr. Alex wants to put down a piece of material to protect the bottom of his toolbox. If the bottom of the box was $\frac{1}{2}$ feet long and $\frac{3}{5}$ feet wide, what is the area that needs to be covered?

(A) $\frac{2}{15}$ (B) $\frac{10}{3}$ (C) $\frac{3}{10}$ (D) $\frac{15}{2}$

11 Sarah is making a dozen cupcakes. The recipe she is using makes 20 cupcakes. It calls for $\frac{1}{6}$ a teaspoon of vanilla.
True or False: If she splits the recipe in half, she would need a $\frac{1}{4}$ teaspoon of vanilla.

(A) True   (B) False

12 Simplify: $5 \div \frac{8}{3} =$ _____.

13 Three people competed in a pie-eating contest. When the time was called, each competitor had eaten two-thirds of the pie in front of them. Name three fractions that are equivalent to $\frac{2}{3}$.

_____

14 Five black ski suit costs $100. How much does one ski suit cost?

(A) $40   (B) $25   (C) $30   (D) $20

15 Mrs. Smith made 18 quarts of punch. If she wanted to pour the punch equally into 4 punch bowls, each bowl would get _____ quarts of punch.

16 Kate had 208 tennis balls. If he wanted to split them equally into 8 buckets, each bucket would have _____ tennis balls.

17 Chris worked at a movie theater. If he had 6 pounds of candy that he wanted to equally put into 42 bags, each bag would have _____ pounds of candy.

4.5 Chapter Review

18 The area of the triangle can be calculated using the formula $A = \frac{1}{2} \times$ Base × Height. In the triangle, the base is $5\frac{1}{2}$ cm long. If the area of the triangle is 33 cm², what is the height of the triangle?

Ⓐ 12 cm Ⓑ 22 cm Ⓒ 10 cm Ⓓ 2 cm

19 The tablecloth is $6\frac{1}{2}$ feet long on all four sides.
True or False: The area the tablecloth covers is 45 sq. ft.

Ⓐ True Ⓑ False

20 The plant grew $\frac{1}{18}$ inches every day.
True or False: After 9 days, the plant grew over 2 inches.

Ⓐ True Ⓑ False

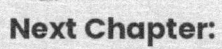

Next Chapter:
Conversions and Interpret Data »

CHAPTER 5

CONVERSIONS AND INTERPRET DATA

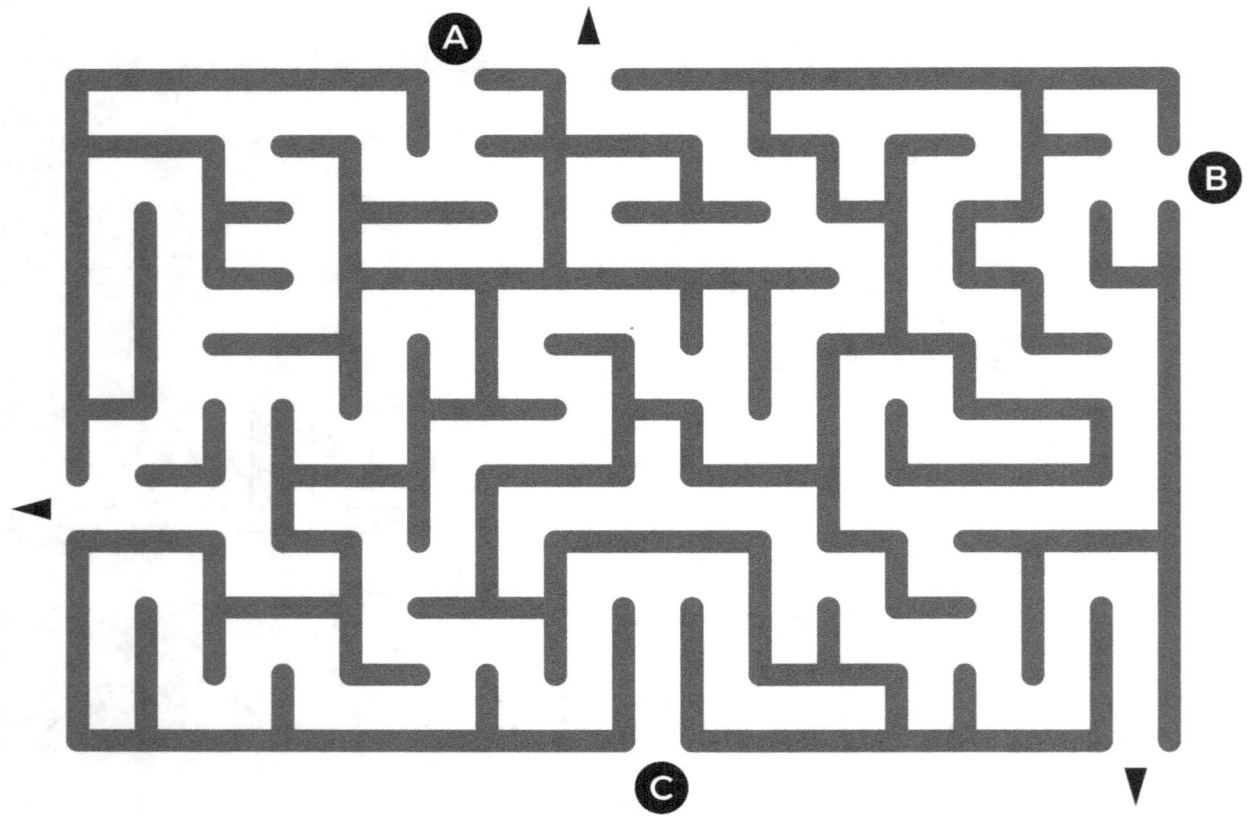

WEIGHT CONVERSION AND LENGTH CONVERSION

Weight conversion involves converting one unit of weight to another. For example, converting pounds to ounces, or grams to kilograms. Length conversion involves converting one unit of length to another. For example, converting meters to centimeters, or inches to feet.

Weight Conversions Customary units:

Pound (lb) = Ounces (oz)
Ton (T) = Pounnd (lb)

The customary weight measurement units are ounces, pounds, and tons.

Metric units of weight:

The metric weight measurement units are milligrams, grams, kilograms, and tons.

Length Conversions Using a Chart
Customary Units:

Lengths and distances in the customary system are measured in inches, feet, yards, and miles.

1 ft = 12 in
1 yd = 3 ft
1 yd = 36 in
1 mi = 5280 ft
1 mi = 1760 yd

WEIGHT CONVERSION AND LENGTH CONVERSION

Metric units of weight:

Length and distances in the metric system are measured in kilometers, meters, decimeters, centimeters, and millimeters.

$$1 \text{ cm} = 10 \text{ mm}$$
$$1 \text{ dm} = 10 \text{ cm}$$
$$1 \text{ m} = 100 \text{ cm}$$
$$1 \text{ m} = 10 \text{ dm}$$
$$1 \text{ km} = 1000 \text{ m}$$

Example: Convert 30 centimeters to meters.

Solution: To convert centimeters into meters, divide the number of centimeters by 100. Therefore,

$$30 \text{ cm} = \frac{30}{100} \text{ m} = 0.3 \text{ m}$$

1 The average length of a blue iguana is 1.4 m . The average length of an ordinary iguana is $\frac{1}{2}$ of the length of a blue iguana. The average length of a sea iguana is $\frac{3}{2}$ of the length of an ordinary iguana. What is the average length, in centimeters, of a sea iguana?

- (A) 115 cm
- (B) 105 cm
- (C) 125 cm
- (D) 100 cm

2 The average weight of an English bulldog is 24.5 kg. The average weight of a collie is $\frac{3}{5}$ of the weight of an English bulldog. The average weight of a poodle is $\frac{3}{7}$ of the weight of the collie. What is the average weight of a poodle in grams?

- (A) 7 kg
- (B) 6 kg
- (C) 6.5 kg
- (D) 6.3 kg

3 Convert 18 feet into inches: _____.

4 Convert 22,000g into kilograms: _____.

5.1   **Weight Conversion and Length Conversion**

5

Together, a pen and a pencil are 38 cm long. Together, the pen and a ruler are 58 cm long. Together, the pencil and the ruler are 46 cm long. How long is each object in millimeters?

6

For the biological project, Melanie caught three insects and weighed them on accurate scales. The weight of the black beetle is 240 mg, the weight of the fly is two times less than the weight of the beetle and the weight of the mosquito is four times less than the weight of the fly. What is the weight of a mosquito in grams?

A) 0.03 g   B) 0.3 g   C) 0.003 g   D) 3 g

7

Helen is 4 feet 6 inches tall. Her brother is 6 inches taller. What is the height of Helen's brother?

A) 5 feet 1 inches   B) 5 feet

C) 6 feet 3 inches   D) 6 feet 1 inches

Weight Conversion and Length Conversion

5.1

8 Joel measures 4 different pencils. This table shows the length of each pencil. What is the combined length of these pencils in meters?

Pencil	Length (centimeters)
A	5.1
B	4.6
C	2.1
D	5.7
E	8

A) 255 m

B) 0.0225 m

C) 0.255 m

D) 2.25 m

9 Convert 48 pounds into ounces: _____.

10 Convert 36 feet into yards: _____.

11 If 6,900g = 69x kg , what is the value of x?

A) x = 1   B) x = 0.01   C) x = 0.2   D) x = 0.1

CONVERSIONS AND INTERPRET DATA

5.1 Weight Conversion and Length
Conversion

12 Two high jumpers made their first attempts. The first jumped 2.65m, the second jumped 2.42 m. How many centimeters higher did the first jumper jump?

(A) 23 cm   (B) 24 cm   (C) 2.3 cm   (D) 2.4 cm

13 Mercy has 6 books that have a combined mass of 9.24 kilograms. Three of the books have a mass of 728 grams. What is the mass of the remaining two books, in grams?

(A) 8,876 grams   (B) 8,654 grams

(C) 8,512 grams   (D) 8,186 grams

14 Marson weighed a pumpkin and found that it had a mass of 10 kg. She cut the pumpkin and gave her friend a 2.5 kg piece. Then she divided the remaining pumpkin into 6 identical parts. How many grams of pumpkin were there in each part?

(A) 2,650 g   (B) 1,250 g

(C) 2,500 g   (D) 2,000 g

15 A box containing 4 identical plates weighs 2kg. If the weight of the box is 440 g, what is the weight of each plate?

(A) 360 g   (B) 440 g   (C) 390 g   (D) 380 g

16 The ceiling height is 10 feet 10 inches. Raising her hands up, Tracy reaches a height of 8 feet 4 inches. How many additional inches does Tracy need to reach the ceiling?

(A) 10 in   (B) 20 in   (C) 30 in   (D) 40 in

17 Cleo is 5 feet 10 inches tall. His sister is 11 inches shorter. What is the height of Cleo's sister?

(A) 4 ft 11 inches   (B) 4 ft 10 inches

(C) 5 ft 11 inches   (D) 5 ft 10 inches.

18 Carey bought a 4 lb bag of strawberries at the market and ate 8 oz of them on the way home. At home, she ate 10 oz of the remaining strawberries. How many ounces of strawberries did Carey have left?

(A) 44 oz   (B) 46 oz   (C) 48 oz   (D) 64 oz

5.1   **Weight Conversion and Length Conversion**

19   A rectangle is 10 inches wide and 12 inches long. What is the perimeter of the rectangle?

_____

20   Kerry measures 4 different insects she found in a park. This table shows the length of each insect. What is the combined length of these insects in meters?

Insect	Length (centimeters)
Butterfly	12.4
Bee	13.7
Grasshopper	14.3
Ladybug	13.2

(A) 53.6 m   (B) 0.0536 m   (C) 5.36 m   (D) 0.536 m

Next Chapter: Time conversion and capacity conversion

TIME CONVERSION AND CAPACITY CONVERSION

Time conversion is the process of converting time from one unit to another. It involves understanding the relationship between different units of time, such as seconds, minutes, hours, days, weeks, months, and years.

Capacity conversion is the process of converting one unit of measurement of volume to another. It involves understanding the relationship between different units of capacity, such as liters, milliliters, gallons, quarts, pints, and cups.

Capacity Conversions Using a Chart

Customary Units:

1 tablespoon = 3 teaspoons
1 fluid ounce = 2 tablespoons
1 cup = 8 fluid ounces
1 pints = 2 cups
1 quart = 2 pints
1 gallon = 4 quart
1 gallon = 128 fluid ounces

The customary capacity or volume measurement units are teaspoons, tablespoons, ounces, cups, pints, quarts, and gallons.

Metric units of weight:

The metric capacity or volume measurement units are milliliters, liters, cm^3 and m^3.

1 L = 100ml
1 kL = 1000L
1 cm^3 = 1 mL
1 m^3 = 1 kL

TIME CONVERSION AND CAPACITY CONVERSION

The metric capacity or volume measurement units are milliliters, liters, cm³ and m³.

Example: Convert 3,000 milliliters to liters.

Solution: To convert milliliters to liters, divide the number of milliliters by 1000. Therefore,

$$3000 \text{ mL} = \frac{3000}{1000} = 3L$$

Time conversions Using a Chart

1 minute = 60 seconds

1 hour - 60 minutes = 3600 seconds

1 day = 24 hour = 1440 minutes = 86400 seconds

1 week = 7 days

1 year = 12 months

1 year = 365 days

Example: Convert

a) 3.5 hours into minutes;

b) 240 seconds into minutes.

Solution:

a) 3.5 hours = 3.5 × 60 = 210 minutes

b) 240 seconds = $\frac{240}{60}$ = 4 minutes

Time Conversion and Capacity
Conversion

5.2

1 Every day Nancy increases the dosage of the antidote by 4 mL. She began to take an antidote in the amount of 0.004 L. Her treatment will stop when she takes 60 mL a day. In how many days will her treatment stop?

(A) 12 days   (B) 13 days   (C) 14 days   (D) 15 days

2 Emma fills a fish tank $\frac{2}{3}$ full. The fish tank has a capacity of 42 liters. How many milliliters of empty space remain in the fish tank?

(A) 12,000   (B) 28,000   (C) 22,000   (D) 32,000

3 If 8 hours x minutes = y hours 130 minutes, then
x = _____ and y = _____.

4 A shoe company produces 425 feet of shoelaces every hour. Each shoelace is 25 inches long. How many shoelaces are produced in 2 hours?

_____

5.2 Time Conversion and Capacity Conversion

5 A large tub holds 40 gallons of water. When the tub is full, it drains at a speed of 80 quarts per minute. How many minutes does it take to drain a full tub?

_____

6 Emily stayed at the hotel for 14 days. Kris was there for 1 week and 6 days. Which of the following statements is true?

(A) Isabella stayed at the hotel 1 day longer

(B) They stayed the same number of days at the hotel

(C) Emily stayed at the hotel 2 days longer

(D) Emily stayed at the hotel 1 day longer

7 A water jug contains 50 pints of water. How many cups of water are in this jug?

(A) 400   (B) 200   (C) 100   (D) 300

8 Alva has a gallon of milk, and she pours 4 ounces of milk into each glass. How many glasses does Alva use?

_____

Time Conversion and Capacity Conversion   5.2

9 A teapot can hold up to 20 cups of tea. Camilla poured out 2.5 pints of tea. How much tea is left in the teapot?

(A) 10 cups   (B) 15 cups   (C) 20 cups   (D) 25 cups

10 Eden was doing Science and Math for 3 hours 30 minutes. If Math homework took Eden 150 minutes how long did Science homework take her?

(A) 60 minutes   (B) 65 minutes
(C) 70 minutes   (D) 75 minutes

11 Together, a bucket and a container can hold 20 L. Two buckets can hold three times as much as six containers. How much, in milliliters, can a bucket hold? How much, in milliliters, can a container hold?

_____

12 Ryan was 5 years 6 months old when he joined the school.
Remi was 6 years 4 months old when she joined the school. How much older was Remi?

(A) 10 months   (B) 12 months
(C) 8 months   (D) 11 months

CONVERSIONS AND INTERPRET DATA

5.2 Time Conversion and Capacity Conversion

13 One push of the fuel pump allows you to fill 16 fluid ounces of fuel into the tank. How many pushes do you need to fill 72 pints of fuel?

_____

14 Jordan played the PlayStation game from 16:50 until 18:15. How many minutes did Jordan played the PlayStation game?

A) 55 minutes   B) 65 minutes

C) 75 minutes   D) 85 minutes

15 Alan has 4 quarts of lemonade. She drinks $\frac{1}{2}$ of it. How many cups of lemonade does Amari have left?

A) 6 cups   B) 8 cups   C) 10 cups   D) 12 cups

16 Convert 350 cm³ into liters: _____.

17 Riley said that in 4 years he will be 118 months old. How old is Riley now?

A) 5 years 10 months   B) 6 years 10 months

C) 5 years 8 months   D) 6 years 8 months

18 Blake would like to serve lemonade in cups. He has 6 bottles with a capacity of 4 pints each. How many cups can Blake fill with lemonade using lemonade from all bottles?

(A) 56 cups

(B) 48 cups

(C) 60 cups

(D) 52 cups

19 Convert $\frac{10}{3}$ hours into hours and minutes _____.

20 For each of her 12 flowerbeds, Peyton needs two quarts of water in order to water each flower bed. How much water does Peyton need to water flowers in all of her flowerbeds?

_____

Next Section: Measuring Data From Survey

153

MEASURING DATA FROM SURVEY

Measuring data from survey involves understanding and applying the concept of statistics. This includes collecting, organizing, analyzing, interpreting, and presenting data.

Identify Data as Numerical or Categorical

You can measure data from a survey by presenting the data as an ordered set or on a line plot.

Then you can determine the minimum or maximum value, the most frequent or least frequent value, how many people took part in a survey, or analyze the data in some other way.

Example: A data set is given: 4, 2, 3, 1, 2, 5, 3, 2, 1, 4, 2, 2, 4, 3, 4, 2

Find:

- minimum value
- maximum value
- least frequent value
- most frequent value
- number of values

Solution: Order data: 1, 1, 2, 2, 2, 2, 2, 2, 3, 3, 3, 4, 4, 4, 4, 5

The minimum value is 1.

The maximum value is 5.

Create a frequency table.

Value	1	2	3	4	5
Frequency	2	6	3	4	1

Least frequent value is 5.

Most frequent value is 2.

Create a line plot.

Count Xs. The total number of values in the data set is 16

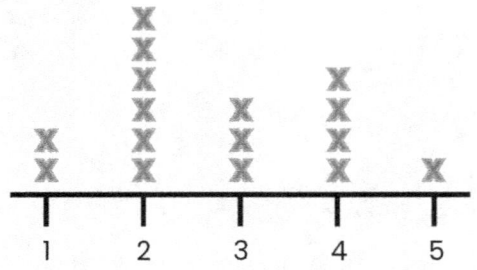

Measuring Data From Survey   **5.3**

1 Data set is given: 2, 6, 3, 1, 5, 2, 1, 3, 2, 6, 4, 5, 1, 4, 5, 5, 5, 2, 7, 6, 7, 4, 1
Find the minimum value in the data set.
The minimum value =

_____.

2 Data set is given: 2, 6, 3, 8, 5, 8, 1, 2, 6, 4, 5, 1, 8, 5, 5, 2, 7, 6, 7, 4, 1,8
Find the maximum value in the data set.
The maximum value =

_____.

3 Data set is given: 2, 5, 3, 1, 5, 2, 1, 3, 2, 4, 5, 1, 4, 5, 5, 5, 2, 7, 6, 7, 4, 1, 4, 7
Find the least frequent value in the data set.
The least frequent value =

_____.

4 Data set is given:
2, 3, 3, 1, 5, 1, 3, 2, 6, 4, 5, 3, 1, 4, 5, 5, 5, 2, 7, 6, 7, 3,4, 1, 4, 7, 3
Find the most frequent value in the data set.
The most frequent value in the data set =

_____

CONVERSIONS AND INTERPRET DATA

5.3   Measuring Data From Survey

5

Data set is given:

2, 3, 3, 1, 5, 1, 3, 2, 6, 4, 5, 3, 1, 4, 5, 5, 5, 2, 7, 6, 7, 3,4, 1, 4, 7, 3

Find the total number of values in the data set.

The total number of Xs =

_____.

6

A student rolls a dice multiple times and the following numbers appear:

2, 4, 5, 1, 1, 1, 6, 3, 4, 2, 5, 4, 2, 4, 5, 2, 3, 1, 4

Find the most frequent value in the data set.

The most frequent value in the data set =

_____.

7

The students received the following grades on the exam:

12, 8, 11, 12, 6, 7, 9, 10, 7, 6, 12, 7, 8, 9, 6, 10, 8, 10, 7, 6, 9, 12, 10, 6, 6, 9, 7, 8, 10, 7, 12, 7, 6, 9, 8, 7

Find the maximum value in the data set.

The maximum value =

_____

8 A teacher recorded the number of siblings of each student in the class:

3, 0, 3, 2, 2, 1, 0, 3, 4, 0, 0, 2, 4, 2, 0, 4, 0

What is the least number of siblings reported in the data set?

_____.

9 Kerry recorded the number of items sold and their prices.

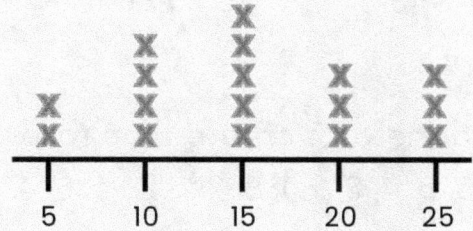

Which of the following statements is true?

(A) The total cost of items with a price of $10 is less than the total cost of items with a price of $20

(B) The total cost of items with a price of $10 is greater than the total cost of items with a price of $20

(C) The total cost of items with a price of $10 is equal to the total cost of items with a price of $20

(D) It is not possible to conclude

5.3 **Measuring Data From Survey**

10 Max recorded the number of apples sold and their prices.

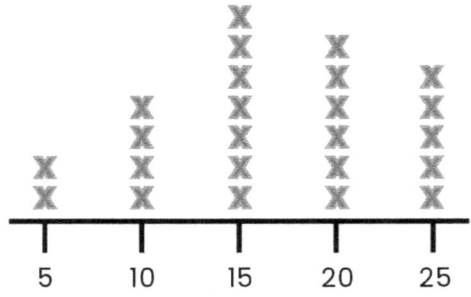

What is the total cost of all items cheaper than $15?

A) $10   B) $40   C) $30   D) $50

11 A random number generator created the following one−digit numbers: 2, 3, 3, 8, 6, 6, 4, 3, 2, 1, 8, 8, 5, 9, 4, 6, 4, 7, 3, 5, 2, 6, 2, 6, 8, 3, 3, 2, 1, 6, 9 , 5

Find the most frequent value in the data set.

The most frequent value in the data set is

_____.

12 Jack rolls a dice numerous times and the following numbers appear: 4, 2, 3, 6, 5, 7, 4, 6, 6, 4, 6, 2, 7, 6, 4, 5, 3, 6, 7, 5, 4, 2, 4, 6, 5, 6, 2, 7, 7, 4, 7, 6, 5, 3

Find the total number of values in the data set

13 A student rolls a dice numerous times and the following numbers appear: 6, 5, 7, 4, 2, 3, 4, 3, 7, 5, 6, 2, 3, 4, 4, 6, 4, 5, 6, 2, 5, 6, 4, 3, 2, 4, 3, 6, 3, 5, 4, 4, 2, 3, 3

Find the maximum value in the data set.

The maximum value is:

_____.

14 The students received the following grades on the exam:
9, 7, 8, 10, 6, 8, 7, 8, 10, 8, 9, 10, 7, 6, 9, 6, 8, 9, 7, 10, 8, 6, 7, 7, 10 , 8, 9, 6, 8, 9, 8, 7, 10, 9, 8, 10

Find the minimum value in the data set.

The minimum value is:

_____.

15 Marson recorded the points scored by football players:
6, 10, 12, 6, 6, 11, 8, 11, 10, 7, 7, 12 ,8, 9, 11, 6, 6, 8, 6

How many football players scored points?

Count the number of Xs:

_____.

5.3   **Measuring Data From Survey**

16 The teacher recorded the number of siblings of each student in the class:

4, 2, 1, 4, 3, 3, 0, 2, 2, 1, 4, 0, 1, 2, 1, 3, 3, 1, 3, 2, 2, 3, 2, 3, 2, 4, 1, 1, 2, 3, 4

How many students took part in the survey?

_____.

17 Jack recorded the number of cars for each household on the street: 1, 3, 1, 0, 2, 3, 2, 3, 2, 0, 2, 0, 2, 3, 1, 3, 0, 3, 0, 3, 3, 2, 0, 2

What is the highest number of cars from a household on the street?

(A) 0   (B) 1   (C) 2   (D) 3

18 Emily recorded the number of goals by handball players:
5, 3, 4, 2, 2, 1, 2, 1, 3, 1, 4, 3, 1, 3, 1, 5, 4, 3, 2, 1
What is the lowest number of goals for a handball player?
The lowest number of goals for a handball player is:

_____

19 Henry recorded the points scored by basketball players:

6, 10, 12, 6, 6, 11, 8, 11, 10, 7, 7, 12 ,8, 9, 11, 6, 6, 8, 6

What is the highest score by a basketball player?

The highest score for a basketball player is = _____ points.

20 Alvan measured the weight of the goat to the nearest tens of kilograms.

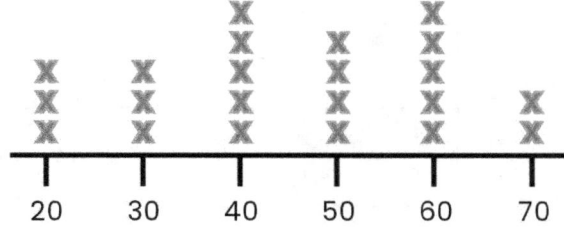

Which of the following statements is true?

(A) Goats with a weight of 40 kg are equal in weight to pigs with a weight of 50 kg

(B) Goats with a weight of 40 kg are heavier than pigs with a weight of 50 kg

(C) Goats with a weight of 40 kg are lighter than pigs with a weight of 50 kg

(D) It is not possible to conclude

Next Section: Interpret Graphs

INTERPRET GRAPHS

Interpreting graphs is the ability to read, understand and analyze data represented in graphical form. Graphs are visual representations of data that can help to identify patterns, trends, and relationships between variables. The different types of graphs commonly used include bar graphs, line graphs, scatter plots, and pie charts.

Identify Data as Numerical or Categorical

Data can be categorical or numerical.

Categorical data can be divided into specific groups: type of flowers, movie genre, favorite color, etc.

An example of a graph with categorical data is shown below.

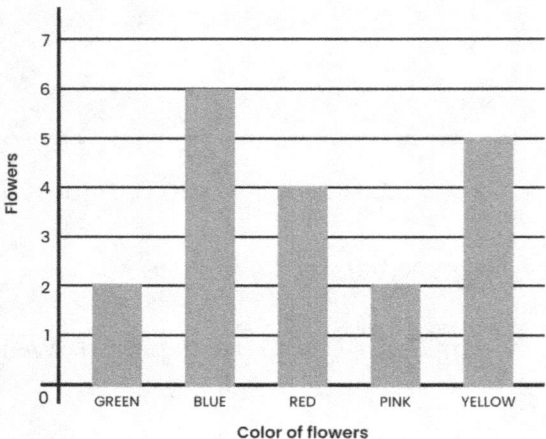

Numerical data can be discrete or continuous.

Discrete data is counted: number of people, number of cars, number of pages, etc.

Continuous data is measured: weight, temperature, speed, etc.

An example of a graph with numerical continuous data is shown below.

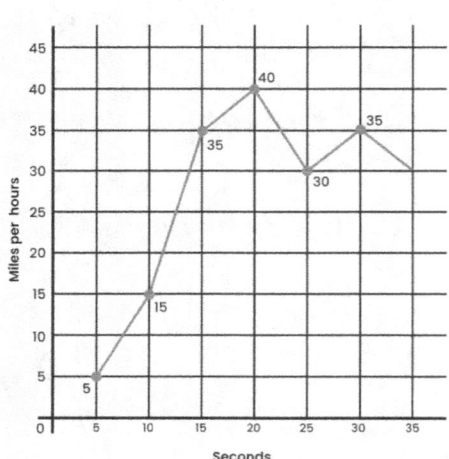

Interpret Graphs 5.4

1 Is the graph numerical or categorical?

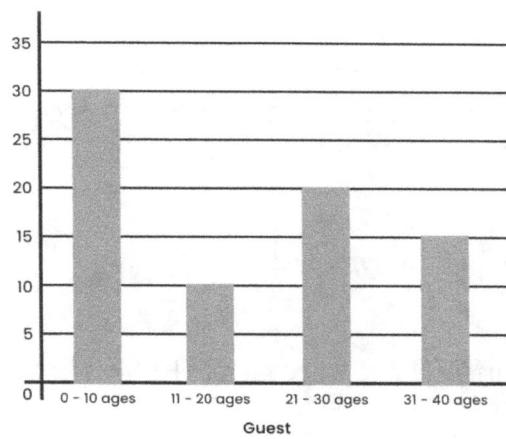

Guest

_____

2 Draw a bar graph using the given data.

Name of the fruit	Orange	Apple	Grapes	Banana	Kiwi
Number of students	48	25	32	10	20

5.4 Interpret Graphs

3 This list shows the number of miles Oliver runs on various days in the month of May.

$$2\frac{1}{7}, 2\frac{1}{6}, 2\frac{1}{2}, 2\frac{1}{4}, 2\frac{1}{3}, 2\frac{1}{8}, 2\frac{1}{6}, 2\frac{1}{4}, 2\frac{1}{3}$$

Oliver is making a line plot of this data. How many data points will be on the line plot?

A) 9   B) 8   C) 7   D) 10

4 This line plot shows the age range of the students in Mr. Cruz's class.

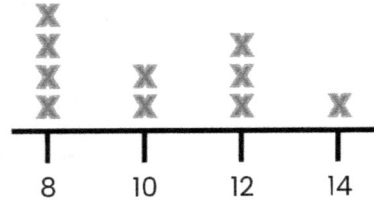

How many students are 12 and 14 years old?

A) 4   B) 5   C) 6   D) 8

5 This line plot displays the data collected on the weight of cats.

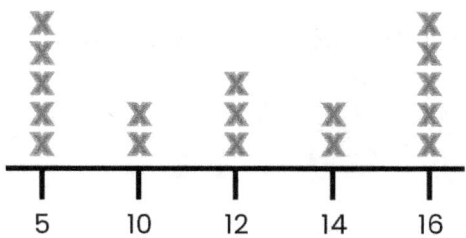

What is the difference between the weight of the heaviest cats and the lightest cats?

(A) 8 pounds   (B) 10 pounds   (C) 11 pounds   (D) 16 pounds

6 This line plot displays the data collected on the length of insects.

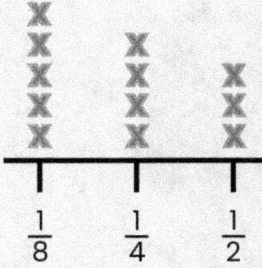

What is the combined length of the insects that are $\frac{1}{4}$ inch long?

(A) $\frac{1}{2}$ (B) 1   (C) $\frac{1}{4}$ (D) 2

5.4   Interpret Graphs

7   Complete a line plot created from the data set.

2, 3, 3, 4, 5, 6, 4, 3, 4, 5, 3, 2, 3, 6, 2, 4 , 5, 4

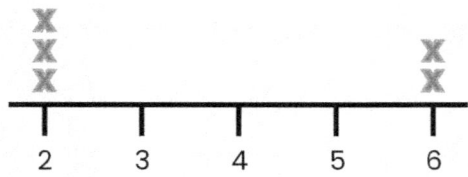

8   The pie chart shows the students favorite flavor of ice cream.

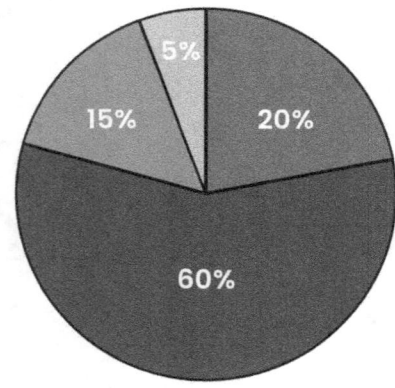

- Vanilla – 20%
- Strawberry – 60%
- Chocolate – 15%
- Orange – 5%

Is the graph numerical or categorical?

_____

9 How many crew members are there in total?

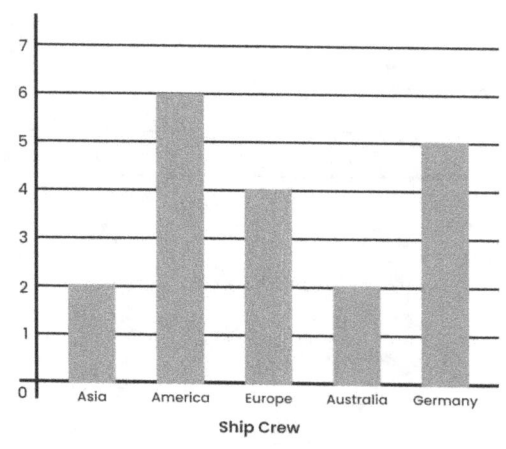

Ship Crew

(A) 21

(B) 20

(C) 17

(D) 19

10 Are there students with no pets?

Number of pets	0	1	2	3	4
Number of students	6	7	3	3	1

(A) Yes   (B) No

11 The pie chart shows the color of jersey that the basketball team most prefers.

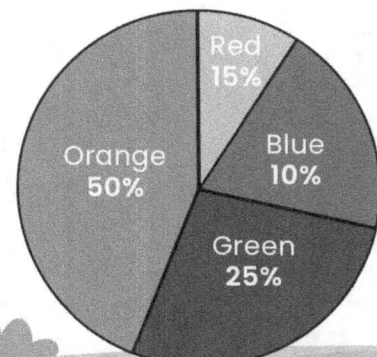

Which color jersey received the most votes?

(A) Green   (B) Red

(C) Blue   (D) Orange

5.4 Interpret Graphs

12 Are there students with no siblings?

Number of siblings	0	1	2	3	5
Number of students	6	9	4	6	1

Ⓐ Yes　　　Ⓑ No

13 Which month has the most visitors to the planetarium?

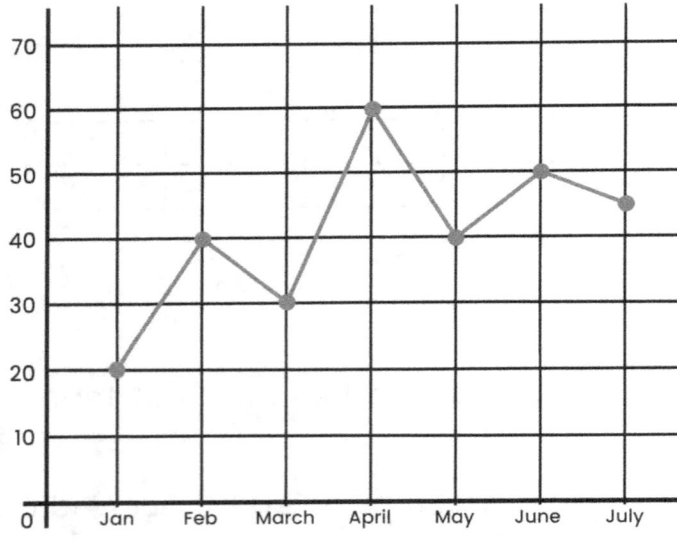

Ⓐ June

Ⓑ March

Ⓒ April

Ⓓ July

14 This line plot shows the temperatures recorded in the first six days of March.

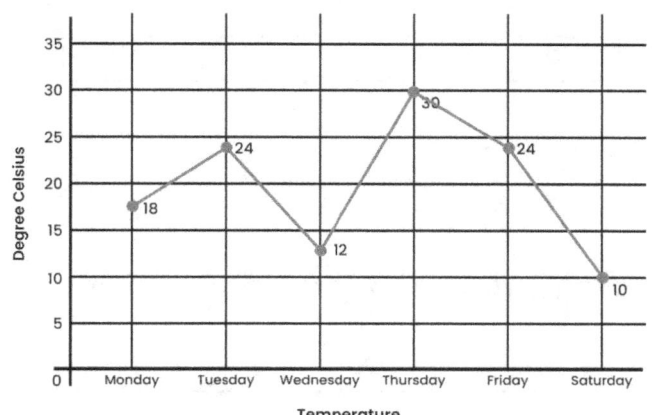

What was the average temperature on these six days?

(A) 20°C   (B) 18.3°C

(C) 19.7°C   (D) 17.7°C

15 This line plot shows the temperatures recorded in the first six months of last year.

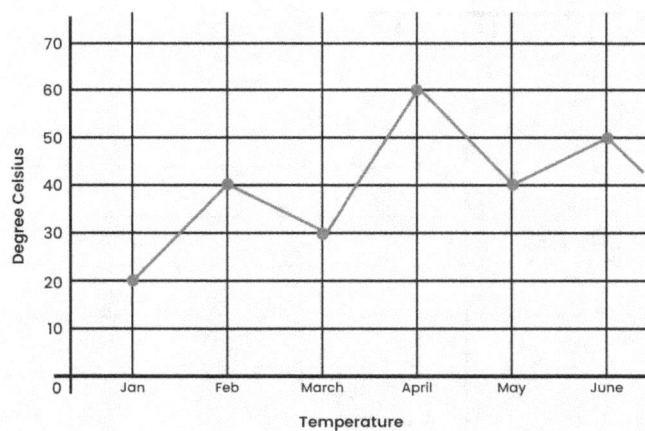

What was the least amount of temperature change between two months?

(A) 2°C   (B) 6°C

(C) 8°C   (D) 10°C

5.4 Interpret Graphs

16 Are there students with 4 pets?

Number of pets	0	1	2	3	4
Number of students	6	7	3	3	1

Ⓐ Yes   Ⓑ No

17 Complete a line plot that represents data reported in the following table:

Value	1	2	3	4	5
Frequency	5	3	1	2	3

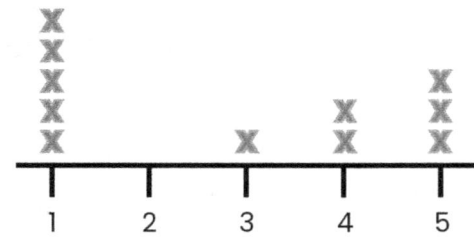

18 How many crew members are there in Asia and America?

Ⓐ 18   Ⓑ 19

Ⓒ 20   Ⓓ 21

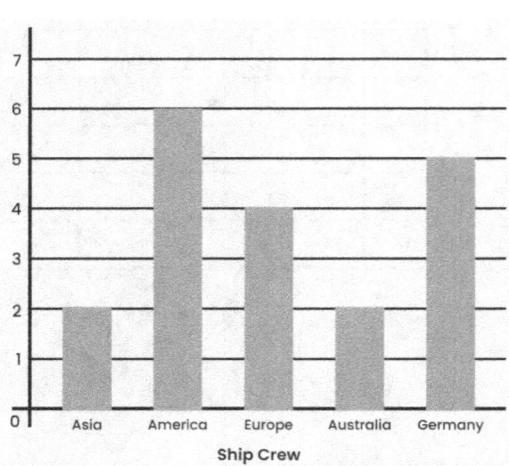

19 A group of students are playing snake ladder, and a dice is rolled 50 times. Which number does the dice land on most often?

1 – 15%; 2 – 20%; 3 – 10%;
4 – 25% ; 5 – 5%; 6 – 25%

(A) 4 (B) 2 (C) 6 (D) 1

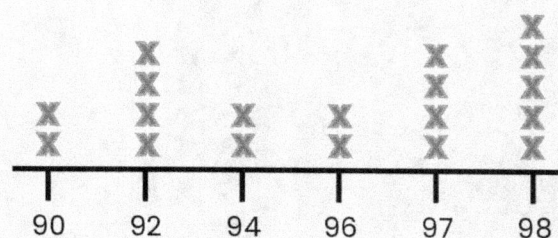

20 This line plot shows the temperatures recorded in California during a few weeks.

Next Section: Chapter Review

CONVERSIONS AND INTERPRET DATA

5.5   Chapter Review

1 Aubrey buys a 6-pound bag of oranges. The oranges weigh 12 ounces each. How many oranges are in the bag?

(A) 8   (B) 10   (C) 12   (D) 9

2 Rachel buys a 5-pound bag of apples. The apples weigh between 5.1 and 5.5 ounces each. Approximately how many apples are in the bag?

(A) 12   (B) 10

(C) 15   (D) 16

3 Peter buys a 8-pound bag of carrots. The carrots weigh 8 ounces each. How many carrots are in the bag?

(A) 12   (B) 10

(C) 15   (D) 16

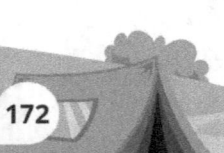

4 Dr. Paul uses this line plot to display the amount of growth her patients have had in one year.

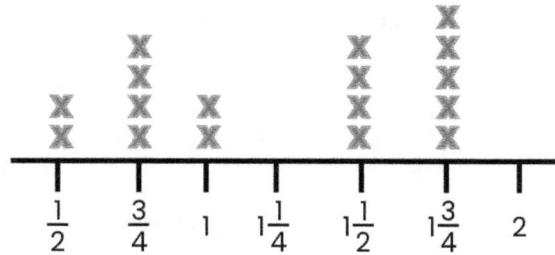

Which of the following is true?

(A) Dr. Paul has 12 patients

(B) No patient grew $1\frac{1}{4}$ or 2 inches

(C) The greatest amount of growth is 4 inches

(D) Most patients grew at least 1 inch

5 Lucy keeps track of how much paper is recycled by her class each week. The data is shown in this table:

Week	1	2	3	4	5	6	7
Amount of Paper (Pounds)	$\frac{1}{2}$	$\frac{1}{4}$	$\frac{3}{2}$	$\frac{1}{2}$	$\frac{1}{4}$	$\frac{2}{5}$	$3\frac{1}{3}$

Loria plans to use this data to create a line plot. How many data points will be on the line plot?

5.5 Chapter Review

6 Two apples and three pears weigh 2 kg 200 grams. Three apples and two peaches weigh 2.5 kg. Two pears and three peaches weigh 0.8 kg. How much, in grams, do one apple, one pear, and one peach weigh?

- (A) 1000 grams
- (B) 1100 grams
- (C) 2500 grams
- (D) 2100 grams

7 If 10 quarts = 16x fluid ounces, what is the value of x ?

- (A) 20
- (B) 25
- (C) 30
- (D) 35

8 Mr. Jones' car weighs 2.6 tons. What is the weight of his car in pounds?

- (A) 2,200 pounds
- (B) 3,200 pounds
- (C) 4,200 pounds
- (D) 5,200 pounds

9 A truck can carry up to 14,000 kilograms of supplies. What is the maximum number of supplies (in tons) the truck can carry?

- (A) 1.4 tons
- (B) 1.4 tons
- (C) 4 tons
- (D) 5 tons

10 Riley makes necklaces using beads that are 12 millimeters in diameter. What is the length of the necklace if Riley uses 36 beads?

A) 0.432 cm

B) 432 cm

C) 4.32 cm

D) 43.2 cm

11 Avery's goal was to bike 2.5 kilometers yesterday. She biked 700 meters from her house to the store, and then biked 760 meters to the library. How many more meters does she need to bike to reach her goal?

A) 1,060 m

B) 1,050 m

C) 1,040 m

D) 1,030 m

12 Quinn bought 10 gallons of juice for the party. She poured it into 2.5 - quart jars. How many jars did Quinn fill with juice?

A) 10 jars

B) 12 jars

C) 14 jars

D) 16 jars

5.5   **Chapter Review**

13 First, Mrs. Morgan watched two episodes of her favorite TV series, which lasted 40 minutes each and then a cooking show that lasted 1 hour and 40 minutes. How much time did Mrs. Morgan spend watching TV?

(A) 1 hour 50 minutes   (B) 2 hours 20 minutes

(C) 3 hours   (D) 4 hours

14 Cleo's backpack weighs 3.5 pounds when it is empty. Cleo's backpack weighs 8 pounds when it has books and notebooks inside of it. How much do the books and notebooks weigh in Cleo's backpack?

(A) 72 ounces   (B) 82 ounces

(C) 74 ounces   (D) 84 ounces

15 Max drinks 1 cup of water every 180 minutes. How many pints of water does he drink per day?
(Assume Max is not sleeping the whole day)

(A) 2 pints   (B) 4 pints

(C) 6 pints   (D) 8 pints

16 This line plot shows the weight of 12 kiwis. How would you determine the difference between the heaviest and the lightest kiwi?

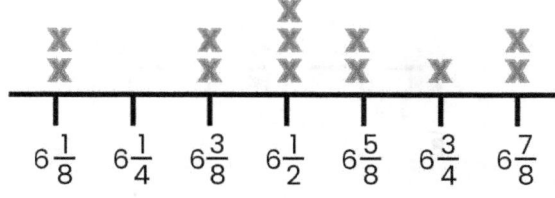

Weight of kiwis (Ounces)

_____

17 If 20 quarts = 16x fluid ounces, what is the value of x ?

A) 20 B) 40 C) 30 D) 50

18 This line plot displays the amount of juice consumed by the students in a class.

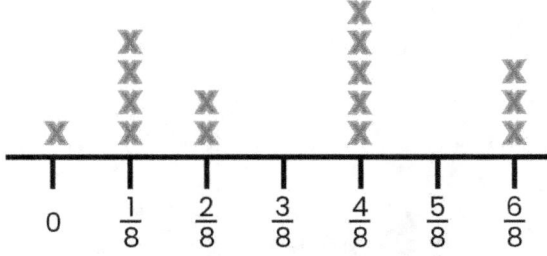

Quart of juice consumed

Write 3-4 sentences describing the data represented in this line plot.

_____

19 This line plot displays the length of some leaves Cruz collected.

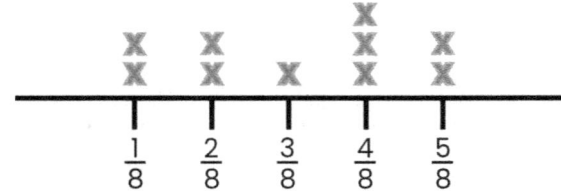

Leaf of length (Inches)

How many leaves did Cruz collect?

(A) 10   (B) 9   (C) 8   (D) 7

20 The data given below shows the average rainfall from Week 1 to Week 4 during the month of May. Draw a pie chart to represent this information.

Week of May	1	2	3	4
Average rainfall	20cm	40cm	30cm	10cm

Next Chapter:
Measurement: Volumes

CHAPTER 6

MEASUREMENT VOLUMES

COUNTING AND MULTIPLICATION FOR CUBES

Counting and multiplication for cubes refer to the understanding of the relationship between the number of cubes and the total volume of a three-dimensional figure. It involves using cubes to visually represent and understand multiplication and the concept of volume.

Count Cubes to Determine Volume

The volume is expressed in cubic units, and can be represented by unit cubes.

If you completely fill a prism with unit cubes and count the number of cubes, you will get the volume of the prism.

Relate Volume to Multiplication

The volume is expressed in cubic units, and can be represented by unit cubes.

If you completely fill a prism with unit cubes and count the number of cubes, you will get the volume of the prism.

You can count the number of cubes using multiplication. The unit cubes in a prism are arranged in layers. Count the number of cubes in one layer and multiply by the number of layers to find the volume of the prism.

COUNTING AND MULTIPLICATION FOR CUBES

Example:

Find the volume of the prism shown below using the unit cubes.

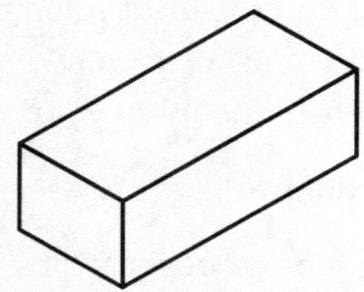

Fill the prism with unit cubes.

Count the cubes.

There are 8 cubes in the top layer, and the same number of cubes are in the bottom layer.

Therefore, the volume of the prism is 16 cubic units.

If the volume of the cube is 1 cubic inch, we say that the volume of the prism is 16 cubic inches.

If the volume of the cube is 1 cubic foot, we say that the volume of the prism is 16 cubic feet.

If the volume of the cube is 1 cubic yard, we say that the volume of the prism is 16 cubic yards.

And so on. We can use any unit to express volume. We just call it – a cubic unit.

Counting and Multiplication For Cubes | **6.1**

1 Find the number of cubes needed to make each rectangular prism. You can use unit cubes or you can count the cubes by looking at the drawing.

(A) 6   (B) 12   (C) 8   (D) 4

2 Find the number of cubes needed to make each rectangular prism. You can use unit cubes or you can count the cubes by looking at the drawing.

(A) 16   (B) 20   (C) 12   (D) 14

3 The volume of the small cube is 1 cubic inch. What is the volume of the prism?

(A) 16 cubic inches   (B) 12 cubic inches

(C) 24 cubic inches   (D) 30 cubic inches

6.1 **Counting and Multiplication For Cubes**

4 Select the prism with the greater volume.

 (A)

(B)

5 Fill in the blank:

The volume of the prism is

_____ cubic units.

6 The washing machine can be completely filled with the cubes shown below. The volume of each cube is 1 cubic foot. What is the volume of the washing machine?

 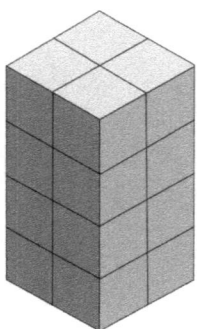

(A) 16 cubic inches   (B) 12 cubic inches

(C) 20 cubic inches   (D) 15 cubic inches

7 The wardrobe can be completely filled with the cubes shown below. The volume of each cube is 1 cubic foot. What is the volume of the wardrobe?

(A) 20 cubic feet

(B) 28 cubic feet

(C) 18 cubic feet

(D) 25 cubic feet

8 The red prism is partially filled with unit cubes. Count the visible and missing cubes to find the volume of the prism in terms of cubic feet.

(A) 38 cubic feet

(B) 28 cubic feet

(C) 48 cubic feet

(D) 25 cubic feet

MEASUREMENT: VOLUMES

9   Fill in the blank:

The volume of the prism is

_____ cubic units.

---

10   Use multiplication to find the number of cubes needed to make each rectangular prism.

Number of Layers		Number of Cubes in One Layer		Volume
	×		=	

Ⓐ 6   Ⓑ 16   Ⓒ 12   Ⓓ 10

---

11   Use multiplication to find the number of cubes needed to make each rectangular prism.

Number of Layers		Number of Cubes in One Layer		Volume
	×		=	

Ⓐ 6   Ⓑ 16   Ⓒ 12   Ⓓ 10

Counting and Multiplication For Cubes   6.1

12   Which product represents the volume of the prism?

(A) 3 × 4   (B) 4 × 4

(C) 3 × 5   (D) 3 × 6

13   Find the volume of the prism as a product of the number of layers and the number of cubes in each layer.

_____ × _____ = _____.

(A) 2×7=14   (B) 2×8=16

(C) 3×8=24   (D) 3×6=18

14   Multiply the number of layers and the number of cubes in each layer to find the volume of each prism. Then select the prism with the greater volume.

(A)    (B)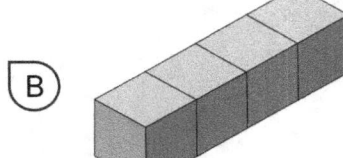

6.1 **Counting and Multiplication For Cubes**

15 Multiply the number of layers and the number of cubes in each layer to find the volume of each prism. Then select the prism with the greater volume.

Ⓐ

Ⓑ

16 Fill in the blanks:

There are _____ layers with _____ cubes in each layer.

The volume of the prism is _____ cubic units.

17 The book can be completely filled with the cubes shown below. The volume of each cube is 1 cubic foot. Find the volume of the book.

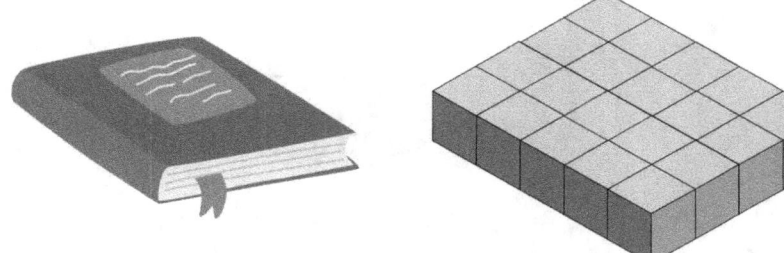

Number of Layers		Number of Cubes in One Layer		Volume
	×		=	

(A) 1×20=20   (B) 1×15=15   (C) 2×5=10   (D) 1×25=25

18 The red prism is partially filled with unit cubes. Find the number of layers and the number of cubes in each layer. Find the volume of the prism in cubic units.

_____ × _____ = _____.

(A) 2×12=24 cubic units

(B) 4×12=48 cubic units

(C) 3×12=36 cubic units

(D) 2×11=22 cubic units

6.1 **Counting and Multiplication For Cubes**

---

19 Find the volume of the prism as a product of the number of layers and the number of cubes in each layer.

_____ × _____ = _____ cubic units.

(A) 5×2=10 cubic units

(B) 4×2=8 cubic units

(C) 3×2=6 cubic units

(D) 5×3=15 cubic units

---

20 Find the number of cubes needed to make each rectangular prism. You can use unit cubes or you can count the cubes by looking at the drawing.

(A) 12   (B) 15

(C) 20   (D) 10

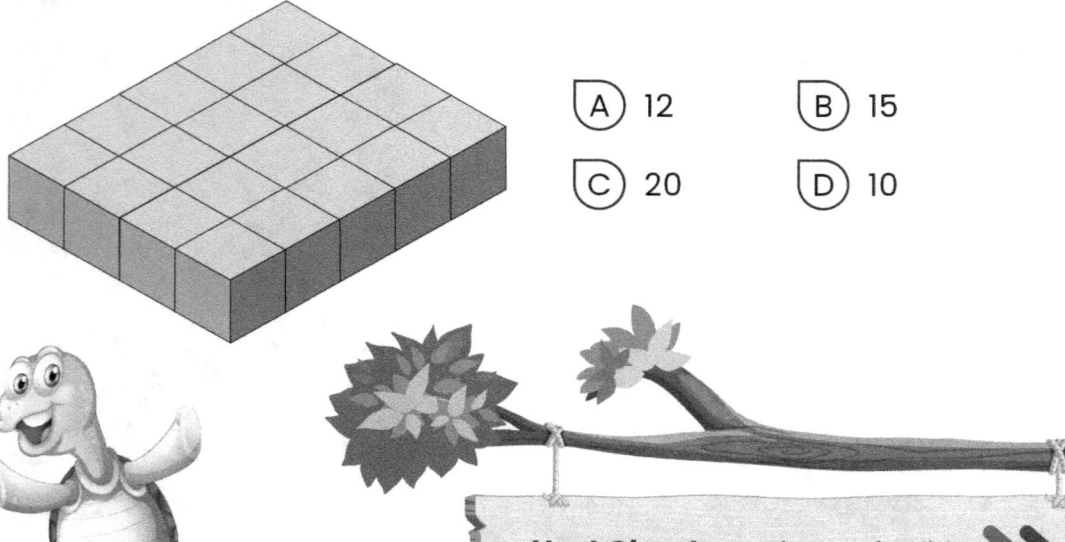

Next Chapter: Volume of Solids »

VOLUME OF SOLIDS

The volume of a solid is the amount of space occupied by the object. For three-dimensional objects, such as cubes, rectangular prisms, cylinders, cones, and spheres, volume is typically measured in cubic units such as cubic centimeters (cm^3) or cubic meters (m^3).

If the solid consists of two or more prisms, then the volume of the solid is equal to the sum of the volume of all the prisms.

Example: Find the volume of the solid shown below.

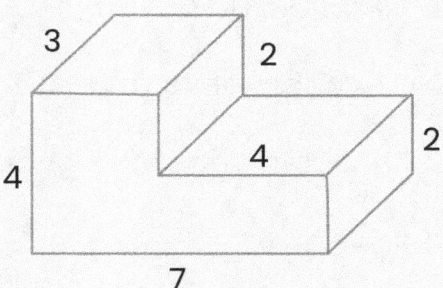

Solution: The solid consists of two prisms: red and green.

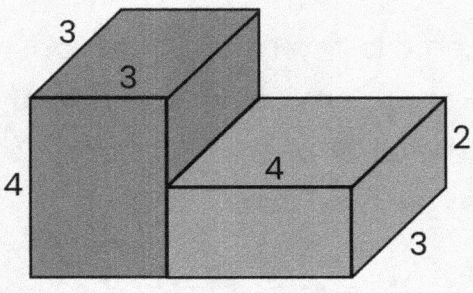

The volume of the red prism is 3×3×4 = 36 cubic units.
The volume of the green prism is 4×3×2 = 24 cubic units.
The volume of the solid is equal to the sum of the volume of the red and green prisms: 36+24 = 60 cubic units.

6.2 Volume of Solids

1 Lisa fills two rectangular prisms with 66 unit cubes.
Both prisms have 3 layers of cubes. The number of cubes in the first layer of the smaller rectangular prism is 6. What is the volume of both prisms?

- A) 10 cubic units and 42 cubic units
- B) 18 cubic units and 48 cubic units
- C) 24 cubic units and 32 cubic units
- D) 14 cubic units and 48 cubic units

2 Leo fills two rectangular prisms with 108 unit cubes.
Both prisms have 4 layers of cubes. The number of cubes in the first layer of the smaller rectangular prism is 9. What is the volume of both prisms?

- A) 20 cubic units and 42 cubic units
- B) 36 cubic units and 72 cubic units
- C) 34 cubic units and 52 cubic units
- D) 24 cubic units and 68 cubic units

3 Tom is filling a box with centimeter cubes. The height of the box is 42 centimeters, and he can fit 48 cubes in the base of the box. How many cubes will fill the box?

(A) 2016   (B) 2015   (C) 2014   (D) 2013

4 Which tables show the dimensions of a box that can be filled completely with 1200-centimeter cubes?

(A)

Length	Width	Height
25	16	3

(B)

Length	Width	Height
20	15	2

(C)

Length	Width	Height
10	15	2

(D)

Length	Width	Height
10	15	5

5 Aaron is filling a box with centimeter cubes. The height of the box is 30 centimeters, and he can fit 36 cubes in the base of the box. How many cubes will fill the box?

(A) 1680   (B) 86   (C) 1080   (D) 66

6.2 Volume of Solids

6 Robert is measuring a cereal box with centimeter cubes. The box is filled to the halfway point when it has 300 cubes in it. The cereal box has a height of 20 centimeters.

Which picture represents one layer of cubes inside Robert's cereal box?

Ⓐ

Ⓑ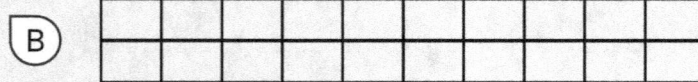

Ⓒ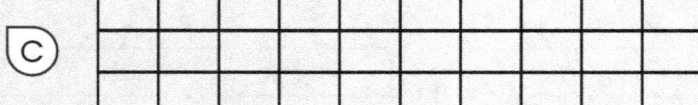

Ⓓ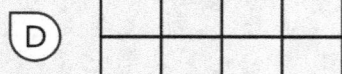

7 Myra wants to fill this box with $\frac{1}{2}$ inch cubes. How many cubes are needed to fill this box?

The box is 6 inches in length, 4 inches in height, and 2 inches in width. How many cubes are needed to fill this box?

Ⓐ 384 cubes

Ⓑ 415 cubes

Ⓒ 56 cubes

Ⓓ 100 cubes

8 A company packs 600 smaller boxes inside large crates to be shipped to stores. Each small box is in the shape of a cube and has edge lengths of 0.8 feet. The large crate is also in the shape of a cube with each side as a length of 4 feet. How many crates are needed to ship these boxes?

(A) 3   (B) 5   (C) 416   (D) 212

9 Which prism has the greatest volume?

	Length (in.)	Width (in.)	Height (in.)
Prism A	10	2	2
Prism B	4	1	5
Prism C	6	5	2
Prism D	3	4	4

(A) Prism A   (B) Prism B   (C) Prism C   (D) Prism D

10 Which Prism has the smallest volume?

	Length (in.)	Width (in.)	Height (in.)
Prism A	10	2	2
Prism B	4	1	5
Prism C	6	5	2
Prism D	3	4	4

(A) Prism A   (B) Prism B   (C) Prism C   (D) Prism D

6.2 Volume of Solids

11 Find the volume of the solid.

(A) 12 cubic units   (B) 8 cubic units

(C) 16 cubic units   (D) 10 cubic units

12 Which sum represents the volume of the solid?

(A) V = 6+10 cubic units

(B) V = 8+8 cubic units

(C) V = 8+10 cubic units

(D) V = 4+10 cubic units

13 Find the volume of the solid as a sum of the volumes of prisms it consists of.

_____ × _____ = _____

(A) 12 + 8 = 20   (B) 12 + 10 = 22

(C) 10 + 8 = 18   (D) 12 + 12 = 24

14 Select the solid with greater volume.

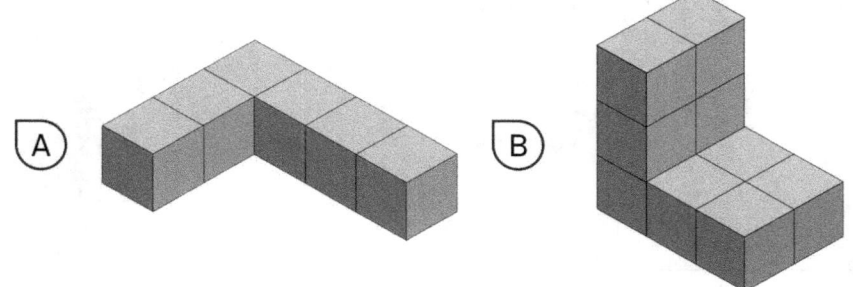

15 Fill in the blanks.

The volume of the solid is

_____ cubic units.

16 A company packs 1000 smaller boxes inside large crates to be shipped to stores. Each small box is in the shape of a cube and has edge lengths of 0.4 feet. The large crate is also in the shape of a cube with each side as a length of 2 feet. How many crates are needed to ship these boxes?

(A) 8   (B) 16   (C) 26   (D) 32

6.2   **Volume of Solids**

17 Sam is making blocks of steel. How much steel does he need for each digit? Each cube is 2 inches high.

_____

18 Sarah is making blocks of steel. How much steel does he need for each digit? Each cube is 3 inches high.

A. 459 cubic inches

B. 350 cubic inches

C. 315 cubic inches

D. 415 cubic inches

19 Edward is making digits of steel. How much steel does he need for each digit? Each cube is 5 inches high.

A. 1000 cubic inches   B. 1110 cubic inches

C. 990 cubic inches   D. 850 cubic inches

20 Fill in the blanks.

The volume of the solid is _____ cubic units.

Next Section:
Word Problems Using Formulas

WORD PROBLEMS USING FORMULAS

Lesson Introduction:

We can use formulas to find the volume of a prism.

The volume of any solid is the product of the area of a base (B) and the height (h) of the solid.

$$V = Bh$$

In the case of a rectangular prism the volume is equal to the product of its dimensions.

$$V = lwh$$

Example:

Find the volume of the rectangular prism with a base area of 12 in^2 and height of 4 in.

Solution:

B = 12 in^2, h = 4 in.

V = Bh = 12 ×4 in = 48 in^3.

Word Problems Using Formulas   **6.3**

1 Find the volume of the rectangular prism given its base area and height.

$$B = 14 \text{ in}^2, h = 6 \text{ in}$$

(A) 84   (B) 76   (C) 66   (D) 68

2 Find the volume of the rectangular prism given its base area and height.

$$B = 20 \text{ in}^2, h = 5 \text{ in}$$

(A) 84   (B) 100   (C) 96   (D) 78

3 Find the volume of the rectangular prism given its dimensions.

$$l = 4, w = 8, h = 3 \text{ in}$$

(A) 85 in^2 (B) 110 in^2 (C) 96 in^2 (D) 100 in^2

4 Fill in the blanks to find the volume of the prism shown.

V = _____ × _____ × _____ = _____ cubic units.

6.3   **Word Problems Using Formulas**

---

5 Find the height of the prism given its volume and base area.

$$V = 160, B = 20$$

(A) 8   (B) 12   (C) 10   (D) 16

---

6 Find the height of the prism given its volume and base area.

$$V = 280, B = 14$$

(A) 12   (B) 20   (C) 10   (D) 16

---

7 The base area of the open drawer is 20 square inches, and its height is 6 inches. Find the volume of the drawer.

(A) 60   (B) 100

(C) 55   (D) 120

---

8 Find the base area of the prism given its volume and height.

$$V = 560, h = 20$$

(A) 28   (B) 20   (C) 16   (D) 18

Word Problems Using Formulas — 6.3

9 The base area of the cupboard is 11 square feet, and its volume is 440 cubic feet. What is the height of the cupboard?

(A) 28　　(B) 40　　(C) 36　　(D) 48

10 If you triple the width and length of a rectangular prism, how many times does its volume increase?

(A) 10　　(B) 9　　(C) 6　　(D) 8

11 Find the volume of the rectangular prism given its base area and height.

$$B = 20 \text{ in}^2, h = 11 \text{ in}$$

(A) 110　　(B) 220　　(C) 215　　(D) 250

12 Find the volume of the rectangular prism given its base area and height.

$$B = 55 \text{ in}^2, h = 22 \text{ in}$$

(A) 1110　　(B) 1220　　(C) 1210　　(D) 1250

6.3 Word Problems Using Formulas

---

13 Find the height of the prism given its volume and base area.

$$V = 560, B = 40$$

(A) 22   (B) 12   (C) 14   (D) 16

---

14 Find the height of the prism given its volume and base area.

$$V = 450, B = 30$$

(A) 22   (B) 12   (C) 14   (D) 15

---

15 Find the volume of the rectangular prism given its dimensions.

$$l = 12, w = 24, h = 6 \text{ in}$$

(A) 1728 in²   (B) 1510 in²   (C) 916 in²   (D) 1700 in²

---

16 Fill in the blanks to find the volume of the prism shown.

V = _____ × _____ × _____ = _____ cubic units.

17 Find the base of the prism given its volume and height.

$$V = 465, h = 15$$

(A) 22   (B) 32   (C) 31   (D) 25

18 Find the volume of the rectangular prism given its dimensions.

$$l = 10, w = 15, h = 5 \text{ in}$$

(A) 728 in²   (B) 750 in²   (C) 715 in²   (D) 700 in²

19 Find the base of the prism given its volume and height.

$$V = 560, h = 14$$

(A) 42   (B) 40   (C) 36   (D) 20

20 If you triple the width and height of a rectangular prism, how many times does its volume increase?

(A) 8   (B) 9   (C) 4   (D) 5

Next Section: Chapter Review

6.4 Chapter Review

1 Find the number of cubes needed to make each rectangular prism. You can use unit cubes or you can count the cubes by looking at the drawing.

(A) 6   (B) 12   (C) 8   (D) 4

2 The volume of the small cube is 1 cubic inch. What is the volume of the cube?

(A) 32   (B) 22   (C) 16   (D) 30

3 Fill in the blank.

The volume of the prism is _____ cubic units.

4 Use multiplication to find the number of cubes needed to make each rectangular prism.

Number of Layers		Number of Cubes in One Layer		Volume
	×		=	

(A) 6   (B) 16   (C) 12   (D) 10

5 Find the volume of the prism as a product of the number of layers and the number of cubes in each layer.

_____ × _____ = _____

(A) 2×24 = 48

(B) 2×8 = 16

(C) 3×8 = 24

(D) 3×6 = 18

6.4   **Chapter Review**

6   Find the number of cubes needed to make each rectangular prism. You can use unit cubes or you can count the cubes by looking at the drawing.

(A) 12   (B) 16   (C) 20   (D) 10

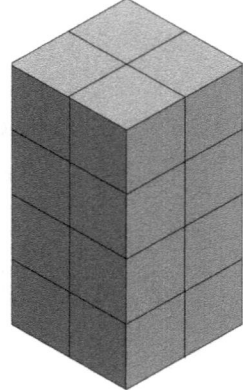

7   Eda fills two rectangular prisms with 44 unit cubes.
Both prisms have 2 layers of cubes. The number of cubes in the first layer of the smaller rectangular prism is 4.
What is the volume of both prisms?

(A) 8 cubic units and 36 cubic units

(B) 18 cubic units and 48 cubic units

(C) 24 cubic units and 32 cubic units

(D) 14 cubic units and 48 cubic units

8   Amy is filling a box with centimeter cubes. The height of the box is 40 centimeters, and he can fit 56 cubes in the base of the box. How many cubes will fill the box?

(A) 2240   (B) 86   (C) 1080   (D) 96

9

Lisa is making blocks of steel. How much steel does she need for each digit? Each cube is 6 inches high.

_____ cubic inches.

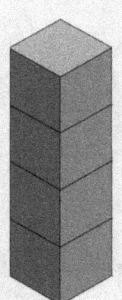

10

Sam is making blocks of steel. How much steel does he need for each digit?
Each cube is 4 inches high.

(A) 320 cubic inches   (B) 550 cubic inches

(C) 615 cubic inches   (D) 415 cubic inches

11

Find the volume of the rectangular prism given its base area and height.

$$B = 15 \text{ in}^2, h = 6 \text{ in}$$

(A) 84   (B) 90   (C) 66   (D) 68

6.4   Chapter Review

---

12 Find the volume of the rectangular prism given its dimensions.

$$l = 7, w = 14, h = 5 \text{ in}$$

(A) 385 in²   (B) 110 in²   (C) 490 in²   (D) 590 in²

---

13 Find the height of the prism given its volume and base area.

$$V = 250, B = 25$$

(A) 8   (B) 12   (C) 10   (D) 16

---

14 Find the base area of the prism given its volume and height.

$$V = 480, h = 16$$

(A) 12   (B) 20   (C) 10   (D) 30

---

15 If the width and length of a rectangular prism are 4 times, how many times does its volume increase?

(A) 10   (B) 9   (C) 16   (D) 8

16 The base area of the mirror is 10 square feet, and its volume is 550 cubic feet. What is the height of the mirror?

(A) 55   (B) 32

(C) 66   (D) 25

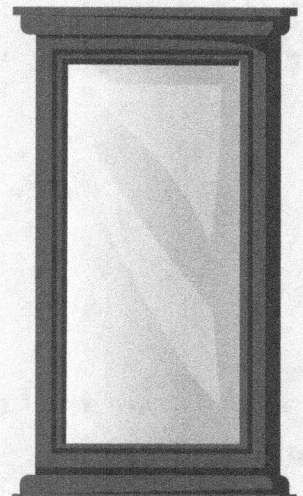

17 Find the volume of the rectangular prism given its base area and height.

$$B = 30 \text{ in}^2, h = 16 \text{ in}$$

(A) 410   (B) 450   (C) 480   (D) 550

18 Find the volume of the rectangular prism given its dimensions.

$$l = 10 \text{ in}, w = 30 \text{ in}, h = 7 \text{ in}$$

(A) 1728 in²   (B) 2100 in²

(C) 916 in²   (D) 1700 in²

6.4   **Chapter Review**

19 Find the base of the prism given its volume and height.

$$V = 300, h = 15$$

(A) 20   (B) 32   (C) 31   (D) 25

20 Find the volume of the rectangular prism given its base area and height.

$$B = 8 \text{ in}^2, h = 4 \text{ in}$$

(A) 11   (B) 32   (C) 25   (D) 34

Next Chapter:
Geometric Measurement

CHAPTER 7

GEOMETRIC MEASUREMENT

FIND THE WAY

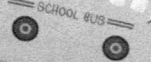

PROPERTIES OF SIDES, ANGLES, AND SYMMETRY

Properties of sides and angles

Lesson Introduction:

Quadrilaterals are closed 2-D shapes with sides, angles, and vertices.

Name of the quadrilateral	Properties of sides	Properties of angles
Parallelogram	• Two pairs of parallel opposite sides • Two pairs of equal opposite sides	• Two pairs of parallel opposite angles • Every two consecutive angles add upto 180°
Rectangle	• Two pairs of opposite parallel sides • Two pairs of equal opposite sides • Every two adjacent sides are perpendicular	• Four right angles
Square	• Two pairs of opposite parallel sides • Four equal sides • Every two adjacent sides are perpendicular	• Four right angles
Rhombus	• Two pairs of parallel opposite sides • Four equal sides	• Two pairs of opposite parallel angles • Every two consecutive angles add up to 180°
Trapezoid	One pair of opposite parallel sides. Note: Isosceles trapezoid has one pair of not parallel equal sides.	Two angles adjacent to each are, not parallel sides add up to 180°. Note: Isosceles trapezoid has an angle adjacent to the bases that are equal sides.

PROPERTIES OF SIDES, ANGLES, AND SYMMETRY

Properties of symmetry

A line of symmetry divides a figure into two equal parts, each of which is the mirror image of the other.

The main task is to learn to distinguish how many lines of symmetry a figure has.

There are figures that have no lines of symmetry, for example a scalene triangle has no lines of symmetry.

There are figures that have many lines of symmetry, for example the circle has infinitely many lines of symmetry.

Example: If the perimeter of the rhombus is 168° in, what is the length of each side of the rhombus?

Solution: Each rhombus has four equal sides, therefore:
Perimeter of the rhombus = 4 (Sides)
If the perimeter of the rhombus is 168 in, then:

$$168 \text{ in} = 4(\text{Sides}) \Rightarrow \text{Side} = \frac{168}{4} = 42 \text{ in.}$$

1 If the length of the side of the square is 12 cm, what is the perimeter of the square?

(A) 24   (B) 48   (C) 36   (D) 60

2 If the perimeter of the square is 72 in, what is the length of each side of the square?

(A) 32   (B) 46   (C) 38   (D) 18

3 If the length of the side of the rhombus is 23 ft, what is the perimeter of the rhombus?

(A) 92 ft   (B) 84 ft   (C) 98 ft   (D) 76 ft

4 In a parallelogram, the longest side is 19 cm long, the shortest side is 11 cm long. What is the perimeter of the parallelogram?

(A) 40   (B) 55   (C) 60   (D) 86

5 If the perimeter of a rhombus is 92 in, what is the length of each side of the rhombus?

(A) 23   (B) 17   (C) 35   (D) 51

7.1   **Properties of Sides, Angles, and Symmetry**

6 In a parallelogram, the longest side is 20 cm long, and its perimeter equals 58 cm. What is the length of the shortest side of the parallelogram?

A) 17   B) 6   C) 11   D) 9

7 In a parallelogram, the shortest side is 8 in long, and its perimeter equals 48 in. What is the length of the longest side of the parallelogram?

A) 24   B) 16   C) 20   D) 18

8 In an isosceles trapezoid, two bases have lengths of 25 in and 17 in. If the perimeter of the trapezoid is 68 in, what is the length of each of the non-parallel sides?

A) 34in   B) 23in   C) 13in   D) 19in

9 In a rectangle, the longest side is 24 cm long and the shortest side is 16 cm long. What is the area of the rectangle?

A) 384 cm²   B) 342 cm²   C) 426 cm²   D) 486 cm²

Properties of Sides, Angles, and Symmetry **7.1**

10 In a rectangle, the longest side is 6 in long and its area equals 30 in². What is the length of the shortest side of the rectangle?

(A) 20 in   (B) 15 in   (C) 10 in   (D) 5 in

11 If quadrilateral PQRS is an isosceles trapezoid, what is the measure of angle R?

(A) 30°   (B) 40°

(C) 60°   (D) 80°

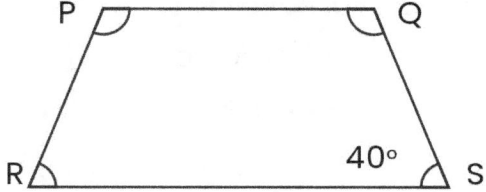

12 If quadrilateral STUV is a rhombus, what is the measure of angle V?

(A) 70°   (B) 50°

(C) 90°   (D) 60°

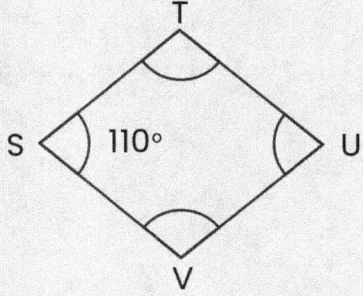

13 In a rhombus the opposite angles are equal.

(A) True   (B) False

GEOMETRIC MEASUREMENT

7.1 Properties of Sides, Angles, and Symmetry

14 Mary drew a triangle in her notebook. She measured two of its angles and came up with 60° and 75°. What would the measure of the third angle be?

(A) 60° (B) 55° (C) 45° (D) 75°

15 Rachel drew a quadrilateral in her notebook. She measured two of its angles and came up with 90° each. What would the measure of the remaining angles be if these angles were equal also?

(A) 180° (B) 90° (C) 60° (D) 120°

16 Sofia drew a triangle. She measured two of its angles and came up with 75° each. What would the measure of the third angle be?

(A) 145° (B) 85° (C) 120° (D) 30°

17 What is the measure of angle B in quadrilateral ABCD?

(A) 80° (B) 85°
(C) 90° (D) 95°

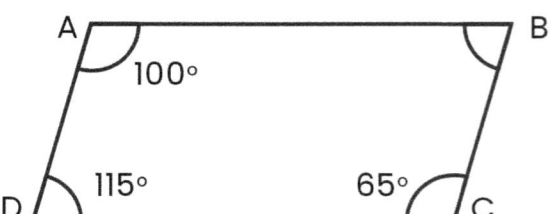

A   100°   B
D   115°   65°   C

18 How many lines of symmetry does the regular hexagon below have?

(A) 12

(B) 10

(C) 6

(D) 9

19 Which of the following statements is false?

(A) A parallelogram has no lines of symmetry.

(B) A trapezoid has four lines of symmetry.

(C) A square has four lines of symmetry.

(D) An equilateral triangle has three lines of symmetry.

20 James is playing with a kite. How many lines of symmetry does the kite have?

(A) 1

(B) 2

(C) 4

(D) 0

Next Section: Area of Rectangles, Squares, Rhombuses, and Trapezoids ≫

AREA OF RECTANGLES, SQUARES, RHOMBUSES, AND TRAPEZOIDS

The area of a rectangle is found by multiplying its length by its width. The area of a square is found by squaring its side length. The area of a rhombus can be found by multiplying the lengths of its diagonals and dividing by 2. The area of a trapezoid is found by multiplying the average of the parallel sides (the height) by the distance between the parallel sides (the length of the base)

A <u>rhombus</u> is a parallelogram with four equal sides.

A <u>rectangle</u> is a parallelogram with four right angles.

A <u>square</u> is a rectangle with four equal sides.

Properties:

- The diagonals of a rhombus bisect one another.
- The diagonals of a rhombus bisect rhombus's angles.
- The diagonals of a rhombus are perpendicular.

A <u>trapezoid</u> is a quadrilateral with only one pair of parallel sides.

The <u>perimeter</u> of a quadrilateral is the distance around the quadrilateral.

Area:

Area of rhombus = Side×Height

$\qquad\qquad$ = 1/2 × Diagonal 1 × Diagonal 2

Area of trapezoid = Average Width × Height

Area of rectangle = Length × Width

Area of square = side^2

Example:

Find the area of the rectangle:

Solution:

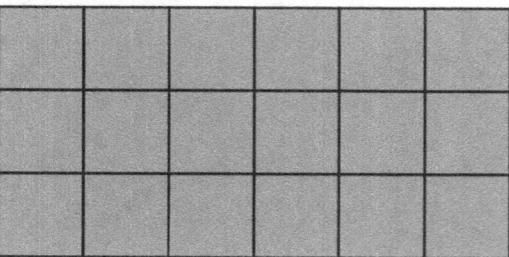

Length = 6 units

Width = 3 units

Area = 6×3 = 18 un^2

Area of Rectangles, Squares, Rhombuses, and Trapezoids **7.2**

1 What is the area of the square below?

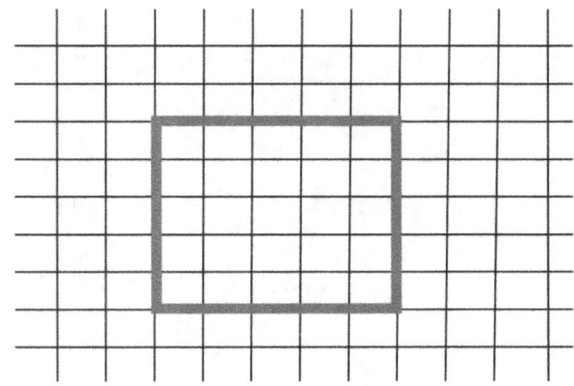

(A) 49   (B) 25

(C) 36   (D) 64

2 What is the area of the rectangle below?

(A) 35   (B) 21

(C) 28   (D) 56

3 What is the area of a square with a side measuring 8 cm?

(A) 64 cm²   (B) 90 cm²   (C) 36 cm²   (D) 135 cm²

4 What is the area of a rectangle with sides measuring 11 cm and 9 cm?

(A) 82 cm²   (B) 110 cm²   (C) 99 cm²   (D) 124 cm²

7.2 Area of Rectangles, Squares, Rhombuses, and Trapezoids

5 What is the area of a rectangle with sides measuring 75 mm and 4 cm?

A) 71 cm²   B) 53 cm²   C) 80 cm²   D) 30 cm²

6 Which of the following rectangles have the greatest area?

A) Rectangle measuring 14 cm by 12 cm

B) Rectangle measuring 17 cm by 3 cm

C) Rectangle measuring 7 cm by 15 cm

D) Rectangle measuring 21 cm by 6 cm

7 Which of the following rectangles have the smallest area?

A) Rectangle measuring 24 cm by 32 cm

B) Rectangle measuring 27 cm by 33 cm

C) Rectangle measuring 31 cm by 21 cm

D) Rectangle measuring 29 cm by 29 cm

8 Jack wants to cover the bedroom floor with carpet. If the bedroom measures 9 meters by 5 meters, how much carpet does Jack need?

(A) 42 m² (B) 45 m² (C) 50 m² (D) 62 m²

9 Zane bought a square shape cake. If the width of the cake is 55 cm, what is the area of the cake?

(A) 3,275 cm² (B) 2,950 cm² (C) 3,156 cm² (D) 3,025 cm²

10 Jett bought a large piece of cloth, measuring 8 feet wide and 14 feet long. What is the area of the cloth?

(A) 112 ft² (B) 108 ft² (C) 132 ft² (D) 154 ft²

11 What is the area of the rhombus with diagonals measuring 6 cm and 9 cm?

(A) 6 cm² (B) 27 cm² (C) 54 cm² (D) 16 cm²

12 What is the area of the rhombus with side and height measuring 12 cm and 10 cm respectively?

(A) 90 cm² (B) 180 cm² (C) 60 cm² (D) 120 cm²

7.2 Area of Rectangles, Squares, Rhombuses, and Trapezoids

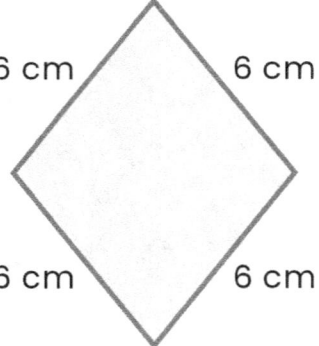

6 cm   6 cm

6 cm   6 cm

13 What is the area of the rhombus below?

(A) 54 cm²   (B) 42 cm²

(C) 24 cm²   (D) 36 cm²

14 What is the area of the trapezoid with average width and height measuring 10 cm and 9 cm respectively?

(A) 70 cm²   (B) 50 cm²   (C) 45 cm²   (D) 90 cm²

15 What is the area of the trapezoid with bases and height measuring 9 cm, 5 cm and 2 cm respectively?

(A) 14 cm²   (B) 45 cm²   (C) 18 cm²   (D) 10 cm²

16 Which of the following trapezoids has the greatest area?

(A) Trapezoid with bases measuring 16 cm and 8 cm and height of 5 cm

(B) Trapezoid with bases measuring 11 cm and 11 cm and height of 3 cm

(C) Trapezoid with bases measuring 14 cm and 10 cm and height of 9 cm

(D) Trapezoid with bases measuring 15 cm and 12 cm and height of 4 cm

Area of Rectangles, Squares, Rhombuses, and Trapezoids **7.2**

17 Which of the following rhombuses has the smallest area?

A) Rhombus with a side measuring 16 cm and height of 8 cm.

B) Rhombus with diagonals measuring 24 cm and height of 14 cm.

C) Rhombus with side measuring 17 cm and height of 13 cm.

D) Rhombus with diagonals measuring 20 cm and height of 18 cm.

18 Madeline drew the shape of a trapezoid. The smaller base of the trapezoid is 60 cm long, the greater base of the trapezoid is 120 cm long and the height of the trapezoid is 30 cm. What is the area of the trapezoid?

A) 1,800 cm²   B) 2,700 cm²   C) 3,600 cm²   D) 4,800 cm²

19 Julia bought trapezoidal shape door mats. One door mat has to be 50 cm high and have the average width of 85 cm. What will be the area of the door mat?

A) 24 m²

B) 4,750 cm²

C) 35 m²

D) 4,250 cm²

7.2 Area of Rectangles, Squares, Rhombuses, and Trapezoids

20 Gianna cut the cloth in the shape of a right trapezoid with parallel sides of 30 cm and 36 cm and two other sides 13 cm and 19 cm. What is the area of the trapezoid?

(A) 396 cm²   (B) 487 cm²   (C) 429 cm²   (D) 534 cm²

Next Section: The Perimeter of Rectangles, Squares, Rhombuses, and Trapezoids »

THE PERIMETER OF RECTANGLES, SQUARES, RHOMBUSES, AND TRAPEZOIDS

The perimeter of a shape is the total length of its sides. For rectangles, squares, rhombuses, and trapezoids, the perimeter is the sum of the lengths of all of its sides.

A <u>rhombus</u> is a parallelogram with four equal sides.

A <u>rectangle</u> is a parallelogram with four right angles.

A <u>square</u> is a rectangle with four equal sides.

Properties:

The diagonals of a rhombus bisect one another.

The diagonals of a rhombus bisect rhombus's angles.

The diagonals of a rhombus are perpendicular.

A trapezoid is a quadrilateral with only one pair of parallel sides.

The perimeter of a quadrilateral is the distance around the quadrilateral.

Perimeter:

Perimeter of rectangle = 2(Length+Width)

Perimeter of square = 2(Side)

Perimeter of rhombus = 4(Side)

Perimeter of trapezoid = Sum of all Sides .

Example:

Find the perimeter of the rectangle

Solution:

Length = 6 units

Width = 3 units

Perimeter 26 + 3 = 2×9 = 18 un.

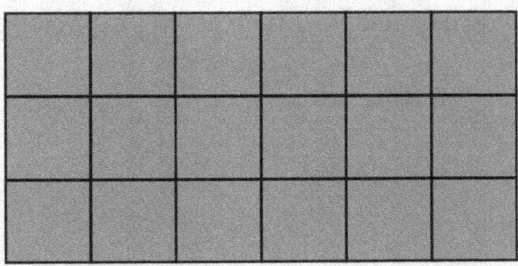

7.3 The Perimeter of Rectangles, Squares, Rhombuses, and Trapezoids

1 What is the perimeter of the square below?

A) 32 units
B) 20 units
C) 35 units
D) 64 units

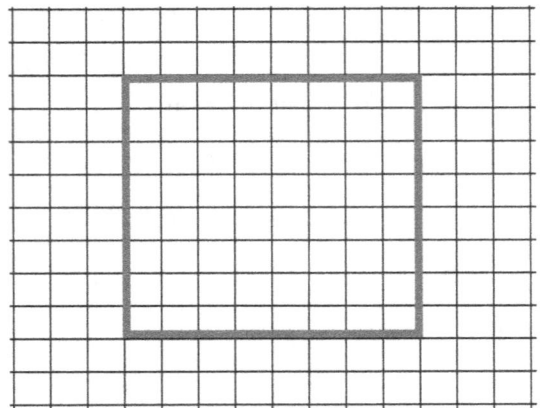

2 What is the perimeter of a square with a side measuring 11 cm?

A) 54 cm
B) 40 cm
C) 44 cm
D) 55 cm

3 What is the perimeter of a rectangle with sides measuring 6 cm and 8 cm?

A) 28 cm
B) 12 cm
C) 16 cm
D) 48 cm

4 Which of the following squares has a perimeter of 16 units?

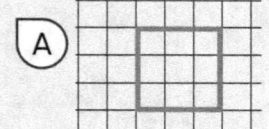 A
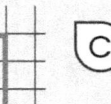 B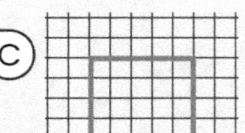
 C
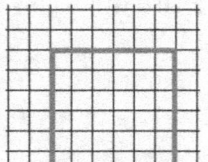 D

The Perimeter of Rectangles, Squares, Rhombuses, and Trapezoids | 7.3

5 Which of the following rectangles have the smallest perimeter?

(A) Rectangle measuring 5 cm and 3 cm

(B) Rectangle measuring 8 cm and 7 cm

(C) Rectangle measuring 12 cm and 13 cm

(D) Rectangle measuring 9 cm and 3 cm

6 Which of the following squares have the greatest perimeter?

(A) Square side measuring 21 cm

(B) Square side measuring 19 cm

(C) Square side measuring 12 cm

(D) Square side measuring 23 cm

7 Benjamin bought a carpet. The size of the carpet is 12m by 7m. What is the perimeter of the carpet?

(A) 19 cm   (B) 38 m   (C) 14 cm   (D) 24 m

8 How many meters of lace do you need to line a rectangular bed measuring 100 cm by 80 cm?

(A) 2.7 m   (B) 4.8 m   (C) 3.6 m   (D) 2.8 m

7.3 The Perimeter of Rectangles, Squares, Rhombuses, and Trapezoids

9 Ethan used 52 cm of cloth to design a rectangular curtain. If the curtain is 18 cm long, how wide is the curtain?

(A) 8 cm   (B) 10 cm   (C) 4 cm   (D) 12 cm

10 A rectangle with an area of 160 square centimeters has the same side as a square. If the perimeter of the square is 80 centimeters, what could be the length of another side of the rectangle?

(A) 20 cm   (B) 16 cm   (C) 10 cm   (D) 8 cm

11 What is the perimeter of the rhombus below?

(A) 15 cm   (B) 28 cm

(C) 30 cm   (D) 42 cm

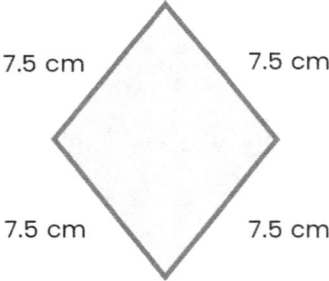

7.5 cm   7.5 cm

7.5 cm   7.5 cm

12 What is the perimeter of the trapezoid below?

(A) 26 cm   (B) 33 cm

(C) 36 cm   (D) 78 cm

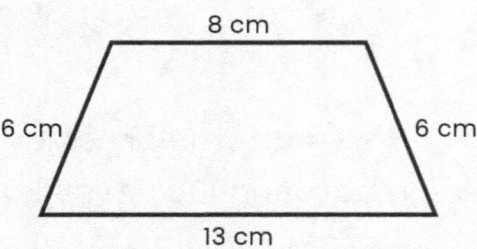

8 cm

6 cm   6 cm

13 cm

13 What is the perimeter of a rhombus with a side measuring 4.7 m?

(A) 18.8 m   (B) 24.6 m   (C) 32.4 m   (D) 42.2 m

14 What is the perimeter of a trapezoid with sides measuring 14 cm, 12 cm, 10 cm, and 8 cm?

(A) 22 cm   (B) 33 cm   (C) 44 cm   (D) 77 cm

15 What is the perimeter of a trapezoid with bases measuring 4.6 cm and 7 cm and legs measuring 8.4 cm and 9 cm?

(A) 17 cm   (B) 41 cm   (C) 73 cm   (D) 29 cm

16 Which of the following trapezoids have the greatest perimeter?

(A) Trapezoid with sides measuring 31 cm, 27 cm, 24 cm, and 21 cm

(B) Trapezoid with sides measuring 35 cm, 33 cm, 30 cm, and 27 cm

(C) Trapezoid with sides measuring 30 cm, 26 cm, 21 cm, and 18 cm

(D) Trapezoid with sides measuring 32 cm, 28 cm, 22 cm, and 15 cm

7.3 The Perimeter of Rectangles, Squares, Rhombuses, and Trapezoids

17 Which of the following rhombuses have the smallest perimeter?

(A) Rhombus with side measuring 27 cm

(B) Rhombus with side measuring 21 cm

(C) Rhombus with side measuring 14 cm

(D) Rhombus with side measuring 19 cm

18 The garden has a trapezoidal base. Sides of the base are 24, 26, 28, 28 feet long. What is the perimeter of the base of the garden?

(A) 121 ft   (B) 98 ft   (C) 118 ft   (D) 106 ft

19 How many meters of lace do you need to line a bed cloth in the shape of a rhombus with a side of 1.8 m?

(A) 7.2 m   (B) 4.1 m   (C) 7.3 m   (D) 2.9 m

20 What is the perimeter of the rhombus with a side measuring 99 mm?

(A) 8.86 cm   (B) 3.96 cm   (C) 2.14 cm   (D) 4.34 cm

Next Chapter: Coordinate Plane and Graph Points

COORDINATE PLANE AND GRAPH POINTS

The coordinate plane is a two-dimensional plane formed by two perpendicular number lines known as the x-axis and y-axis.Graphing a point involves moving to the location of the point and marking it with a dot.

A coordinate plane consists of two perpendicular number lines used to graph pairs of numbers. The lines intersect at each line's zero, called the origin of the coordinate plane. Each line is an axis.

- x-axis: horizontal (left-to-right) number line;
- y-axis: vertical (up-and-down) number line.

You need two numbers to locate a point on a coordinate plane. These two numbers are called coordinates of the point. Coordinates are written as two numbers inside of parentheses.

The first number is the x-coordinate. The x-coordinate tells the distance to travel on the x-axis from the origin.

The second number is the y-coordinate. The y-coordinate tells the distance to travel on the y-axis from the origin.

Example: What are the coordinates of points A and B on the coordinate plane below?

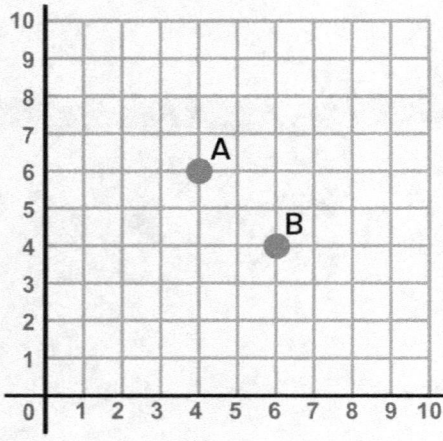

Solution:

Point A: From zero, we move 4 units to the right and 6 units up, so the coordinates of the point A are (4,6).

Point B: From zero, we move 6 units to the right and 4 units up, so the coordinates of the point B are 6,4.

1 What is the x-coordinate of Point B?

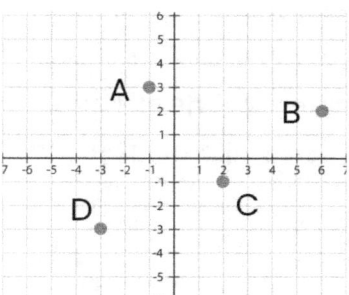

(A) 8

(B) 3

(C) 6

(D) 7

2 What is the y-coordinate of the Point C?

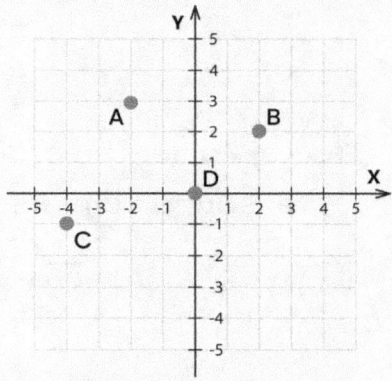

(A) −1

(B) 3

(C) 2

(D) −4

3 Which ordered pair represents Point S?

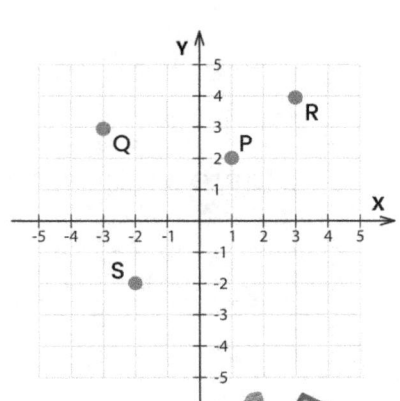

(A) (2, 4)

(B) (−1, 3)

(C) (−5, 3)

(D) (−2, −2)

7.4 Coordinate Plane and Graph Points

4 **True or False:** The ordered pair representing Point P is (3, −4).

Ⓐ True   Ⓑ False

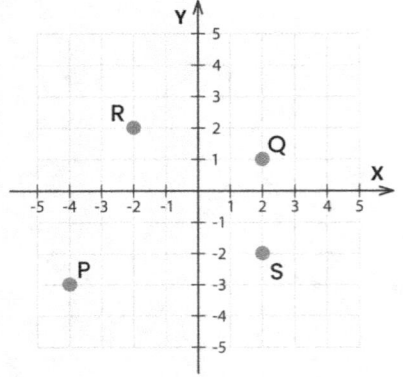

5 **True or False:** The ordered pair representing Point R is (4, 3).

Ⓐ True   Ⓑ False

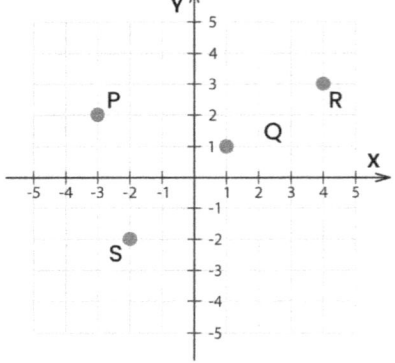

6 The ordered pair representing Point A is

_____ .

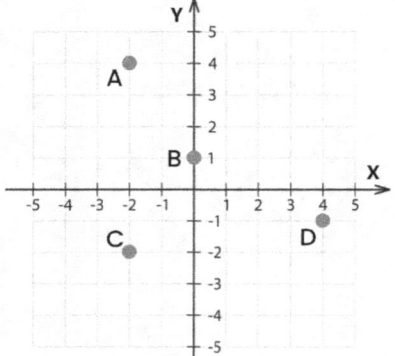

7 The ordered pair representing Point Z is

_____.

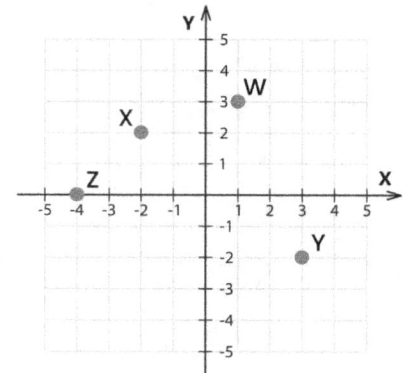

8 The ordered pair representing Point T is

_____.

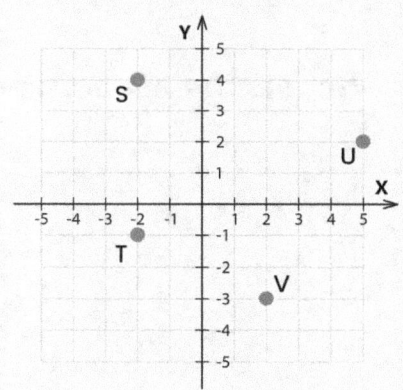

9 The ordered pair representing Point F is

_____.

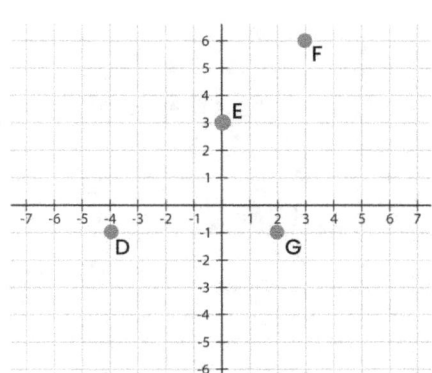

7.4 **Coordinate Plane and Graph Points**

10 The ordered pair representing Point K is

_____.

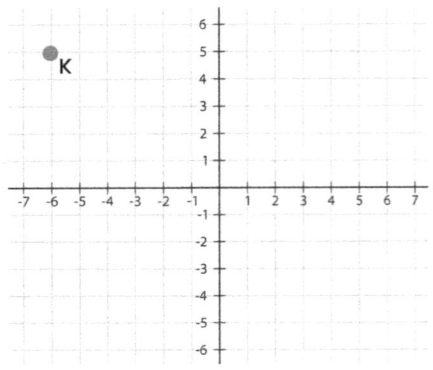

11 What is the X-coordinate of point G?

(A) 2   (B) −2

(C) 3   (D) 5

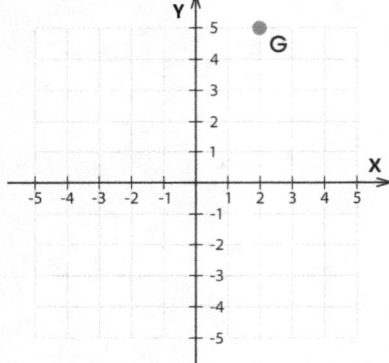

12 What are the coordinates of D?

(A) (1, 1)   (B) (2, 1)

(C) (−1, 1)   (D) (1, −1)

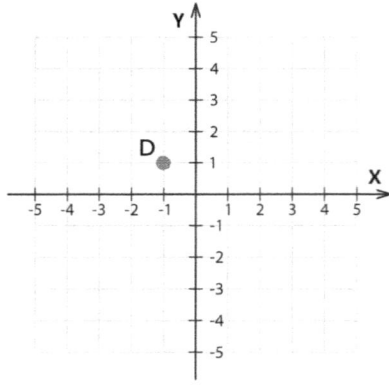

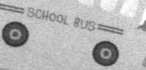

13 Which point can be found on the coordinate plane?

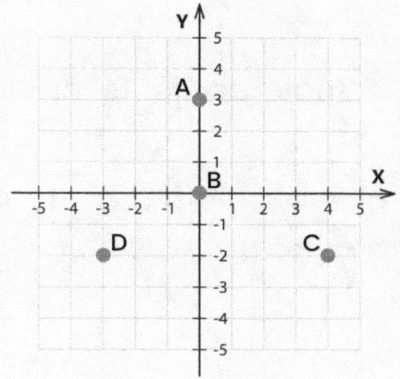

(A) (-1, 5) (B) (0, 0)

(C) (4, 3) (D) (1, 1)

14 Which point cannot be found on the coordinate plane?

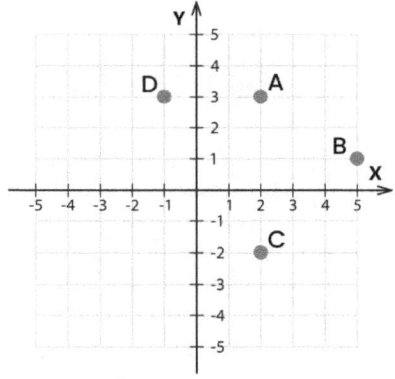

(A) (2, 3) (B) (-1, 3)

(C) (5, 1) (D) (-2, -2)

15 What number is missing?

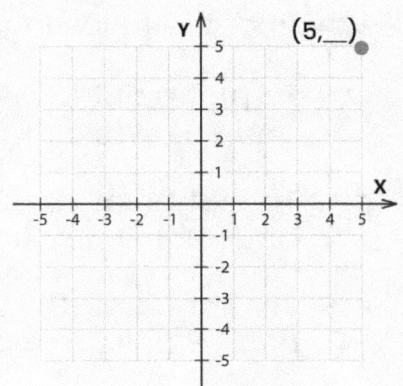

(A) (5) (B) (7)

(C) (8) (D) (-5)

7.4 Coordinate Plane and Graph Points

16 What number is missing?

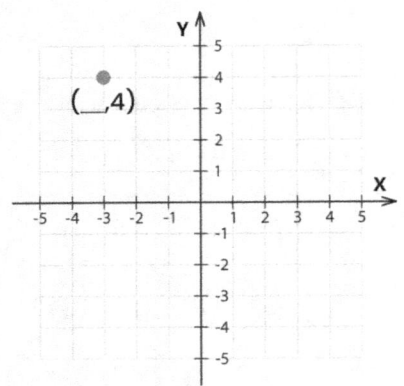

(A) 3

(B) 4

(C) −3

(D) −4

17 What number is missing?

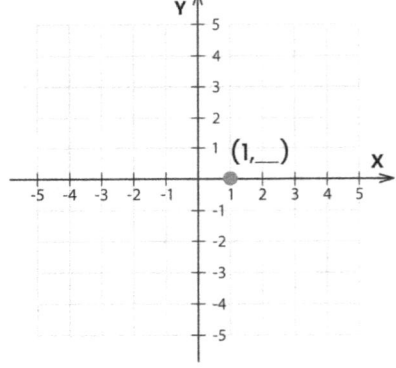

(A) 1

(B) 0

(C) 2

(D) −1

18 Which of the following statements is true about point (3, −9) ?

(A) To plot point (3, −9),we need to move 3 units left and −9 units up from the origin

(B) To plot point (3, −9),we need to move 3 units right and −9 units up from the origin

(C) To plot point (3, −9),we need to move 3 units left and −9 units down from the origin

(D) To plot point (3, −9),we need to move 3 units right and −9 units down from the origin

Coordinate Plane and Graph Points   **7.4**

19 Which of the following statements is true about point (2, 8) ?

(A) Lies on the axis x- axis

(B) Lies on the axis y-axis

(C) Has x- coordinate smaller than y- axis

(D) Has y- coordinate smaller than x- axis

20 Which of the following statements is true about points (5, 2) and (1, 2)?

(A) Have the same x-coordinates

(B) y-coordinate of the first point is the same as y-coordinate of the second point

(C) Have the alternate y-coordinates

(D) x-coordinate of the first point is the same as y-coordinate of the second point

Next Section: Chapter Review ≫

 **7.5** Chapter Review

1 In a parallelogram, the shortest side is 4 cm long, and the perimeter equals to 20 cm. What is the length of the longest side of the parallelogram?

Ⓐ 4 cm Ⓑ 16 cm Ⓒ 6 cm Ⓓ 12 cm

2 In a rectangle, the length is 10 in, and the area equals 80 in2. What is the width of the rectangle?

Ⓐ 18 in Ⓑ 12 in Ⓒ 15 in Ⓓ 8 in

3 Logan drew a triangle in his notebook. He measured two of its angles and came up with 50° and 55°. What would the measure of the third angle be?

Ⓐ 80° Ⓑ 75° Ⓒ 95° Ⓓ 105°

4 How many lines of symmetry does the 4-pointed star below have?

Ⓐ 4 Ⓑ 6 Ⓒ 8 Ⓓ 10

5 What is the area of the square below?

A 49 sq. units   B 36 sq. units

C 81 sq. units   D 100 sq. units

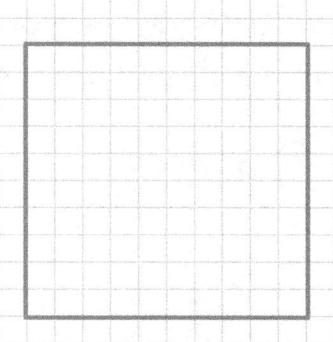

6 What is the area of the rectangle below?

A 50 sq.units   B 60 sq. units

C 120 sq.units   D 10 sq.units

7 What is the area of the rectangle with sides measuring 15 cm and 11 cm?

A 152 cm²   B 125 cm²   C 165 cm²   D 111 cm²

7.5 Chapter Review

8 What is the area of the rhombus with side and height measuring 17 cm and 21 cm respectively?

(A) 357 cm² (B) 257 cm² (C) 326 cm² (D) 296 cm²

9 Which of the following trapezoids has the smallest area?

(A) Trapezoid with bases measuring 6 cm and 8 cm and height of 5 cm

(B) Trapezoid with bases measuring 10 cm and 6 cm and height of 3 cm

(C) Trapezoid with bases measuring 4 cm and 2 cm and height of 6 cm

(D) Trapezoid with bases measuring 7 cm and 9 cm and height of 4 cm

10 What is the perimeter of the square with a side measuring 31 cm?

(A) 98 cm (B) 124 cm (C) 84 cm (D) 132 cm

11 Susan bought a table. The size of the table is 100 cm by 65 cm. What is the perimeter of the table?

(A) 190 cm (B) 280 cm (C) 165 cm (D) 330 cm

12 What is the perimeter of the rhombus with a side measuring 8.5 m?

A 64 m   B 32 m   C 34 m   D 25 m

13 What is the perimeter of a trapezoid with bases measuring 8 cm and 14 cm and legs measuring 12 cm and 11 cm?

A 45 cm   B 23 cm   C 37 cm   D 34 cm

14 Which of the following rhombuses have the greatest perimeter?

A Rhombus with side measuring 29 cm

B Rhombus with side measuring 31 cm

C Rhombus with side measuring 24 cm

D Rhombus with side measuring 39 cm

7.5 Chapter Review

15 Create a point on the graph to represent the coordinates (5, 3)

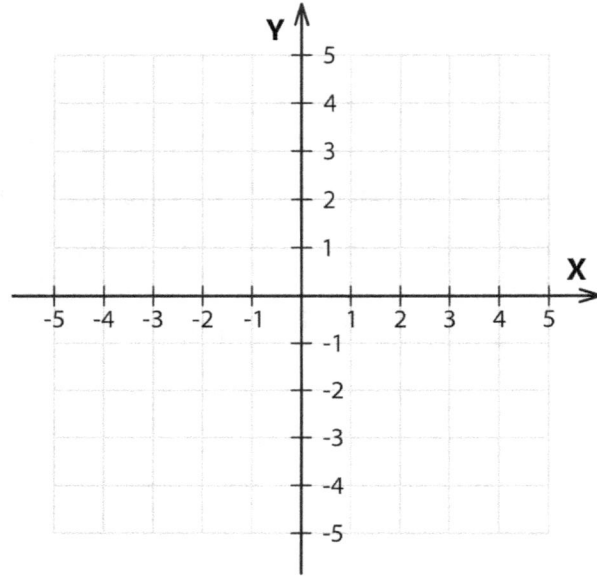

16 What are the coordinates of point F?

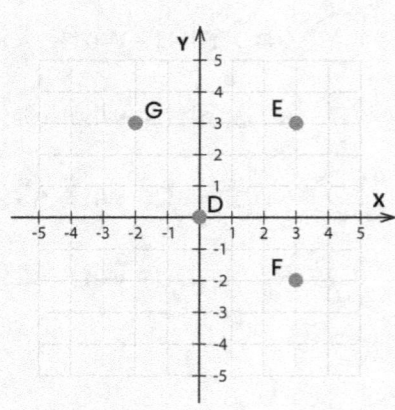

A) (4, 0) B) (3, −2)

C) (2, 7) D) (−2, 5)

17 **True or False:** A regular heptagon has 8 sides.

A) True   B) False

18 The perimeter of a rhombus is the same as the perimeter of a rectangle. If the width of a rectangle is 4 cm smaller than its length, which of the following statements is true?

A) The width of the rectangle is 4 cm smaller than the side of the rhombus

B) The width of the rectangle is the same as the side of the rhombus

C) The width of the rectangle is 2 cm smaller than the side of the rhombus

D) The width of the rectangle is 2 cm greater than the side of the rhombus

19 The area of a square is 256 cm². A rectangle has the same width as the side of the square and a length that is 8 cm longer than the side of the square. What is the area of the rectangle? What is the perimeter of the rectangle?

7.5   **Chapter Review**

20   The smaller base of the trapezoid is the same as its height. The greater base of the trapezoid is twice the smaller base. If the area of the trapezoid is 96 in², what is the height of the trapezoid?

(A) 8 in   (B) 12 in   (C) 16 in   (D) 20 in

Next Chapter:
Comprehensive Assessment 1 & 2 »

COMPREHENSIVE ASSESSMENT

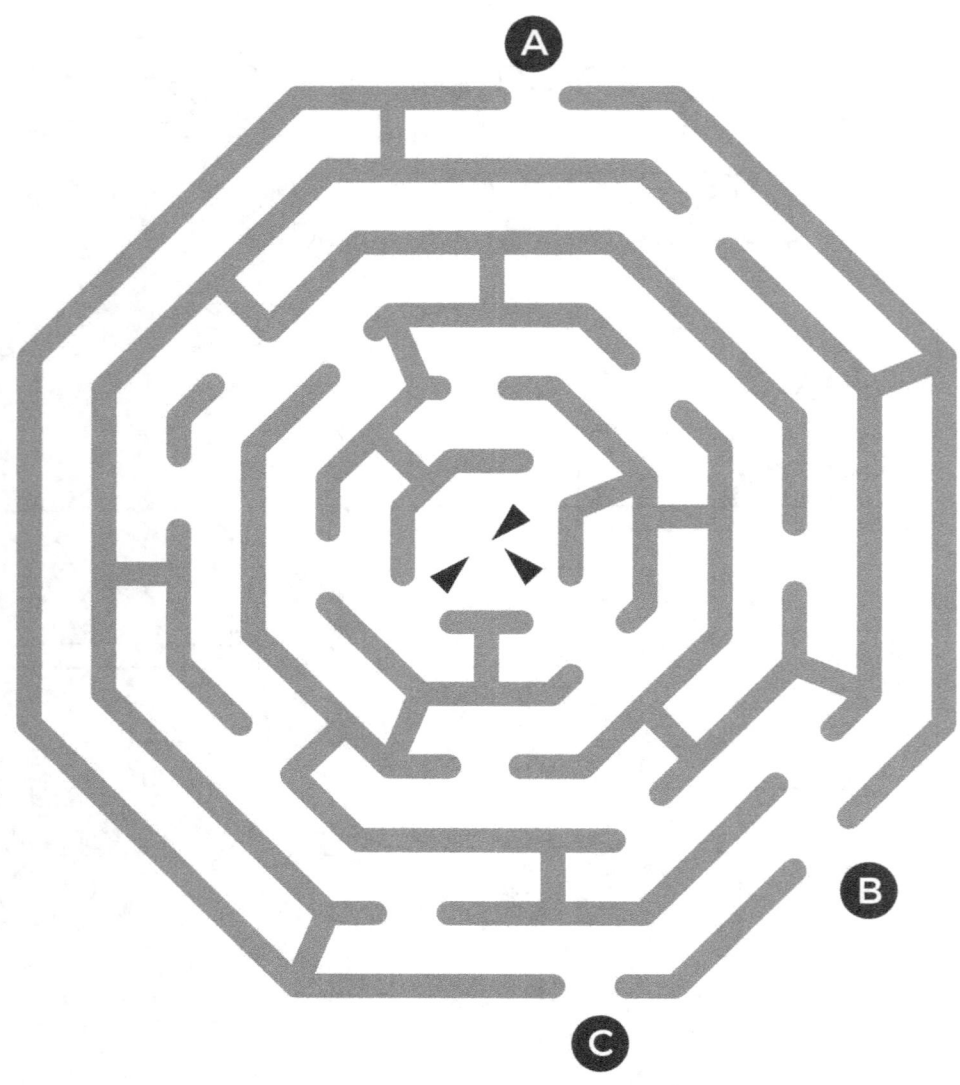

1 Jessy writes an expression that has a value of 21. Which expression has the parentheses and brackets in the correct place?

(A) $3 \times [56 \div (3+5)]$

(B) $3 \times [56 \div 3 + 5]$

(C) $[3 \times (56 \div 3 + 5)]$

(D) $3 \times 56 \div 3 + 5$

2 Tim goes to the book fair where paperback books are $2.75 and hardback books are $6. Tim buys six paperback books and three hardback books. How much change will Tim receive from a $40 bill?

(A) $7.50

(B) $10.25

(C) $13.25

(D) $5.50

3 This expression has a value of 250. What is the value of k?

$$k + 8 \times 6$$

(A) 220

(B) 230

(C) 202

(D) 240

4 Does the expression $8 \times 632 + 92$ show eight times the sum of six hundred and thirty-two and ninety-two? Why or why not?

_____

5 John has 70 yards of ribbon. He wants to use 4-yard ribbon pieces to wrap 5 boxes and 6-yard ribbon pieces to wrap 7 boxes. Which expression can be used to find the amount of ribbon John has left after wrapping his boxes?

(A) 70 - (4×5) + (6×7)   (B) 70 - (4×5) - (6×7)

(C) 70 + (4×5) - (6×7)   (D) 70 - (4+5) - (6+7)

6 What operators should be added to this expression has a value of 2350?

$$\{[7000 \_\_ 55 (200 \_\_ 120)] \_\_ 250\}$$

(A) {[7000 - 55(200 - 120)] + 250}

(B) {[7000 - 55(200 - 120)] - 250}

(C) {[7000 - 55(200 + 120)] + 250}

(D) {[7000 - 55(200 - 120)] + 250}

7 The high school band had 5,700 raffle tickets to sell. There are 1,900 band members. How many raffle tickets will each band member be required to sell?

(A) 4   (B) 5   (C) 2   (D) 3

8 Edwin trained football athletes for 55 hours in week one, 75 hours in week two, and 156 hours in week three. Each athlete trains for 22 hours. How many athletes did Edwin train?

(A) 13   (B) 36   (C) 20   (D) 18

9 Maria and Mercy are training to run a marathon. Maria ran for 12.9 minutes. Mercy ran for 8 times as long, how long did the girls run in total?

(A) 75 minutes   (B) 79.5 minutes

(C) 116.1 minutes   (D) 69 minutes

10 A delivery truck is driven 120 miles per hour for 8 hours each day. How many miles will it have traveled in 3 days?

(A) 1800   (B) 2880   (C) 1000   (D) 1500

11 True or False: The equivalent form of 4,920 is 49.2×10^4.

(A) True   (B) False

12 There are 520,950 gallons of water in an Olympic size swimming pool. Which expression below correctly matches the amount of water in an Olympic size swimming pool?

(A) 520.95×10^2 gallons   (B) 52.095×10^4 gallons

(C) 5.2095×10^4 gallons   (D) 520.95×10^3 gallons

13 Round the following number to the nearest tenth: 75.593

(A) 75.6   (B) 75.5   (C) 75.59   (D) 75.52

14 Choose the correct comparison for the decimals.

0.998 _____ 0.762

(A) >   (B) <   (C) =

15 Represent a number 15.65 as the sum of two decimals if:
- digits in the ones place are different;
- digits in the tenths place are the same;
- the difference of digits in the hundredths place is 1.

How many different solutions can you find?

(A) 6.48 + 9.17   (B) 4.12 + 9.22

(C) 6.18 + 9.47   (D) 5.22 + 7.17

16 Find the missing number in the pattern below.
6.72, 7.50, 8.28, _____, 9.84

(A) 9.06   (B) 9.11   (C) 9.21   (D) 9.03

17 Compare the products without multiplying.
15.27 × 323.18 and 7.025 × 283.5

(A) 15.27 × 323.18 > 7.025 × 283.5

(B) 15.27 × 323.18 < 7.025 × 283.5

(C) 15.27 × 323.18 = 7.025 × 283.5

18 Edwin went to school for 25 days in October. If he paid $ 5.20 for lunch each day, about how much did he pay for lunch in October?

(A) $179   (B) $152   (C) $125   (D) $188

19 Find two missing digits.

20 . _____ ÷ _____ . 2 = 3

How many solutions can you find?

_____

20 Jonny charges $8.40 per hour to babysit toddlers. If Jonny earns $42, how many hours does he spend babysitting?

(A) 6 hours   (B) 4 hours   (C) 5 hours   (D) 3 hours

21 Write the decimal using base-ten numerals.

Five hundred thirty-two and two hundred seventy-nine thousandths

_____

22 A teacher wrote 95.08 on the board. Four students named the number in different ways. Who is incorrect?

(A) Riya – Ninety-five and eight-hundredths

(B) Tim – $95\frac{8}{100}$

(C) Angel – Ninety-five and eight-tenths

(D) Jack – $90 + 5 + \frac{8}{100}$

23 Find the missing numbers

$$\frac{5}{16} + \frac{}{16} = \frac{1}{8} + \frac{1}{4}$$

24 Solve for x.

$$\frac{3}{6} + x = \frac{5}{3}$$

(A) $\frac{3}{4}$ (B) $\frac{1}{6}$ (C) $\frac{2}{3}$ (D) $\frac{3}{4}$

25 Simplify: $\frac{7}{4} \times \frac{8}{5}$

(A) $\frac{35}{12}$ (B) $\frac{14}{5}$ (C) $\frac{15}{28}$ (D) $\frac{9}{10}$

26 Sherlock collected 56 pebbles on the beach. If $\frac{1}{7}$ of the pebbles were white, how many of the pebbles were white?

(A) 6 pebbles (B) 5 pebbles (C) 8 pebbles (D) 7 pebbles

27 Randy said that $\frac{3}{8} \times \frac{5}{7}$ is the same as $\frac{3}{5} \times \frac{8}{7}$. Is she correct? Explain.

_____

28 Elizabeth cleaned rooms for $\frac{15}{18}$ of an hour. Doing it, she listened to the music for $\frac{3}{5}$ of the time and half of the time she was listening to the music, she used headphones. How long did Elizabeth use headphones?

(A) $\frac{3}{5}$ hour (B) $\frac{1}{4}$ hour (C) $\frac{3}{8}$ hour (D) $\frac{3}{10}$ hour

29 David is filling a box with centimeter cubes. The height of the box is 25 centimeters, and he can fit 30 cubes in the base of the box. How many cubes will fill the box?

(A) 680   (B) 86   (C) 750   (D) 650

30 Mike wants to fill this box with $\frac{1}{2}$ inch cubes. How many cubes are needed to fill this box? The cube is 7 inches in length, 5 inches in height and 3 inches in width. How many cubes are needed to fill this box?

(A) 840 cubes   (B) 415 cubes   (C) 560 cubes   (D) 1000 cubes

31 In a parallelogram, the longest side is 23 cm long and the shortest side is 13 cm long. What is the perimeter of the parallelogram?

(A) 40   (B) 55   (C) 72   (D) 86

32 In an isosceles trapezoid, two bases have lengths of 35 in and 19 in. If the perimeter of the trapezoid is 72 in, what is the length of each non-parallel side?

(A) 34 in   (B) 23 in   (C) 9 in   (D) 19 in

33 Which of the following rectangles has the greatest area?

(A) Rectangle measuring 13 cm by 11 cm

(B) Rectangle measuring 17 cm by 3 cm

(C) Rectangle measuring 17 cm by 15 cm

(D) Rectangle measuring 23 cm by 8 cm

34 What is the area of the trapezoid with bases and height measuring 12 cm, 8 cm, and 3 cm respectively?

(A) 30 cm²   (B) 32 cm²   (C) 28 cm²   (D) 22 cm²

35 Eden used 72 cm of cloth to design a rectangular curtain. If the curtain is 28 cm long, how wide is the curtain?

(A) 4 cm   (B) 10 cm   (C) 8 cm   (D) 12 cm

36 A rectangle with an area of 207 square centimeters has the same side as a square. If the perimeter of the square is 92 centimeters, what could be the length of another side of the rectangle?

(A) 20 cm   (B) 16 cm   (C) 10 cm   (D) 9 cm

37 The perimeter of a rhombus is the same as the perimeter of a rectangle. If the width of the rectangle is 8 cm smaller than its length, which of the following statements is true?

(A) The width of the rectangle is 4 cm smaller than the side of the rhombus

(B) The width of the rectangle is the same as the side of the rhombus

(C) The width of the rectangle is 2 cm smaller than the side of the rhombus

(D) The width of the rectangle is 2 cm greater than the side of the rhombus

38 The area of a square is 225 cm². A rectangle has the same width as the side of the square and the length that is 9 cm longer than the side of the square. What is the area of the rectangle? What is the perimeter of the rectangle?

_____

39 Find the base area of the prism given its volume and height.

$$V = 330, h = 15$$

(A) 12   (B) 22   (C) 10   (D) 16

40 If you double the width and length of a rectangular prism, how many times does its volume increase?

(A) 10   (B) 4   (C) 6   (D) 8

41 Find the volume of the rectangular prism given its dimensions.

l = 13, w = 22, h = 9 in

(A) 1728 in²   (B) 2100 in²   (C) 2574 in²   (D) 1700 in²

42 Find the number of cubes needed to make each rectangular prism. You can use unit cubes or you can count the cubes by looking at the drawing.

(A) 12   (B) 15   (C) 20   (D) 10

43 Melissa wants to buy a notebook for $8, a binder for $10, and a pack of pens for $8. She paid with $58. How much change will Melissa receive?

(A) $32   (B) $22   (C) $20   (D) $24

44 **True or False:** The equivalent form of 33,220 is 332.2×10^2.

(A) True   (B) False

45 **True or False:** A rule for this table could be x = y – 8.

x	12	26	40
y	20	34	48

Next Chapter: Assessment – 2 ≫

COMPREHENSIVE ASSESSMENT

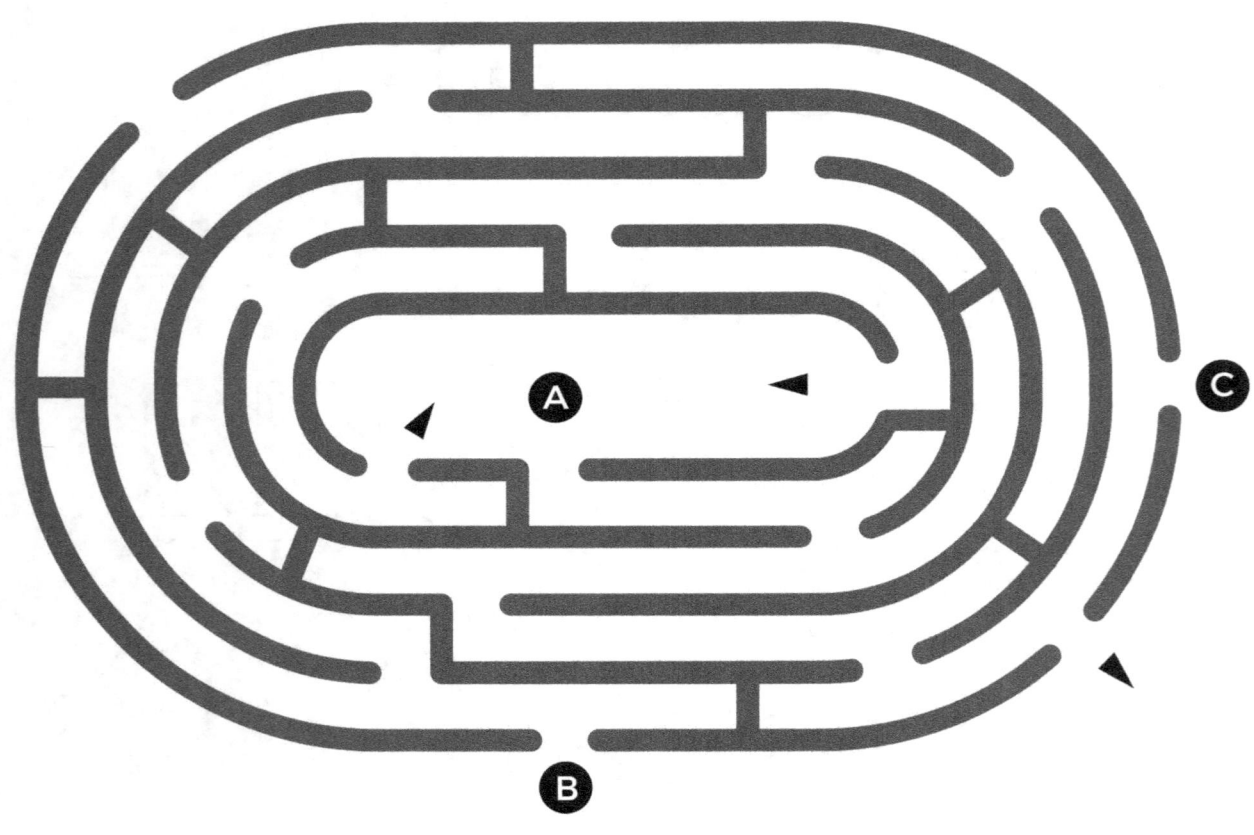

1 James writes an expression that has a value of 40. Where should he place the parentheses to make this expression have a value of 40?

$$30 \times 20 \div 20 - 5$$

(A) Around 30 times 20

(B) Around 20 divided by 20

(C) Around 20 minus 5

(D) Around 20 divided by 20 minus 5

2 In a mall, there are 8 floors. Each floor has 35 shops. 230 of the shops are being used. How many shops are empty?

(A) 35   (B) 50   (C) 40   (D) 45

3 The expression $7 \times (3216 + 175)$ means:

(A) Seven times 3216 and 175

(B) Seven times more than 3216 minus 175

(C) Seven more than 3216 and 175

(D) Seven times the sum of 3216 and 175

4 Which ordered pair is missing in the function table?

x	5	10	15	?
y	10	20	30	?

(A) (20, 40)   (B) (17,40)

(C) (16, 40)   (D) (40, 17)

5 A triangle has these 3 side lengths:

- Side A is 35 cm long
- Side B is 10 cm shorter than Side A
- Side C is 8 cm longer than Side B

$$\{35 + (35 - 10) + (35 - 10 + 8)\}$$

Does this expression represent the sum of the side lengths? Explain your thinking.

_____

6 Angel buys 7 pizzas for 12 dollars. She also buys 5 french fries for 3 dollars each, and 6 Pepsi sodas for 3 dollars each. Which expression shows the amount of money Angel spends on pizza, french fries, and Pepsi?

A) $(7×12) + (5×3) × (6×3)$

B) $12 + (5×3) + (6×3)$

C) $(7+15) + (5×3) + (6×3)$

D) $12 + (5×3) × (6×3)$

7 Jonny can allow 5,60 minutes for guitar class this month. There are 80 children signed up for class. How many minutes will each child be allowed?

A) 7   B) 6   C) 8   D) 9

8 Mary baked 8 dozen cookies day 1. She increased her baking by 30 times on day 2 . She increased the baking from day 2 by 40 times for day 3. How many dozen cookies did Mary bake over all three days?

_____

9 Mr. Peter must buy glue sticks and scissors for the school. Each child must have one of each. The glue sticks are sold in boxes of 50 and the scissors in boxes of 42. He plans to buy 100 boxes of each. There are 4,000 students at the school. Will he have enough glue sticks and scissors? Explain.

_____

10 There are multiple questions on a game show. There are seven 75-point questions and five 75-point questions. How many points are there in each episode?

(A) 900   (B) 400   (C) 800   (D) 500

11 Find the missing value: $? \times 10^4 = 93.69$.

(A) 0.0009369   (B) 0.009369   (C) 0.09369   (D) 0.9369

12 Jerry is simplifying this: $600 \div [10^2 \times 3]$. Jerry thinks the answer is 2. Do you agree or disagree? Why?

_____

13 There was a competition at school to determine who ran the most in one month. Who ran the most miles?

(A) Nicki – 72.15 miles

(B) James – 72.159 miles

(C) Olivia – 72.13 miles

(D) Angel – 72.153 miles

14 Mr. Peter weighed two chickens on the farm. One of them weighed 8.32 lbs. The other weighed less. What is the possible weight of the second chicken?

(A) 8.88

(B) 8.64

(C) 8.59

(D) 8.10

15 Which two decimals have the sum of 10.10 and the difference of 1.60? (Use the length model for the calculation)

_____

16 The width of the rectangle is 21.75 cm. The length of the rectangle is 8.82 cm longer than its width. What is the perimeter of the rectangle?

(A) 102.01 cm   (B) 101.88 cm   (C) 106.2 cm   (D) 104.64 cm

17 Solve the equation: $(3.8x - 0.8) \div 0.9 = 52.7$.

(A) 12.69   (B) 12.3   (C) 12   (D) 12.4445

18 What is the area of the trapezoid with bases and height measuring 21 cm, 9 cm, and 5 cm respectively?

(A) 75 cm²   (B) 72 cm²   (C) 87 cm²   (D) 82 cm²

19 Edward used 97.2 grams of butter to bake some batches of cookies. If one batch of cookies requires 24.3 g of butter, how many batches of cookies did Edward bake?

(A) 6   (B) 4   (C) 5   (D) 3

20 Find two numbers a and b, if $a - b = 15.83$ and $b = 0.38a$.

a = _____.

b = _____

21 Compare by filling in the box using the >, <, or = symbol.

Seven hundred thirty-nine and three hundred seventy-four thousandths		Seven hundred thirty-nine and two hundred fifty-five thousandths

22 Mercy is a cow who weighs 808.82 lbs. What is the value of the 2?

(A) 20   (B) $\frac{2}{10}$ (C) $\frac{2}{100}$ (D) $\frac{2}{1000}$

23 **True or False:** $5\frac{1}{2} + 2 = \frac{7}{2}$.

(A) True   (B) False

24 Kerry spent $2\frac{2}{8}$ hours in the training class, which is $1\frac{1}{2}$ hours longer than she had planned. How long was the training class scheduled?

(A) $1\frac{5}{4}$ hours   (B) $1\frac{1}{4}$ hours   (C) $2\frac{3}{4}$ hours   (D) $1\frac{3}{4}$ hours

25 There were $\frac{1}{5}$ of ice cream bars left over from the dinner party. If the ice cream bars were divided equally among 11 people, what fraction of the ice cream bars would each person get to eat?

(A) $\frac{1}{64}$ of the ice cream bars   (B) $\frac{1}{55}$ of the ice cream bars

(C) $\frac{1}{49}$ of the ice cream bars   (D) $\frac{1}{48}$ of the ice cream bars

26 Jack's dog eats $3\frac{1}{2}$ cups of dog food each day. How much dog food will Jack's dog in $4\frac{1}{2}$ days?

(A) $15\frac{3}{4}$ (B) $7\frac{7}{8}$ (C) $6\frac{7}{8}$ (D) $6\frac{6}{8}$

27 Mark walked $\frac{5}{10}$ of a mile. Peter walked $\frac{5}{7}$ of the way with Mark. Jessy walked $\frac{3}{7}$ of the way with Mark. Who walked the furthest with Mark?

_____

28 Ellisa picked $\frac{7}{10}$ of a pound of kiwi. She gave $\frac{1}{8}$ of the kiwi to her mother. How many pounds of kiwi did Ellisa give to her mother?

(A) $\frac{3}{10}$ (B) $\frac{7}{80}$ (C) $\frac{11}{40}$ (D) $\frac{1}{4}$

29 In a parallelogram, the shortest side is 12 in long, and its perimeter equals 52 in. What is the length of the longest side of the parallelogram?

(A) 24   (B) 14   (C) 20   (D) 18

30 Blessy drew a triangle. She measured two of its angles and came up with 85° each. What would the measure of the third angle be?

(A) 45°   (B) 75°   (C) 30°   (D) 10°

31 What is the area of the rectangle with a side measuring 95 mm and 6 cm?

(A) 71 cm²   (B) 53 cm²   (C) 80 cm²   (D) 57 cm²

32 The ordered pair representing Point D is

_____.

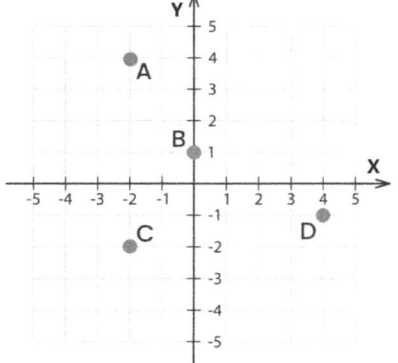

33 Which of the following rectangles have the smallest area?

(A) Rectangle measuring 25 cm by 35 cm

(B) Rectangle measuring 23 cm by 38 cm

(C) Rectangle measuring 33 cm by 25 cm

(D) Rectangle measuring 23 cm by 23 cm

34 Which of the following rhombuses have the smallest area?

(A) Rhombus with side measuring 18 cm and height of 10 cm

(B) Rhombus with diagonals measuring 28 cm and height of 18 cm

(C) Rhombus with side measuring 15 cm and height of 17 cm

(D) Rhombus with diagonals measuring 26 cm and height of 22 cm

35 What is the perimeter of the square below?

(A) 32 units   (B) 20 units

(C) 35 units   (D) 64 units

36 Edward used 68 cm of cloth to design a rectangular curtain. If the curtain is 22 cm long, how wide is the curtain?

(A) 8 cm   (B) 10 cm   (C) 4 cm   (D) 12 cm

---

37 Fill in the blank.

The volume of the prism is _____ cubic units.

---

38 **True or False:** The ordered pair representing Point P is (−3, 2).

(A) True   (B) False

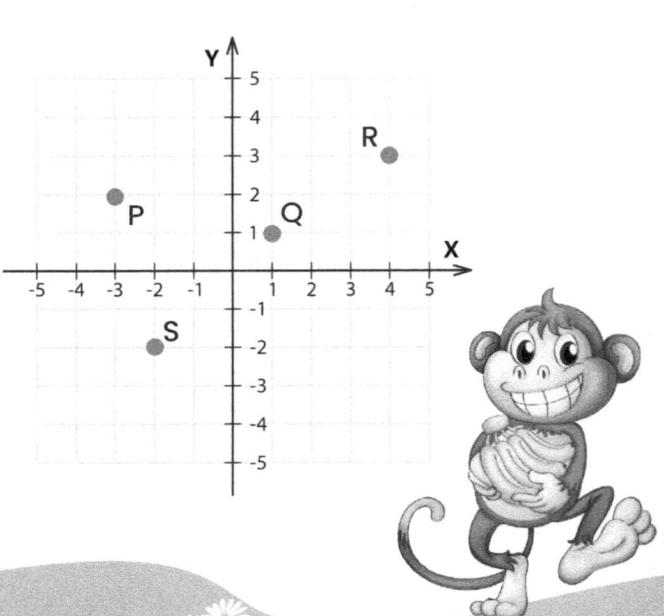

39 A company packs 700 smaller boxes inside large crates to be shipped to stores. Each small box is in the shape of a cube and has edge lengths of 0.5 feet. The large crate is also in the shape of a cube and each side has a length of 3 feet. How many crates are needed to ship these boxes?

(A) 3   (B) 4   (C) 6   (D) 5

40 Find the height of the prism given its volume and base area.
$$V = 195, B = 15$$

(A) 13   (B) 12   (C) 10   (D) 16

41 Find the volume of the prism as a product of the number of layers and the number of cubes in each layer.

 × _____ = _____.

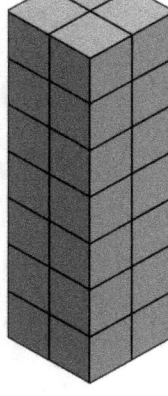

(A) 2×7 = 14

(B) 7×4 = 28

(C) 3×8 = 24

(D) 3×6 = 18

42 Which symbol should be used to compare the two expressions?
$$18 + [35 \div (6+ 1)]_____9 + (5 \times 14) - 8$$

(A) >   (B) <   (C) =   (D) Not enough information

43 The Sirsa family has 6 members. Four of the members have a motorbike and a car each. The other two members have only a car. How many vehicles do they have altogether?

(A) 7   (B) 6   (C) 10   (D) 5

44 Simplify the expression.

$$\{200 \div [5 \times (6+8+6)]\} + 30$$

(A) 32   (B) 44   (C) 48   (D) 46

45 Robert trained athletes for 75 hours in week one, 85 hours in week two, and 220 hours in week three. Each athlete trains for 20 hours. How many athletes did Robert train?

(A) 22   (B) 36   (C) 20   (D) 19

Next Chapter:
Answers & Explanations

ANSWER AND EXPLANATION

TABLE OF CONTENTS

TABLE OF CONTENTS

1.NUMERICAL EXPRESSIONS

1.1 PARENTHESES IN MATH EXPRESSIONS

1. Answer: A
Explanation: The number of multiple-choice questions = 20
Points for each question = 5
The number of short questions = 7
Points for each short question = 6
Total score = (5×20) + (6×7).

2. Answer: Add 6 and 12 or multiply 18 and 4.
Explanation: Answers must include a reasonable explanation such as, "Mary should add 6 and 12 first because they are inside parentheses." However, in this expression, multiplying 18 by 4 will not affect the answer.

3. Answer: B
Explanation: 9 minus 4 is 5, 5 times 12 is 60.
12 × (9-4) = 12 × 5 = 60.

4. Answer: C
Explanation: The order of operations requires parentheses first. 10 plus 2 is 12. Then, 12 times 5 is 60 and 60 plus 14 is 74.
14 + [5 × (10 + 2)] = 14 + [5×12] = 14 + 60 = 74.

5. Answer: C
Explanation: If he subtracts 16 from 20 first, the expression will equal 50, so he should place the parentheses around 20-16.
20 × 20 ÷ (20 - 16) = 400 ÷ 4 = 100.

6. Answer: B
Explanation: The left expression is simplified as follows:
15 + [25 ÷ (4+1)] = 15 + [25÷5] = 15 + 5 = 20
The right expression is simplified as follows:
7 + (4×12) - 9 = 6 + 48 - 9 = 45
The missing symbol is <

7. Answer: He is incorrect. Multiply first.
Explanation: Answers must include a reasonable explanation such as, "I would tell him that, to follow the correct order of operations, he should multiply first. He should multiply 64 by 2 and then add 8."

8. Answer: Multiply 7 and 8
Explanation: Answers must include a reasonable explanation such as, "Olivia should multiply 7 and 8 first. According to the order of operations, we multiply first since there are no parentheses."

9. Answer: Disagree
Explanation: Answers must include a reasonable explanation such as, "I disagree. She must subtract 15-6 is inside parentheses first." The correct order of operations require the operation inside the parentheses to be performed first.

10. Answer: A
Explanation: To equal 14, the expression must include 2 × 7. The number 49 divided by 7 equals 7, so 2+5 must be performed first. Then 2 × 7 = 14.

11. Answer: D
Explanation: Each box has 2 rows of 7 colored pencils, so the expression must add 7 and 7 first and then multiply the answer by 12.

12. Answer: B
Explanation: 9 minus 4 is 5, 5 times 15 is 75.
15 × (9-4) = 15 × 5 = 75.

13. Answer: A
Explanation: Emma scored: 45 - 25 = 20.
Dane scored half as many points as Emma = 20 ÷ 2 = 10.

14. Answer: D
Explanation: Total amount of items Mercy bought = 4 + 6 + 4 = 14
Mercy paid with $38
Expression = 38 - (4+6+4) = 38-14 = 24.

15. Answer: A
Explanation:
5 added to 3 first, then 8 multiply by 3
Expression $(5+3) \times 3 = 8 \times 3 = 24$.

16. Answer: A
Explanation: Three of the members have a motorbike and a car each = 3×2
Another member has only a car = 1×1
Total number of vehicles
$(3 \times 2) + (1 \times 1) = 6 + 1 = 7$

17. Answer: D
Explanation: One dining table set includes items $(4 + 5 + 1)$
Total items needed to set all 10 tables
$= 10 \times (4 + 5 + 1) = 10 \times 10 = 100$.

18. Answer: B
Explanation: 8 divided by 2 first, then 4 multiply by 9
Expression $(8 \div 2) \times 9 = 4 \times 9 = 36$.

19. Answer: A
Explanation:
Correct answer is $8 \times (9 - 4) = 8 \times 5 = 40$
So, Mylan's solution is not correct.

20. Answer: A
Explanation:
Tara buys five paperbacks = 5×1.75
Tara buys two hardbacks = 2×5
Tara receives = $30 - [(5 \times 1.75) + (2 \times 5)]$
$= 30 - [8.75 + 10] = 30 - 18.75 = 11.25$.

1.2 VARIABLES AND EXPRESSIONS

1. Answer: C
Explanation: Let z represent cookies, and a week contains 7 days.
Total number of cookies = $7 \times z$.

2. Answer: C
Explanation: $x \div (-25 + 20) + 13 = 20x \div 8 = 20$
$x = 160$.

3. Answer: B
Explanation: Given $G(70 - 40) = 90$
$G(30) = 90$
$G = 90 \div 30 = 3$.

4. Answer: C
Explanation: Given $k + 5 \times 10 = 300$
$k + 50 = 300$
$k = 300 - 50 = 250$.

5. Answer: A
Explanation: One week=7 days
n weeks $7 \times n = 7n$
David exercised one time a day for n week
$= 1 \times 7n = 7n$.

6. Answer: Disagree
Explanation: Answers must include a reasonable explanation such as, "Disagree, if the expression is correct, the words should be half as much, not three times as much. OR The expression should be $(655 - 346) \times 3$.

7. Answer: A quantity eight times the sum of sixty-six and two hundred thirty-two
Explanation: Answers must include a reasonable explanation such as, "$(66+232) \times 8$ can be written as "eight times the sum of 66 and 232."

8. Answer: No
Explanation: Answers must include a reasonable explanation such as, "No, the expression would need a parenthesis around $585 + 89$ to show seven times a sum. As written, it shows 7 times $585 + 89$.

9. Answer: D
Explanation: The expression $5 \times (4586 + 182)$ means 5 times more than the sum of 4586 and 182. When an expression includes a number within a parenthesis that includes a + or a - , it means the number times a sum or a difference.

ANSWERS AND EXPLANATIONS

10. Answer: B
Explanation: The words require 23 and 4 to be added first, which means they are inside a set of parentheses. Then the sum is multiplied by 5.

11. Answer: A
Explanation: The numbers 19 and 4 are multiplied first, then add the difference of 8 and 2.

12. Answer: 50 ÷ (6+2)
Explanation: The expression $50 \div (6+2)$ shows that 50 is divided by the sum of 6 and 2.

13. Answer: True
Explanation: The expression $(1994 - 77) \div 2$ can be written as the difference of 1,994and 77 then divided by 2.

14. Answer: False
Explanation: To match the words, the expression needs to have parentheses. It should be $33 \times (15 + 658)$.

15. Answer: D
Explanation: The numbers for x in the points are 10, 8, and 6. This means the rule for x is subtract 2.

16. Answer: C
Explanation: The rule for x is add 3, so to find the x in the point before another point, subtract 3 from the x-value. The rule for y is add 4, so to find the y in the point before another point, subtract 7 from the y-value. The ordered pair before (5, 6) is (2, 2).

17. Answer: B
Explanation: The rule for x is add 3 to find the next x, and the rule for y is add 10 to find the next y. The next ordered pair is $(14 + 3, 30+10) = (17,40)$.

18. Answer: True
Explanation: The table follows the pattern of x is always 4 less than y.

19. Answer: A
Explanation: To find the next point, start with (8, 40). The next point is found using the rule: $(8 \times 2, 408)$ which results in (16, 5).

20. Answer: D
Explanation: Using the rule, one option to find y is to write the equation $y = 4x$. Then, if $y = 20$, solve for x. The solution is 5.

1.3 MULTI-STEP EXPRESSIONS

1. Answer: C
Explanation: Given expression is
$= (20-18) + (31+17) \times 4$
$= (2) + (48) \times 2$
$= 2 + 96$
$= 98.$

2. Answer: D
Explanation: Given expression is
$= 100 \div [5 \times (2+2+6)] \} + 40$
$= \{100 \div [5 \times (10)] \} + 40$
$= \{100 \div [50] \} + 40$
$= 2 + 40$
$= 42.$

3. Answer: B
Explanation: Given expression is
$= 90 - \{(9 \times 10) - [5 + (5 \times 5)] \}$
$= 90 - \{(90) - [5 + (25)] \}$
$= 90 - \{(90) - [30] \}$
$= 90 - 60$
$= 30.$

4. Answer: A
Explanation: Logan buys 5 oranges for 85 cents = 5×85
Logan 4 bananas for 38 cents each = 4×38
The amount of money he has spent on oranges and bananas $5 \times 85 + (4 \times 38)$.

5. Answer: A
Explanation: Mr. James has 64 yards of ribbon. He wants to use 6-yard ribbon pieces to wrap 3 boxes = 6 × 3 and 4 -yard ribbon pieces to wrap 9 boxes = 4 × 9
Therefore, The amount of ribbon Mr. James has left after wrapping = 64 - (6×3) + (4×9).

6. Answer: A
Explanation:
The given expression is [40 - (14-7) - 4 × 8]
In the rule, step 1 is inside the brackets. Subtract 7 from 14. And the second step is multiplication, which is multiplying 4 and 8.

7. Answer: C
The given expression 42 - 23 + 6 (18-9)
In the rule, step 1 is inside the brackets. Subtract 9 from 18. And the second step is multiplication, which is to multiply 6 by the difference from Step 1.

8. Answer: C
Explanation: The total cost of 6 hardback books = 6 × 3. The total cost of 12 paperback books = 12 × 2.5. Therefore, the amount of money Isabella could spend on the books = (6×3) + (12×2.5) = 18 + 30 = 48.

9. Answer: A
Explanation: Given expression is
= {9000 ___ 65(240 ___ 120) ___ 100}
= {9000 - 65(240 -120) + 100}
= 9000 - 65 × 120 + 100
= 9000 - 7800 + 100
= 1200 + 100
= 1300

10. Answer: C
Explanation: Olivia has $88.
She buys 4 notebooks for $8 each = 4 × 8
She also buys a backpack for $24 and a calculator for $35 = 24 + 35
The amount of money she spends
= 4 × 8 + 24 + 35.

11. Answer: D
Explanation: Given [22 ___ 8 ___ (5 ___ 9)]
= [22 × 8 - (5 × 9) = 176 - 45 = 131.

12. Answer: B
Explanation: Noah walks 4 miles every day for 6 days each week = 4 × 6
Therefore, the total number of miles Noah walks in half of a year = (4×6) × (52÷2)
= 24 × 26
= 624 miles.

13. Answer: No
Explanation: Left Side =
4 × [5+(7-3)] = 4 × 5 + 4 = 4 × 9 = 36 and
Right Side = 4 × [5 - (7-3)] = 4×(5-4) = 4×1=4
Therefore, Left Side Right Side.

14. Answer: D
Explanation: Yes
Side A = 20 cm
Side B = 20 - 8 cm
Side C = (20-8) + 4 cm
Perimeter of the triangle =
{20 + (20-8) + (20-8+4)} = {20+12+16} = 48.

15. Answer: Answers will vary
Explanation: Sample response: multiply 7 and 2, then subtract the product from 9.

16. Answer: Answers may vary.
Explanation: Sample response:
= [(20-11) × 8 + (9-5)]
= [(9) × 8 + (4)]
= [72 + 4] = 76.

17. Answer: B
Explanation: Amount Ms. Mia has left
= [600 + (600×2)] - ($\frac{600×2}{2}$)] = 600 + 1200 - $\frac{1200}{2}$] = 1800 - 600 = 1200.

18. Answer: D
Explanation: Cost of 8 pencils = 8 × 27 cents
Cost of 6 erasers = 88 cents
Cost of 5 notepads = 5 × 92 cents
Total amount spent = (8×27) + 88 + (5×92)
= 216 + 88 + 460 = 764 cents.

19. Answer: A
Explanation: Total amount paid = $300
Cost of 6 shirts = 6 × $30
Cost of 12 pairs of socks = $20
Cost of 4 hats = $32
Amount remaining =
300 - [(6×30) + 20 + 32] = 300 - 232 = 68.

20. Answer: A
Explanation:
Emma buys 6 burgers for 15 dollars = 6 × 15
She also buys 4 large fries for 3 dollars each
= 4 × 3
and 6 milkshakes for 4 dollars each = 6 × 4
Expression of Emma spends on burgers, fries, and milkshakes = (6×15) + (4×3) + (6×4).

1.4 CHAPTER REVIEW

1. Answer: Yes
Explanation: Answers must include a reasonable explanation such as, "Yes, the difference means to subtract, so subtract 225 from 4365 in parentheses. Then, to find half of that, divide by 2."

2. Answer: A
Explanation: The product of one-fifth and one-third $= \frac{1}{5} \times \frac{1}{3}$
The difference of five-ninths and one-half
$= \frac{5}{9} - \frac{1}{2}$
Therefore, the numerical expression is
$= (\frac{1}{5} \times \frac{1}{3}) - (\frac{5}{9} - \frac{1}{2})$.

3. Answer: +
Explanation: Sum of two number means add them with a + sign.

4. Answer: A
Explanation: Given, there are 348 markers in a bin. Five packages of 9 markers are added to the bin Therefore, the expression is
348 + (5×9).

5. Answer: (3, 6), (4, 7) and (5, 8)
Explanation: The relationship between x and y, is y = x + 3. The next point is at (3, 3 + 3) or at (3, 6). Then, the next point is at (4, 4 + 3) or at (4, 7), and the third point is at (5, 5 + 3) or at (5, 8).

6. Answer: A
Explanation: Four and fifty hundredth = 4.50
And the difference of sixteen and fifteen
= 16-15.Therefore, the expression =
4.50 - (16-15).

7. Answer: 3, 13, 4, 14 and (5, 15)
Explanation: The first point is (2, 12) and the relationship between x and y is y = 10 + x. The next point is at (3, 3 + 10) or at (3, 13). Then, the next point is at (4, 4 + 10) or at (4, 14), and the third point is at (5, 5 +10) or at (5, 15).

8. Answer: B
Explanation: 640,000 ÷ (799+1) = 640,000 ÷ 800 = 800 = Left Side.
640,000 ÷ (79+1) = 640,000 ÷ 80 = 8000 = Right Side. Left Side < Right Side.

9. Answer: 30
Explanation: Answers must include a reasonable explanation such as, "The number 30 is missing from the pattern. Each value is 6 larger than the previous one".

10. Answer: C
Explanation: There are 60 minutes in one hour and 60 seconds in one minute. The result is found by multiplying the number of hours by 8.15 × 60 × 60.

11. Answer: B
Explanation: In the table, y is always 14 more than x, so 1 plus 14 is 15.

12. Answer: A
Explanation: Subtract the amount of time spent on science and math homework from two hours to determine the amount of time left.Therefore, the expression is 2 - $(\frac{1}{8}+\frac{1}{4})$.

13. Answer: C
Explanation: If the rule is (x + 4, y + 7), then the sequence will be (4, 6), (8, 13), (12, 20).

14. Answer: D
Explanation: Find the sum (total) for the pencils and pens. Divide this amount by 36 Therefore, the expression is $\frac{300+80}{36}$.

15. Answer: A
Explanation: If the y-value is 33 more than the x-value, then the x-value is 33 less than the y-value. Thus, 55 minus 33 is 22.

16. Answer: Multiply 6 by the difference between 14 and 7.
Explanation: Multiply 6 by the difference between 14 and 7.

17. Answer: 12 × (25+12)
Explanation: Answers must include a reasonable explanation such as, "Add 25 and 12 first to figure out how many writing utensils are on each table. Then, multiply that number by 12 to get the total number of writing utensils.
The expression is 12 × (25+12)."

18. Answer: D
Explanation: 48 × ($\frac{3}{4}$×30). If $\frac{1}{4}$ of the offices have windows, this means $\frac{3}{4}$ of the offices do not have windows.

19. Answer: I agree, Leo is correct.
Explanation: Answers must include a reasonable explanation such as, "I agree, the addition of 12 and 50 is inside the parentheses so it must be performed first."

20. Answer: D
Explanation: Write an equation:
10 + (n × 5) = 55. Subtract 10 from both sides leaving (n × 5) = 45. Divide both sides by 5. The solution is n = 9.

2. PLACE VALUE

2.1 PATTERNS IN MULTIPLYING AND DIVIDING

1. Answer: A
Explanation: Given 40 × 70 can be expressed as 10 × 4 × 10 × 7. By using the property, 100(4×7) = 100 × 28 = 2800.

2. Answer: D
Explanation: Given 810 ÷90 can be expressed as 81 × 10 ÷ 9 × 10.
By using the property (81 ÷ 9) = 9

3. Answer: A
Explanation: Number of cards in a page = 30 cards. Number of pages = 80 pages
Total number of cards = 30×80 = 2,400 cards.

4. Answer: B
Explanation: Given 1800 ÷ 60 can be expressed as 180 × 10 ÷ 6 × 10.
Divide both the numerator and denominator by 10 to get, 180 ÷ 6 = 30.

5. Answer: C
Explanation:
60 times larger, that is 60 × 6 = 360.

6. Answer: A
Explanation: Let the unknown number be x
6, 400 ÷ x = 8
x = 6400 ÷ 8 = 800.

7. Answer: A
Explanation: Let y be the unknown number
70 × y = 4,900
y = 4,900 ÷ 70 = 70.

8. Answer: D
Explanation: Let m be the missing number.
m ÷ 440 = 20
m = 440 × 20 = 8800.

9. Answer: A
Explanation: Let m be the missing number
$m \times 40 = 3,600$; $m = 3,600 \div 40 = 90$.

10. Answer: C
Explanation:
Total number of raffle tickets = 4,400
Number of band members = 2,200
Number of tickets per band member = $4,400 \div 2,200 = 2$.

11. Answer: B
Explanation: Liam had 60 pieces of taffy.
Henry had 20 times more taffy $= 60 \times 20 = 1200$.

12. Answer: A
Explanation:
Total number of minutes = 45,000
Number of children = 900
Number of minutes per child = $45,000 \div 900 = 50$.

13. Answer: 1000
Explanation: Tom had 40 pieces of cake.
Jerry had 25 times more cake $= 40 \times 25 = 1000$.

14. Answer: D
Explanation: Total hours Robert trained
athletes = $75 + 85 + 200 = 360$.
Each athlete trained for 20 hours each
$360 \div 20 = 18$.

15. Answer: 9,000 and 7,800
Explanation: Given, the pet shop has 30 times more pet supplies than the department store.
- Bones: $300 \times 30 = 9,000$
- Toys: $260 \times 30 = 7,800$.

16. Answer: 7,389
Explanation: Given Marion baked 9 dozen cookies day 1
She increased her baking by 20 times on day 2: $9 \times 20 = 180$.
She increased the baking from day 2 by 40 times for day 3: $180 \times 40 = 7,200$.
Total dozen cookies: $9 + 180 + 7,200 = 7,389$.

17. Answer: 10 boxes
Explanation: Total batches of slime:
$190 + 140 + 270 = 600$.
Total number of boxes Jodie need:
$600 \div 60 = 10$.

18. Answer: D
Explanation: Given, Alva printed 60 photos in week one.
She printed 20 times more for the next week:
$60 \times 20 = 1,200$.
Then she increased that amount 20 times again for week three: $1,200 \times 20 = 24,000$.
Total photos she prints week two and week three combined: $1,200 + 24,000 = 25,200$.

19. Answer: Yes
Explanation: Required quantity = $30 \times 30 = 900$
Available quantity = 1000
There are enough markers for all the students.

20. Answer: 29,400
Explanation: Amount of wood David used = 600
Jase builds another model plane and uses 50 times more wood = $600 \times 50 = 30,000$
Therefore, the answer is $30,000 - 600 = 29,400$.

2.2 MULTIPLYING AND DIVIDING BY 10

1. Answer: $134.60 and $7.70
Explanation: Given that the Records by Ethan is a new shop, they plan to mark everything up 10 times over the original price.
Headphones –
Original price: $13.46 \times 10 = \$134.60$
Posters – Original price: $0.77 \times 10 = \$7.70$.

2. Answer: B
Explanation: The total hours Jacob trained golfers = $40 + 55 + 135 = 230$
Number of golfers Jacob trained = $230 \div 10 = 23$.

3. Answer: A
Explanation: When dividing, the problem is dividend ÷ divisor = quotient. In this problem, let the divisor be n. Now, substituting the values, you get 640 ÷ n = 10. What number times 10 gives you 640? The answer is 64.

4. Answer: B
Explanation: Dividing is dividend divided by divisor equals quotient. This problem is 90 ÷ 10, so the quotient is 9.

5. Answer: C
Explanation: When dividing, the problem is dividend divided by the divisor to equal the quotient.. In this problem,
you know n ÷ 10=55. Consider what number divided by 10 is 55. The answer is 550.

6. Answer: Yes
Explanation:
Number of glue sticks per box: 52
Mr. Noah plans to purchase 100 boxes of glue sticks
Total number of glue sticks : 52 × 100 = 5200
Number of students at the school : 5000
They have enough glue sticks.

7. Answer: 87
Explanation: When dividing, the problem is dividend divided by the divisor to equal quotient. In this problem, 870 ÷ n = 10. You need to determine what number will go into 870, 10 times. The answer is 87.

8. Answer: D
Explanation: Divide 43,000 ÷ 100. Then, the answer is 430.

9. Answer: A
Explanation: Multiply 6 × 100 and 4 × 100 and then add the answers get 600 + 400 = 1000.

10. Answer: D
Explanation: Multiply 100 × 10 × 6 = 6,000.

11. Answer: $2,626
Explanation: Owen spent $26 on cards
He bought baseball jersey for 100 times -
$26 × 100 = $2,600
Add them together $26 + $2600 = $2,626.

12. Answer: A
Explanation: Divide 494.7 ÷ 100 = 4.947.

13. Answer: C
Explanation: Ella ran 6.9 minutes
Daisy ran 10 times as long: 6.9 × 10 = 69 minutes. The combined total would be
6.9 + 69 = 75.9 minutes.

14. Answer: $45,200
Explanation: Add 440 + 12, then multiply that result by 100. That is, 452 × 100 = 45,200.

15. Answer: 10,000
Explanation: First find the total number of students by multiplying 100 and 20.
100 × 20 = 2000. Then multiply 2000 with 5 to find a total number of letters.
2000 × 5 = 10,000.

16. Answer: A
Explanation:
Number of chips with Creed = 3,300
Number of chips with Cruz = 33
Creed's number has two more zeros than Cruz's. Creed has 100 times more than Cruz.

17. Answer: C
Explanation: Total number of minutes = 4,500
Number of children = 100
Number of minutes per child = 4,500÷100=45.

18. Answer: A
Explanation: Multiply 56 × 2.

19. Answer: B
Explanation: Multiply 100, 9, 2 in any order. 100 times 2 is 200; 200 times 9 is 1,800.

20. Answer: C
Explanation: Multiply 38 × 100 = 3,800.

2.3 EXPONENTS

1. Answer: D
Here, 4 is multiplied 5 times.
That is 4^5.

2. Answer: B
Explanation: Because the exponent of 10 is 3, add 3 zeros to 325 when multiplying:
$325 \times 1000 = 3,25,000$.

3. Answer: 8,000,000
Explanation: The exponent of 10 is the same as the number of zeros for the place value. Add six zeros because you are multiplying by 10 six times.

4. Answer: A
Explanation: Because the exponent of 10 is 4, add 4 zeros to 645 when multiplying:
$645 \times 10,000 = 6,450,000$.

5. Answer: B
Explanation: The correct statement is $78.22 \div 10$ because $78.22 \div 100 = 0.7822$.

6. Answer: B
Explanation: The decimal place was moved 2 places to the left. Thus, to retain the original value, multiply by 100. The given expression $(93.6 \times 10,000)$ is 936,000.

7. Answer: D
Explanation: The decimal place was moved 3 places to the left. Thus, to retain the original value, multiply by 1,000:
$440.75 \times 1,000 = 440,750$.

8. Answer: D
Explanation: The number 10^4 is 10,000, so $2 \times 10,000 = 20,000$.

9. Answer: B
Explanation: The decimal moves over four places to the right.

10. Answer: A
Explanation: The decimal moves over two places to the right.

11. Answer: C
Explanation: Because the exponent of 10 is 4, move the decimal 4 places to the right:
$5.8 \times 10,000 = 58,000$.

12. Answer: A
Explanation: Because the exponent of 10 is 0, do not add any zeros to 455: $455 \times 1 = 455$
Multiplying by 10^0 is the same as multiplying by 1.

13. Answer: Agree
Explanation: Given $300 \div [10^2 \times 3] =$
$300 \div [100 \times 3] = 300 \div 300 = 1$
Therefore, Olivia got the correct answer.

14. Answer: 99^0, 10^1, 4^2, 5^2, 6^2, 7^4.
Explanation:
$6^2 = 6 \times 6 = 36$, $7^4 = 7 \times 7 \times 7 \times 7 = 2401$, $10^1 = 10$,
$99^0 = 1$, $4^2 = 4 \times 4 = 16$, $5^2 = 25$
$1 < 10 < 16 < 25 < 36 < 2401$.

15. Answer: 4^4, 3^4, 2^6, 6^2
Explanation: $2^6 = 64$, $3^4 = 81$, $4^4 = 256$, $6^2 = 36$
$256 > 81 > 64 > 36$.

16. Answer: Peter
Explanation: Let a^b be an exponent number. Here a is the base. The base number is used as a factor in multiplying itself.

17. Answer: C
Explanation: $54 \times 9 = 486$
$486 \div 10^4 = 0.0486$
While dividing, the decimal moves to the left the number of places of the exponent.

18. Answer: A
Explanation: $6 \times 6 \times 6 = 216$, that is $6^3 = 216$
Therefore, the missing exponent is 3.

19. Answer: C
Explanation: 9×9=81, that is 92=81
Therefore, the missing base is 9.

20. Answer: Answer will vary
Explanation:

Exponential form	Expanded form	Standard form
2^5	2×2×2×2×2	32

2.4 COMPARING AND ROUNDING DECIMALS

1. Answer: B
The 8 makes the 6 roundups.

2. Answer: 0.85, 0.86, 0.87, 0.88.
Explanation: Rounded to the nearest hundredth 0.87, 0.86, 0.88, 0.85. In increasing order, they are 0.85, 0.86, 0.87, 0.88.

3. Answer: A
Explanation: 6.66 x 10 = 66.6. Multiplying by 10 moves the decimal one place to the right.

4. Answer: B
Explanation: 4.38 times 100 is 438. Multiplying by 100 moves the decimal two places to the right.

5. Answer: C
Explanation: Dividing by 10 moves the decimal one place to the left.
78.69 ÷ 10 = 7.869

6. Answer: C
Explanation: The number 4 leaves the number 5 stay the same.

7. Answer: A
Explanation: The 8 in the hundredth-place rounds the 4 up.

8. Answer: B
Explanation: Given 0.889 ___ 0.998
Multiply both sides by 1000 to get 889 and 998, which is <.

9. Answer: C
Explanation: Comparing all students' details James ran the most miles. (Hundredth place is 6 which is the highest value compared to others)

10. Answer: D
Explanation: The 8 rounds the 5 up. Elvis' correct response is 25.6.

11. Answer: <
Explanation: The number 20.033 < 20.303. Compare decimals beginning from the left, one digit at a time.

12. Answer: C
Explanation: When rounding a number, review the place to the right of the digit the number is being rounded to. If the digit if 5 or more, round up, and if the digit is 4 or less, change all digits to the right of that place to 0.

13. Answer: C
Explanation: 45 is less than 50, therefore 9.45 is not be considered far enough.

14. Answer: D
Explanation: 49 is less than 56, therefore 7.49 is the possible weight of the second chicken.

15. Answer: D
Explanation: 99 is more than 65,75 and 79, therefore 87.99 is the possible longest length of wood.

16. Answer: A
Explanation: 30 is less than 45, therefore 67.3 is the possible length of the shorter piece.

17. Answer: 5,754.0378
Explanation:
1,304.0256 + 4,450.0122 = 5,754.0378
Therefore, nearest thousandth: 5,754.038.

18. Answer: B
Explanation: 6.56 + 13.34 = 20.44.

19. Answer: B
Explanation: 2.36 is the value of X because it is the closest value to 2.34.

20. Answer: C
Explanation: 920 is larger than 400, 678 and 288, therefore 67.920 is the largest number.

2.5 CHAPTER REVIEW

1. Answer: C
Explanation: 4,200 ÷ 2 = 2,100
They each ran a total of 2,100.
2,100 ÷ 30 = 70. Therefore, each person runs 70 minutes each day.

2. Answer: 1,100
Explanation: First find the perimeter of the field Perimeter = 2 (length + width) = 2 (20,000+2,000) = 44,000. Now, divide the perimeter by 40 as there are fence posts every 40 feet. 44,000 ÷ 40 = 1,100.

3. Answer: D
Explanation: Compare the decimals beginning with the first place to the right of the decimal point:
48.38 > 48.372 > 48.37>48.36.

4. Answer: B
Explanation: There really is no need to compare the scores above 87. However, compare the decimal values beginning on the left next to the decimal point:
86.03 < 86.3< 86.33 < 86.31

5. Answer: D
Explanation:
Ernest needs 78 buckets of water.
Total capacity of gallons= 78×100=7,800
There are two zeros added.

6. Answer: C
Explanation: The total is 16.255
The 5 rounds the 2 up.

7. Answer: A
Explanation: First, 187 ÷ 8 = 23.375. This number must be rounded up to 24, so there is at least 1 counselor per 8 children.

8. Answer: B
Explanation: The hundredths digit is 9, which is odd, but when rounded the tenth digit is 6, which is even.

9. Answer: C
Explanation: 29 + 16 = 45, which will require 5 bills to pay.

10. Answer: D
Explanation: Multiply 78 × 17 = 1,326.

11. Answer: C
Explanation: 700 × 2 = 1,400
1,400 ÷ 50 = 28. There are 28 types of vegetables in the garden this year.

12. Answer: A
Explanation: 2,200 − 400 = 1,800
1,800 ÷ 10 = 180, There is one zero in ten so drop one zero in 180.

13. Answer: A
Explanation: 24 × 100 = 2,400
2,400 + 24 = 2,424

14. Answer: A
Explanation: 2.5 × 30 = 75
There is one decimal place.

15. Answer: B
Explanation: $700 \div 10 = 70$
Therefore, Jacob can make 70 cheeseburgers.

16. Answer: C
Explanation: Multiply $12 \times 24 = 288$.

17. Answer: D
Explanation: Multiply $44 \times 22 = 968$.

18. Answer: B
Explanation: Divide $75 \div 15 = 5$

19. Answer: B
Explanation: The best way to solve this problem is to reduce both the dividend and the divisor by 10, which makes the problem $850 \div 5$.

20. Answer: 53,000 Or 52,000
Explanation: Round 9.8 to 10 and round 5311 to 5300 and then multiply. Alternatively, Multiply 9.8 and 5311 gives 52,047 and then round 52,047 gives 52,000.

3. DECIMALS

3.1 ADDITION AND SUBTRACTION FOR DECIMALS

1. Answer: A and C
Explanation: Given options:
A. $4.18 + 9.17 = 13.35$
B. $4.12 + 9.22 = 13.32 \neq 13.35$
C. $6.18 + 7.17 = 13.35$
D. $5.22 + 7.17 = 13.29 \neq 13.35$

2. Answer: 20.92 (Answers will vary)
Explanation: 0 is the smallest single digit number. So, to get the smallest sum place 0 in the gaps.

3. Answer: 60.19+4.02=(60+4)+(0.19+0.02).
Explanation: 4 standing in the ones place in 4.02 and 2 standing in the hundredths place. Correct calculation:
$60.19 + 4.02 = (60+4) + (0.19+0.02)$.

4. Answer:
Explanation:

$$5.92 \xrightarrow[+0.92]{-5.00} 3.65 \xrightarrow[-1.98]{+2.73} 1.67$$

5. Answer: B
Explanation: Greatest possible difference = Greatest Decimal − Smallest Decimal
Greatest decimal = 8.76
Smallest decimal = 5.6
Greatest possible difference = $8.76 - 5.6 = 3.16$.

6. Answer: A
Explanation: $5.98 = 5.32 + 0.66$
$6.64 = 5.98 + 0.66$
$7.30 = 6.64 + 0.66$
$7.30 + 0.66 = 7.96$
$7.96 + 0.66 = 8.62$.

7. Answer: C
Explanation: Width = 7.02 cm
Perimeter = 28.42 cm
$28.42 = 7.02 + 7.02 + \text{Length} + \text{Length}$
Length + Length = $28.42 - 7.02 - 7.02$
Length + Length = 14.38
Length = 7.19 cm.

8. Answer: B
Explanation:
Longest side = $3.49 + 2.55 = 6.04$ft
Perimeter = $3.49 + 4.28 + 4.44 + 6.04 = 18.25$ft.

9. Answer: 3.85 and 4.75
Explanation:
Sum − difference = $8.6 - 0.9 = 7.7$
Two equal parts = 7.7
One of these parts = 3.85
1st decimal = 3.85
2nd decimal = $3.85 + 0.9 = 4.75$.

10. Answer: B
Explanation: Monday: 4.14 miles
Tuesday: 4.14 + 0.86 = 5 miles
Thursday: 5 + 0.55 = 5.55 miles
Friday: 5.55 + 0.45 = 6 miles.

11. Answer: C
Explanation: 78.80 - 18.45 - 52.50 = 7.85$.

12. Answer: D
Explanation: Width = 15.65 cm
Length = 15.65 +3.66 = 19.31 cm
Perimeter = 15.65 + 15.65 + 19.31 + 19.31 = 26.9 + 33.98 = 69.92 cm.

13. Answer: A
Explanation: To find the sales tax, subtract $82.86 - $76.32 = $6.54.

14. Answer: B
Explanation: To calculate the change, subtract $49.65 from $60.00 is $10.35.

15. Answer: A
Explanation: 11.76 + 22.55 = 34.31.

16. Answer: D
Explanation: To calculate the crates of cucumbers: 87.99 - 45.86 = 42.13.

17. Answer: A
Explanation: Otis ran 7.7 miles.
Today, Otis ran 2.9 miles more than yesterday = 7.7 + 2.9 = 10.6.

18. Answer: B
Explanation: The first tube weighed 0.24 pounds and the second tube weighed 0.48 pounds.
To calculate, subtract 0.48 - 0.24 = 0.24.

19. Answer: D
Explanation: The fruit salad will weigh = 0.34 + 0.43 + 0.48 = 1.25 kg.

20. Answer: A
Explanation: Correct statement: This week Felix spent 333.65 - 328.44 = 5.21 less.

3.2 MULTIPLICATION AND DIVISION FOR DECIMALS

1. Answer: B
Explanation: To solve the equation, divide 4.9 by 0.7 = 7

2. Answer: B
Explanation: 6.005 × 334.5 ≈ 6 × 330 = 1,980
11.04 × 280.13 ≈ 11 × 280 = 3,080
Therefore, 6.005 × 334.5 < 11.04 × 280.13.

3. Answer: A
Explanation: (1.8x-0.4) = 36.4 × 0.6
1.8x - 0.4 = 21.84
1.8x = 21.84 + 0.4
1.8x = 22.24
x = 12.35.

4. Answer: C
Explanation: First round 3.8 to 4 and multiply by 28. 28 times 4 is 112.

5. Answer: 0.12
Explanation: To solve the equation, divide 1.44 by 12.

6. Answer: A
Explanation: Smallest possible width = 6.1 cm
Smallest possible length = 7.11 cm
Smallest possible area = 6.1 × 7.11 = 43.371 cm^2

7. Answer: 308 ÷ 90
Explanation:
3.08 ÷ 0.9 = 30.8 ÷ 9 = 308 ÷ 90 ≠ 308 ÷ 9.

8. Answer: C
Explanation: £8 = $(8×1.37) = $10.96.

9. Answer: A
Explanation: 124 ÷ 15.5 = 8 days.

10. Answer: B
Explanation: $18.60 × 3 = $55.80.

11. Answer: C
Explanation: 12 ÷ 1.5 = 8 questions.

12. Answer: D
Explanation: Price of one chocolate in the box $5.40 ÷ 60 = $0.09.

13. Answer: A
Explanation: The area of the rectangle = 0.79 × 0.5 = 0.395 m² .

14. Answer: C
Explanation: $23.85 ÷ $2.65 = 9 gallons.

15. Answer: B
Explanation: Tia's weight in pounds:
58 × 2.2 = 127.6 pounds.

16. Answer: D
Explanation: Raisins: 8.6 ÷ 18 = 0.5 kg
Candied fruit: 7.4 ÷ 18 = 0.4 kg
One bag weight: 0.5 + 0.4 = 0.9 kg

17. Answer: A
Explanation: 69.6 - 42.6 = 27 m
One piece length: 27 ÷ 9 = 3 m.

18. Answer: 5.71
Explanation:
14.3 × 0.22 + 0.08 = 14.3 × 0.3 = 4.29
4.29 = 10 - 5.71.

19. Answer: B
Explanation: 1.4 - 0.15 × 7 = 1.4 - 1.05 = 0.35m
Crew has 0.35 m of extra rope.

20. Answer: 8 toy snakes
Explanation: $3.2 ÷ $0.4 = 8 toy snakes.

3.3 DIVIDE DECIMALS USING REPEATED SUBTRACTION

1. Answer: B
Explanation: 0.32 divided by 0.02 is equal to
0.32 ÷ 0.02 = 16
2.5 × x = 16, then x = 16 ÷ 2.5 = 6.4.

2. Answer: A
Explanation: Larger room area = m²
Smaller room area = 54 ÷ 1.5 = 36 m²
Smaller room side = 6 m
Perimeter = 6 × 6 = 36 m.

3. Answer: 12.6 4.2 = 3
Explanation: 12 _____ ≈ 12
12 ÷ 3 = 4,then the divisor is 4.2 and the dividend is 4.2 × 3 = 12.6
Therefore, 12.6 ÷ 4.2 = 3.

4. Answer: A
Explanation:
A. 3.5 ÷ 0.7 = 5,
B. 3.5 ÷ 0.5 ≠ 5,
C. 3.5 ÷ 0.07 ≠ 5,
D. 3.5 ÷ 7 ≠ 5.

5. Answer: C
Explanation:

	2.	5
-	0.	5
	2.	0

1st time

	2.	0
-	0.	5
	1.	5

2nd time

	1.	5
-	0.	5
	1.	5

3rd time

	1.	0
-	0.	5
	0.	5

4th time

	0.	5
-	0.	5
	0.	0

5th time

6. Answer: D
Explanation: 2.8 ÷ 0.7 = 4 remainder is 0.

7. Answer: C
Explanation: 2 ÷ 0.5 = 4 remainder is 0

8. Answer: C
Explanation: $4 ÷ 0.8 = 5$

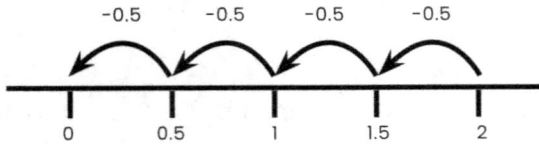

9. Answer: B
Explanation: $34 - 8.5 = 25.5$
$25.5 - 8.5 = 17$
$17 - 8.5 = 8.5$
$8.5 - 8.5 = 0.$

10. Answer: B
Explanation: $10.48 - 2.62 = 7.86$
$7.86 - 2.62 = 5.24$
$5.24 - 2.62 = 2.62$
$2.62 - 2.62 = 0$

11. Answer: D
Explanation: $60.66 - 20.22 = 40.44$
$40.44 - 20.22 = 20.22$
$20.22 - 20.22 = 0$

12. Answer: A
Explanation: $19.2 - 3.2 = 16$
$16 - 3.2 = 12.8$
$12.8 - 3.2 = 9.6$
$9.6 - 3.2 = 6.4$
$6.4 - 3.2 = 3.2$
$3.2 - 3.2 = 0$

13. Answer: D
Explanation: $1.5 - 0.25 = 1.25$
$1.25 - 0.25 = 1$
$1 - 0.25 = 0.75$
$0.75 - 0.25 = 0.50$
$0.50 - 0.25 = 0.25$
$0.25 - 0.25 = 0$

14. Answer: B
Explanation:
Total rate $= 47.9 + 43.5 = 91.4$km/h
Distance $= 639.8$km
Time $= 639.8 ÷ 91.4 = 7$ hours.

15. Answer: 14 and 3.64
Explanation:
If $b = 0.26a$, then $a - 0.26a = 10.36$
$(1-0.26) a = 10.36$
$0.74a = 10.36$
$a = 10.36 ÷ 0.74$
$a = 14$
$b = 0.26 × 14 = 3.64$

16. Answer: C
Explanation: Juice remaining: $4.9 - 0.9 = 4$L
Number of jars filled: $4 ÷ 0.5 = 8$ jars
So Mia fills 8 jars with juice.

17. Answer: A
Explanation:
Weight of the chairs: $12.9 - 4.5 = 8.4$ kg
Number of chairs: $8.4 ÷ 1.2 = 7$ chairs.

18. Answer: D
Explanation: 0.72 of 4: $0.724 = 2.88$
 If 1.8 of a is 2.88 then $1.8a = 2.88$
$a = 2.88 ÷ 1.8 = 1.6$

19. Answer: A
Explanation:
All the remaining answers are near by to the given digit,where as $\frac{9}{100}$ is completely different.

20. Answer: A
Explanation: Right Side:
$(17.6+6.8) ÷ 0.4 = 24.4 ÷ 0.4 = 61$
Left Side: $(176+68) ÷ 4 = 244 ÷ 4 = 61.$

3.4 WRITING DECIMALS USING NUMERALS

1. Answer: 415.152
Explanation: Four hundred fifteen is 415 and one hundred fifty-two thousandths is.152. The decimal place is where the word "and" is when the number is properly written with words.

2. Answer: 69.612
Explanation: Sixty-nine is 69 and six hundred Twelve thousandths is.612. The decimal place is where the word "and" is when the number is properly written with words.

3. Answer: >
Explanation: Left side: Twenty-six and seven hundred thirteen thousandths = 26.713
Right side: Twenty-five and seven hundred fifteen thousandths = 25.715
Therefore: 26.713 > 25.715.

4. Answer: <
Explanation:
Left side: Eight hundred sixteen and one hundred sixty-two thousandths = 816.162
Right side: Eight hundred sixteen and one hundred seventy-one thousandths = 816.171
Therefore: 816.162 < 816.171.

5. Answer: =
Explanation: The two numbers are the same. Thus, 39.916 = 39.916.

6. Answer: C
Explanation: A. Isaac – Sixty-five and six hundredths =65.06
B. Nicki – $65\frac{6}{100}$ = 65.06
C. Ava – sixty-five and six tenths ≠ 65.06
D. Jackie – $60 + 5 + \frac{6}{100}$ = 65.06.

7. Answer: D
Explanation:

A. $40 + 4 + 8 + 9 \neq 44.89$

B. $40 + 4 + \frac{89}{10} \neq 44.89$

C. $40 + 4 + \frac{8}{10} + \frac{9}{10} \neq 44.89$

D. $40 + 4 + \frac{8}{10} + \frac{9}{100} = 44.89$

8. Answer: A
Explanation: 7.095 = 7-ones, 0-tenths, 9-hundredths, 5-thousands.

9. Answer: B
Explanation: 906.87 can be expressed:
$900 + 6 + \frac{8}{10} + \frac{7}{100}$

10. Answer: C
Explanation:
A. Fifty, and fifty-seven ≠ 50.57
B. Fifty, and fifty-seven tenths ≠ 50.57
C. Fifty, and fifty-seven hundredths = 50.57
D. Fifty, fifty-seven ≠ 50.57

11. Answer: B
Explanation: 9.52 = fifty-two hundredths

12. Answer: C
Explanation:
A. Jospin ≠ 54.19
B. Haran ≠ 54.19
C. Nancy = 54.19
D. Benita ≠ 54.19

13. Answer: C
Explanation: $\frac{2}{100}$ is equal to 0.02 . 5000 + $400 + 3 + \frac{2}{100}$ = 5403 + 0.02 = 5403.02

14. Answer: Eighty-seven and six-hundredths
Explanation: 42.12 + 32.44 + 12.5 = 87.06.

15. Answer: B
Explanation:
A. Six million, four hundred three thousand, twenty-three, and eighty-nine thousandths 6,403,023.89
B. Six million, four hundred three thousand, twenty-three, and eighty-nine hundredths =6,403,023.89
C. Six billion, four hundred three thousand, twenty-three, and eighty-nine hundredths 6,403,023.89
D. Six million, four hundred three thousand, twenty-three, and eighty-nine 6,403,023.89

16. Answer: Five hundred, twenty-eight, and four-tenths.
Explanation: $52.84 \times 10 = 528.4$.

17. Answer: $20 + 1 + \frac{59}{100}$
Explanation: $6.16 + 15.43 = 21.59 = 20 + 1 + \frac{59}{100}$

18. Answer: D
Explanation: $9.186 = 9$(ones). 1(tenths) 8(hundredths) 6(thousands)

19. Answer: D
Explanation: $\frac{9}{1000} = 0.0009 \neq 0.009$ (nine thousandths)

20. Answer: D
Explanation:

A. Coral – twenty-three and eighty-five hundredths = 23.85

B. Chris $-20 + 3 + \frac{8}{10} + \frac{5}{100} = 23.85$

C. Azar- $-(2 \times 10) + (3 \times 1) + 8 \times 1\frac{1}{10} + 5 \times \frac{1}{100}$ =23.85

D. Riya – twenty-three and eighty- five tenths $\neq 23.85$

1. Answer: 23.22
Explanation: $2.76 + 1.92 + 18.54 = 23.22$

2. Answer: 1.66
Explanation: $7.6 - 5.94 = 1.66$

3. Answer: B
Explanation: On the first and second day James drove $400.76 + 305.65 = 706.41$ miles. On the third day James drove 776.66 which is not ten times the first and second day of 706.41.

4. Answer: B
Explanation: The shipment contained 10 rolls of white fabric: $10 \times 72.3 = 723$ yards, and 4 rolls of black fabric: $4 \times 112.3 = 449.2$ yards. $449.2 \times 10 = 4492 > 723$

5. Answer: 6, 7, 8, 9
Explanation: 6 is in the ones place, 7 is in the tenths place, 8 is in the hundredths place, 9 is in the thousandths place.

6. Answer: 9.05
Explanation: Multiply the minutes by 100: 5.43 100 = 543. Then divide the product by 60 to convert the time to hours, $543 \div 60 = 9.05$.

7. Answer: A
Explanation:
Kolton has $61.65 to spend on T-shirts
Divide: $61.65 \div 6.85 = 9$ T-shirts

8. Answer: D
Explanation:
Nuts and raisins: $2.9 + 2.25 = 5.15$ kg
Candied fruit: $6 - 5.15 = 0.85$ kg.

9. Answer: B
Explanation:
A. $a \div (b \div c) = 12.54 \div 0.096 = 130.625$ false
B. $a \div b \div c = 5.225 \div 25 = 0.209$ true
C. $(b \div a) \div c = 0.191 \div 25 = 0.0077$ false
D. $c \div (a \div b) = 25 \div 5.225 = 4.78$ false

10. Answer: C
Explanation: $(6.25-1.3) \div 0.55 = 9$ days
(excluding the first day)
Total number of days = 9 + 1 = 10 (including
the first day)

11. Answer: 1.0 kg and 1.5 kg
Explanation: Both brothers' candies = 2.5 –
0.5 = 2.0 kg
Rebels' brothers candies = 2.0 ÷ 2 = 1.0 kg
Rebels' candies = 1.0 + 0.5 = 1.5 kg

12. Answer: B
Explanation: $3.84 \times 2.33 \approx 4 \times 2 = 8$

13. Answer: D
Explanation: Length: 9.24 cm
Width: 6.75 cm
Area: $9.24 \times 6.75 = 62.37$ cm^2

14. Answer: B
Explanation: Multiply L × W × H =
V: $50.5 \times 50.5 \times 160.6 = 409{,}570.15$

15. Answer: A
Explanation: Add: 6.85 + 3.6 = 10.45 L.

16. Answer: 0.033, 0.303, 0.330, 0.333, 0.336
Explanation: Compare decimals beginning
with the first digit on the left.
0.033 < 0.303 < 0.330 < 0.333 < 0.336

17. Answer: 0.772,0.727, 0.707,0.077, 0.071
Explanation: Compare decimals beginning
with the first digit after the decimal point.
0.772 > 0.727 > 0.707> 0.077 > 0.071

18. Answer: 4
Explanation: Add the prices: $19.44 + $42.5
= $61.94, which means he has to give the
cashier (4) $20 bills, which is $80. Three $20
bills are $60.

19. Answer: 4.2476
Explanation: She should have rounded the
last 5 up to 6 because of the 9 in the hundred
thousandth.

20. Answer: D
Explanation:
Small cubes weight: $0.06 \times 14 = 0.84$ kg
Large cubes weight: $0.25 \times 6 = 1.5$ kg
Total weight: 0.84 + 1.5 = 2.34 kg

4. FRACTIONS

4.1 ADDITION AND SUBTRACTION FOR FRACTION AND IMPROPER FRACTION

1. Answer: B
Explanation:
To solve for x, cross multiply: 7x = 84
x = 12.

2. Answer:
Explanation: Smallest numerators and

greatest denominators:
$\frac{5}{7} + \frac{6}{8} = \frac{5}{7} + \frac{3}{4} = \frac{41}{28}$ (smallest)
$\frac{5}{8} + \frac{6}{7} = \frac{35}{56} + \frac{48}{56} = \frac{83}{56}$.

3. Answer: D
Explanation:
To solve for x, cross multiply: 5x = 405. x = 81.

4. Answer: 1
Explanation: $\frac{1}{2} + \frac{1}{6} - \frac{5}{12} = \frac{6+2-5}{12} = \frac{3}{12} = \frac{1}{4}$.

5. Answer: A

Explanation: To change $6\frac{3}{5}$ to an improper fraction, multiply 5 by 6 and add 3 for the numerator of the improper fraction: $\frac{33}{5}$.

6. Answer: C

Explanation: To change $\frac{21}{6}$ to a mixed number, divide 21 by 6 to get the whole number portion. The remainder (1) is the numerator of the fraction portion: $3\frac{3}{6}$.

7. Answer: B

Explanation: To solve for x, subtract $\frac{5}{12}$ from both sides of the equation:

$\frac{3}{4} - \frac{5}{12} = \frac{9-5}{12} = \frac{4}{12} = \frac{1}{3}$.

8. Answer: A

Explanation: Add: $\frac{1}{5} + \frac{2}{3} = \frac{3+10}{12} = \frac{13}{15}$.

9. Answer: B

Explanation: The whole number portion of the mixed number is changed from $2\frac{1}{3} + 1 = \frac{2}{3} - \rightarrow \frac{7}{3} + 1 = \frac{10}{3} \neq \frac{2}{3}$

10. Answer: A

Explanation:

$4\frac{3}{5} + 1 > 1\frac{6}{5} \rightarrow \frac{23}{5} + 1 > \frac{11}{5} \rightarrow \frac{28}{5} > \frac{11}{5}$

Therefore, the given expression is true.

11. Answer: A

Explanation: Numerators: 1, 2, 3

Denominators: 2, 3, 4

Fractions: $\frac{1}{2}, \frac{2}{3}, \frac{3}{4}$

Perimeter $= \frac{1}{2} + \frac{2}{3} + \frac{3}{4} = \frac{12+16+18}{24} = \frac{46}{24} = \frac{23}{12}$

12. Answer: A

Explanation: If there are 16 people and each person will get an equal share, then each person gets to eat one part out of 16 parts, which is 1/16 of the ricotta.

13. Answer: A

Explanation: Second bag:

$2\frac{4}{8} + 2\frac{1}{3} = 4 + (\frac{1}{4} + \frac{1}{3}) = 4\frac{7}{12}$

Together:

$2\frac{4}{8} + 4\frac{7}{12} = 6 + (\frac{1}{4} + \frac{7}{12}) = 6 + (\frac{40}{48}) = 6\frac{5}{6}$

14. Answer: C

Explanation: The problem states that 15 pieces of pizza were eaten. This means that 15/18 of the pizza was eaten, leaving 3/18 of the pizza left over.

15. Answer: D

Explanation: Scheduled time:

$2\frac{6}{14} - 1\frac{1}{2} = (2 - 1) + (\frac{3}{7} + \frac{1}{2}) = 1 + \frac{13}{14} = 1\frac{13}{14}$

16. Answer: B

Explanation: The fractions need to be converted to the common denominator. The mistake made here is that the numerators and denominators were added without finding the common denominators.

17. Answer: B

Explanation: The fractions need to be converted to the common denominator. The mistake made here is that the numerators and denominators were added without finding the common denominators.

18. Answer: $\frac{1}{36}, \frac{41}{36}$

Explanation: Green strip: $\frac{7}{12}$ square yards, yellow strip: $\frac{5}{9}$ square yards

Difference $\frac{7}{12} - \frac{5}{9} = \frac{63-60}{108} = \frac{3}{108} = \frac{1}{36}$

Total area $\frac{7}{12} + \frac{5}{9} = \frac{63+60}{108} = \frac{123}{108} = \frac{41}{36}$

19. Answer: A

Explanation: Total weight of Diana's nut

mixture: $1\frac{1}{3} + \frac{1}{2} + \frac{3}{2} = 1 + (\frac{1}{3} + \frac{1}{2} + \frac{3}{2}) =$

$1 + (\frac{2}{6} + \frac{3}{6} + \frac{9}{6})$

$= 1 + \frac{14}{6} = 1 + \frac{7}{3}$

$= 1 + 2 + \frac{1}{3} = 3\frac{1}{3}$

20. Answer: C

Explanation: Max bakes 1kg pie

$1 - \frac{3}{5} - \frac{1}{5} = \frac{15}{15} - \frac{9}{15} - \frac{5}{15} = \frac{1}{15}$

4.2 MULTIPLICATION AND DIVISION- FRACTION AND IMPROPER FRACTION

1. Answer: A
Explanation: The number 5 divided by 7 is written in fraction form as $5 \div 7 = \frac{5}{7}$

2. Answer: B
Explanation: When multiplying fractions, multiply the numerators and multiply the denominators.

$\frac{5}{3} \times \frac{4}{7} = \frac{5 \times 4}{3 \times 7} = \frac{20}{21}$

3. Answer: C
Explanation: When multiplying fractions, multiply the numerators and multiply the denominators.
$\frac{5}{3} \times \frac{7}{9} = \frac{3 \times 7}{1 \times 9} = \frac{7}{6} = 1\frac{1}{6}$, so they should order 6 buckets.

4. Answer: B

Explanation: Multiply $6\frac{1}{3} \times \frac{1}{3} = \frac{19}{3} \times \frac{1}{3} = \frac{19}{9}$ which is less than 613 because $\frac{19}{9} = \frac{57}{9}$

5. Answer: Less than
Explanation: Since the number 6 is multiplied by a fraction that is less than one, the value decreases. Alternatively: $6 \times \frac{3}{7} = \frac{18}{7}$ which is less than 6

6. Answer: D
Explanation: Multiply: $42 \times \frac{1}{6} = 7$

7. Answer: A
Explanation: Change the mixed number to an improper fraction and multiply. Cross

cancel while multiplying:

$\frac{13}{5} \times \frac{35}{1} = \frac{13 \times 7}{1} = 91$

8. Answer: C
Explanation: Change the mixed number to an improper fraction and multiply. Cross cancel while multiplying:

$\frac{17}{4} \times \frac{24}{1} = \frac{17 \times 6}{1} = 102$

9. Answer: $\frac{3}{20}$
Explanation: To simplify: $\frac{3}{5} \div 4$ find the

reciprocal of 4 and multiply

$\frac{3}{5} \times \frac{1}{4} = \frac{3}{20}$

10. Answer: B
Explanation:
To simplify $\frac{1}{7} \div 8$ you must find the reciprocal of 8 and multiply $\frac{1}{7} \times \frac{1}{8} = \frac{1}{56}$.

11. Answer: D
Explanation: To simplify $\frac{3}{4} \div 6$ you must find the reciprocal of 6 and multiply $\frac{3}{4} \times \frac{1}{6} = \frac{3}{24} = \frac{1}{8}$

12. Answer: A
Explanation: To simplify $\frac{1}{6} \div 2$ you must find the reciprocal of 2 and multiply $\frac{1}{6} \times \frac{1}{2} = \frac{1}{12}$

13. Answer: B
Explanation: To simplify $\frac{1}{4} \div 8$ you must find the reciprocal of 8 and multiply $\frac{1}{4} \times \frac{1}{8} = \frac{1}{32} \ne \frac{1}{8}$

14. Answer: A

Explanation: To simplify $10 \div \frac{1}{5}$ you must find the reciprocal of 10 and multiply $10 \times \frac{5}{1} = 50$

15. Answer: $\frac{7}{12}$ **hours**

Explanation: Kim: $2\frac{1}{3}$ hours

Cruz: $2\frac{1}{3} \times \frac{3}{4} = \frac{7}{3} \times \frac{3}{4} = \frac{7}{4}$ hours

Difference: $\frac{7}{3} - \frac{7}{4} = \frac{28-21}{12} = \frac{7}{12}$

16. Answer: B

Explanation: $3\frac{1}{3} \div 1\frac{1}{3} = \frac{10}{3} \div \frac{4}{3} = \frac{10}{3} \times \frac{3}{4} = \frac{10}{4}$ hours per one flower bed $\frac{10}{4} \times 6 = 15$ hours.

17. Answer: $\frac{25}{16}$

Explanation: Multiply: $1\frac{1}{4} \times 2\frac{1}{2} = \frac{5}{4} \times \frac{5}{4} = \frac{25}{16}$

18. Answer: A

Explanation: $a = \frac{3}{5} \div \frac{2}{b} = a = \frac{3}{5} \times \frac{b}{2} = \frac{3b}{10}$

$\rightarrow 10a = 3b \rightarrow b = \frac{10a}{3}$

19. Answer: B

Explanation: Multiply: $2\frac{1}{4} \times 3\frac{1}{2} = \frac{9}{4} \times \frac{7}{2} = \frac{63}{8} = 7\frac{7}{8}$

20. Answer: 2 pieces

Explanation: $2\frac{3}{6} \div \frac{5}{12} = \frac{15}{6} \div \frac{5}{12} = \frac{15}{6} \times \frac{12}{5} = 6$ pieces

Left wood = 6 − 4 = 2 pieces.

4.3 MULTIPLYING TWO FRACTIONS – AREA MODEL AND LENGTH MODEL

1. Answer: <

Explanation: $\frac{5}{14} \times \frac{2}{3} = \frac{2}{3} \times \frac{5}{14}$

$\frac{2}{3} \times \frac{3}{7} = \frac{2}{3} \times \frac{6}{14}$

$\rightarrow \frac{5}{14} < \frac{6}{14}$, then $\frac{5}{14} \times \frac{2}{3} < \frac{2}{3} \times \frac{5}{14}$

2. Answer: A

Explanation: Yes, this is the associative property of multiplication.

3. Answer: Incorrect

Explanation: $\frac{2}{9} \times \frac{4}{5} = \frac{8}{45} \rightarrow (1)$

$\frac{2}{4} \times \frac{9}{5} = \frac{9}{10} \rightarrow (2)$

$(1) \neq (2)$

4. Answer: C

Explanation: Cleaned windows: $\frac{15}{16}$

Listened to the music: $\frac{15}{16} \times \frac{4}{5} = \frac{3}{4}$ hour

With headphones: $\frac{3}{4} \times \frac{1}{2} = \frac{3}{8}$ hour

5. Answer: A

Explanation: Kiwi: $\frac{5}{6} \times \frac{2}{3} = \frac{5}{9}$ pound

Mangoes: $\left(\frac{1}{6} \times \frac{2}{3}\right) \times \frac{5}{6} = \frac{1}{9} \times \frac{5}{6} = \frac{5}{54}$ pound

Total: $\frac{5}{9} + \frac{5}{54} = \frac{30+5}{54} = \frac{35}{54}$ pound

6. Answer: $\frac{1}{10}$ **of a mile**

Explanation: Mia: $\frac{7}{10}$ of a mile

Liam: $\frac{6}{7} \times \frac{7}{10} = \frac{3}{5}$ of a mile

Jenny: $\frac{5}{7} \times \frac{7}{10} = \frac{1}{2}$ of a mile

Mia walked further $\frac{3}{5} - \frac{1}{2} = \frac{6-5}{10} = \frac{1}{10}$ of a mile.

7. Answer: D

Explanation: Large square side = $\frac{3}{10}$ m

Large square area = $\frac{3}{10} \times \frac{3}{10} = \frac{9}{100}$ m²

Small square side = $\frac{1}{3} \times \frac{3}{10} = \frac{1}{10}$ m²

Small square area = $\frac{1}{10} \times \frac{1}{10} = \frac{1}{100}$ m²

Difference = $\frac{9}{100} - \frac{1}{100} = \frac{8}{100} = \frac{2}{25}$ m²

8. Answer: $\frac{11}{81}$

Explanation: Cross cancel while multiplying:

$\frac{5}{9} \times \frac{11}{45} = \frac{5 \times 11}{9 \times 45} = \frac{1 \times 11}{9 \times 9} = \frac{11}{81}$

9. Answer: A

Explanation: Remaining cards: $1 - \frac{1}{6} = \frac{5}{6}$

Gives to brother: $\frac{1}{2} \times \frac{5}{6} = \frac{5}{12}$

10. Answer: C

Explanation: On a snowy day, $\frac{1}{8}$ of the students miss the school,

Half of these students call the teacher to report about their absence $\frac{1}{2}$

$\frac{1}{2} \times \frac{1}{8} = \frac{1}{16}$

11. Answer: B

Explanation: Multiply: $\frac{9}{10} \times \frac{1}{4} = \frac{9}{40}$

12. Answer: A

Explanation: Amir: $\frac{9}{20}$ of a minute

Omar: $\frac{9}{20} \times \frac{2}{3} = \frac{3}{10}$ of a minute

Difference = $\frac{9}{20} - \frac{3}{10} = \frac{9}{20} - \frac{6}{20} = \frac{3}{20}$ of a minute

13. Answer: B

Explanation: Linda: $\frac{6}{7}$ pound

Lisa: $\frac{6}{7} \times \frac{1}{2} = \frac{3}{7}$ pound

Sam: $\frac{3}{7} \times \frac{1}{2} = \frac{3}{14}$ pound

14. Answer: A

Explanation: Jacob: $\frac{3}{5}$ of a basket

Noah: $\frac{3}{5} \times \frac{2}{3} = \frac{2}{5}$ of a basket

Together: $\frac{3}{5} + \frac{2}{5} = \frac{5}{5} = 1$ basket

15. Answer: $1\frac{3}{15}$ km

Explanation: From school to church: $\frac{12}{15}$ km

From church to home: $\frac{12}{15} \times \frac{1}{2} = \frac{2}{5}$ km

Total distance $\frac{12}{15} + \frac{2}{5} = \frac{12+6}{15} = \frac{18}{15} = 1\frac{3}{15}$ km

16. Answer: $\frac{1}{24}$

Explanation: Multiply $\frac{1}{3} \times \frac{1}{8} = \frac{1}{24}$

17. Answer: $\frac{1}{6}$

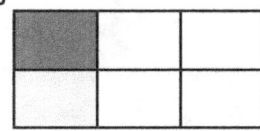

Explanation: $\frac{1}{6}$

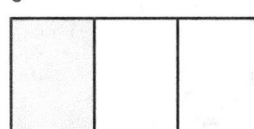

18. Answer: $\frac{5}{16}$

Explanation: Multiply: $\frac{5}{4} \times \frac{1}{4} = \frac{5}{16}$

19. Answer: A

Explanation: $\frac{3}{5} \times \frac{2}{4}$

20. Answer: $\frac{1}{15}$

Explanation: Multiply $\frac{1}{5} \times \frac{1}{3} = \frac{1}{15}$

**4.4 DIVIDE A UNIT FRACTION –
AREA MODEL AND LENGTH MODEL**

1. Answer: A
Explanation: $2 \div \frac{1}{4} = 8$

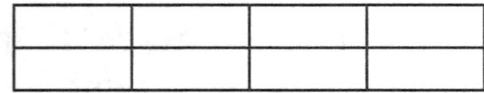

2. Answer: C
Explanation: $3 \div \frac{1}{4} = 12$

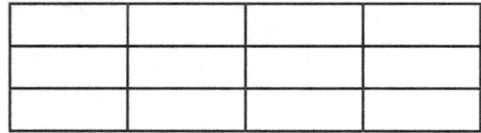

3. Answer: D
Explanation: Let x be the missing digit
$\frac{1}{x} \div 12 = \frac{1}{72} \rightarrow \frac{1}{x} \times \frac{1}{12} = \frac{1}{72}$
$12x = 72 \rightarrow x = 6$

4. Answer: Equal
Explanation: $2 \div \frac{1}{3} = 6$

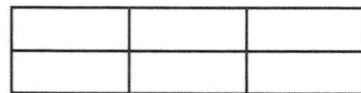

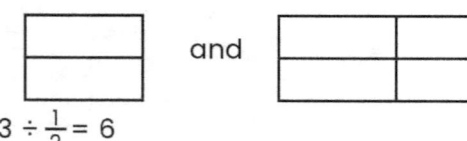   and

$3 \div \frac{1}{2} = 6$

5. Answer: 12
Explanation:

6. Answer: B
Explanation: Length model $3 \div \frac{1}{3} = 9$ and Area model $2 \div \frac{1}{6} = 12$
Both are not equal.

7. Answer: C
Explanation: Divide: $\frac{1}{4} \div 5 = \frac{1}{20}$

8. Answer: Five solutions
Explanation:
$\frac{1}{2} \div \frac{8}{1} = \frac{1}{8} \div \frac{2}{1} = \frac{1}{4} \div \frac{4}{1} = \frac{1}{16} \div \frac{1}{1} = \frac{1}{1} \div \frac{16}{1} = \frac{1}{16}$

9. Answer: 9
Explanation: $9 \div \frac{1}{3} = 9 \times 3 = 27$ which is greater than 25.

10. Answer: A
Explanation: $3 \div \frac{1}{6}$

11. Answer: 18 and 12
Explanation: $18 \div \frac{1}{2} = 36$ and $12 \div \frac{1}{3} = 36$

12. Answer: B
Explanation: $4 \div \frac{1}{8} = 4 \times 8 = 32$ pieces

13. Answer: D
Explanation: $\frac{2}{3} \div 30 = \frac{2}{3} \times \frac{1}{30} = \frac{1}{45}$ stack

14. Answer: C
Explanation: $\frac{1}{12} \div 4 = \frac{1}{12} \times \frac{1}{4} = \frac{1}{48}$

15. Answer: A
Explanation: $6 \div \frac{1}{4} = 6 \times 4 = 24$ km/h

16. Answer: C
Explanation: $\frac{1}{2} \div 14 = \frac{1}{2} \times \frac{1}{14} = \frac{1}{28}$ kg

17. Answer: B
Explanation: $\frac{1}{3} \div 6 = \frac{1}{3} \times \frac{1}{6} = \frac{1}{18}$ pound

18. Answer: B
Explanation: $4 \div \frac{1}{8} = 4 \times 8 = 32$

19. Answer: B
Explanation: $6 \div \frac{1}{3} = 6 \times 3 = 18$

20. Answer: B
Explanation: $5 \div \frac{1}{10} = 5 \times 10 = 50$ photos

1. Answer: C
Explanation: To solve for x, move x by itself to one side of the equation:
$\frac{2}{7} - \frac{1}{14} = x$

$\frac{4-1}{14} = \frac{3}{14} = x$

2. Answer: B
Explanation: Changed into proper fraction:
$x = 2\frac{4}{5} - 2\frac{1}{5} = \frac{14}{5} - \frac{11}{5}$
$x = \frac{3}{5}$

3. Answer: D
Explanation: Change the fractions so they have common denominators and then add them:
$\frac{2}{3} + \frac{4}{9} = \frac{6+4}{9} = \frac{10}{9}$

4. Answer: A
Explanation: In the morning: $\frac{3}{5}$ of the essay
In the evening: $\frac{3}{5} \times \frac{1}{9} = \frac{1}{15}$ of the essay

5. Answer: 3, 24 ÷ 8 and $\frac{24}{8}$
Explanation: The question asks to divide 24 by 8: $24 \div 8 = \frac{24}{8} = 3$

6. Answer: 22 ÷ 12, $\frac{22}{12}$
Explanation: The question asks to divide 22 by 12: $22 \div 12 = \frac{22}{12} = \frac{11}{6} = 1\frac{5}{6}$

7. Answer: B
Explanation: Divide: $8 \div \frac{1}{3} = 8 \times 3 = 24$

8. Answer: $\frac{4}{3}$ or $1\frac{1}{3}$
Explanation: The question asks to divide 8 by 6: $8 \div 6 = \frac{8}{6} = \frac{4}{3} = 1\frac{1}{3}$

9. Answer: A
Explanation: Has: $\frac{5}{9}$ gallon
Used: $\frac{5}{9} \times \frac{3}{7} = \frac{5}{21}$ gallon
Left: $\frac{5}{9} - \frac{5}{21} = \frac{105-45}{189} = \frac{60}{189}$ gallon

10. Answer: C
Explanation: Multiply: $\frac{1}{2} \times \frac{3}{5} = \frac{3}{10}$

11. Answer: A
Explanation: Multiply $\frac{1}{2} \times \frac{1}{2} = \frac{1}{4}$

12. Answer: $\frac{15}{8}$
Explanation: $5 \div \frac{8}{3} = 5 \times \frac{3}{8} = \frac{15}{8}$

13. Answer: $\frac{4}{6}, \frac{6}{9}, \frac{8}{12}$
Explanation: To create an equivalent fraction, divide or multiply the numerator and denominator by the same number.

14. Answer: D
Explanation: Five Black ski suit: $100
So, One suit costs $100 \div 5 = \$20$

15. Answer: $\frac{9}{2}$ or $4\frac{1}{2}$
Explanation: $18 \div 4 = \frac{18}{4} = \frac{9}{2} = 4\frac{1}{2}$

16. Answer: 26
Explanation: $208 \div 8 = \frac{208}{8} = 26$

17. Answer: $\frac{1}{7}$
Explanation: Divide $6 \div 42 = \frac{6}{42} = \frac{1}{7}$

18. Answer: A
Explanation: Base = $5\frac{1}{2}$ cm
$\frac{1}{2} \times$ Base $= \frac{1}{2} \times 5\frac{1}{2} = \frac{1}{2} \times \frac{11}{2} = \frac{11}{4}$ cm
Height = (Area) ÷ ($\frac{1}{2} \times$Base) $= 33 \div \frac{11}{4} =$
$33 \times \frac{11}{4} = 12$ cm

19. Answer: B
Explanation: Multiply $6\frac{1}{2} \times 6\frac{1}{2} = \frac{13}{2} \times \frac{13}{2} = \frac{169}{4}$ not 45

20. Answer: B
Explanation: Multiply $9 \times \frac{1}{18} = \frac{1}{2}$, which is less than 2.

5. CONVERSIONS AND INTERPRET DATA

1. Answer: B
Explanation: 1 m = 100 cm
Blue iguana = 1.4 m = 140 cm
Ordinary iguana = 140 cm × $\frac{1}{2}$ = 70 cm
Sea iguana = 70 cm × $\frac{3}{2}$ = 105 cm

2. Answer: D

Explanation: English bulldog = 24.5 kg

Collie = 24.5 kg × $\frac{3}{5}$ = 14.7 kg

Poodle = 14.7kg × $\frac{3}{7}$ = 6.3 kg

3. Answer: 216 in
Explanation: 1 ft = 12 in
18 ft = 18 × 12 in = 216 in

4. Answer: 22 kg.

Explanation: 1 kg = 1,000 g
22,000 g = $\frac{22000}{1000}$ = 22 kg

5. Answer: 330 mm, 130 mm, 250 mm
Explanation: Pen + Pencil = 38 cm
Pen + Ruler = 58 cm
Pencil + Ruler = 46 cm
2 (Pen 7+ Pencil + Ruler) = 38 cm + 58 cm + 46 cm = 142 cm
Pen + Pencil + Ruler = 71 cm
Ruler = 71 cm - 38 cm = 33×10 = 330mm
Pencil = 71 cm - 58 cm = 13 ×10 = 130 mm
Pen = 71 cm - 46 cm = 25×10 = 250 mm

6. Answer: A
Explanation: Weight of the beetle = 240 mg
Weight of the fly = 240 mg ÷ 2 = 120 mg
1 g = 1,000 mg
Weight of the mosquito = 120 mg ÷ 4 = 30 mg = $\frac{30}{1000}$ g = 0.03 g

7. Answer: B
Explanation: Add 6 inches to 4 feet 6 inches is 4 feet 12 inches, or 5 feet.

8. Answer: C
Explanation: The combined length is 25.5 cm. To convert cm to meters, divide by 100

9. Answer: 768 oz
Explanation: 1 lb = 16 oz
48 lb = 48 × 16 = 768 oz

10. Answer: 12 yd
Explanation: 1 ft = $\frac{1}{3}$ yd
36 ft = 36 × $\frac{1}{3}$ yd = 12 yd

11. Answer: D
Explanation: 1 kg = 1,000 g
6,900g = $\frac{6900}{1000}$ = 6.9kg
6.9 = 69 × 0.1 kg then x = 0.1

12. Answer: A
Explanation: 1 m = 100 cm
2.65 m = 265 cm
2.42 m = 242 cm
First jumper jumps = 265cm - 242 cm =23 cm

13. Answer: C
Explanation: There are 1,000 grams in 1 kilogram. The 6 books have a mass of 9,240 grams. The mass of remaining books subtract 728 from 9,240, giving 8,512.

14. Answer: B
Explanation: 1 kg = 1,000 g
Weight of pumpkin after giving a friend = 10 kg - 2.5 kg = 7.5 kg
Weight of each of the five equal parts = 7.5 kg ÷ 6 = 1.25 kg = 1.25 × 1,000 g = 1,250 g

15. Answer: D
Explanation: 1 kg = 1,000 g
2 kg = 2 × 1,000 g = 2,000 g
Total weight of four plates without the box = 2,000 g - 440 g = 1,560 g
Weight of each plate = 1,560 g ÷ 4 = 390 g.

16. Answer: C
Explanation: 1 ft = 12 in
10 ft 10 in = (10×12+10) in = 130 in
8 ft 4 in = (8×12+4) in = 100 in
Number of additional height =
130 in - 100 in = 30 in

17. Answer: A
Explanation: Subtracting 11 inches from 5 ft 10 inches resulting in 4 ft 11 inches.

18. Answer: B
Explanation: 1 lb = 16 oz
Weight of strawberries bought =
4 lb = 4 × 16 oz = 64 oz
Weight of strawberries left =
64 oz - 8 oz - 10 oz = 46 oz

19. Answer: 3 ft 8 in
Explanation: 1 in = 112ft
Perimeter = 2 (Length +Width) = 2(10+12)=
44 in = 3 ft 8 in.

20. Answer: D
Explanation: The combined length is 53.6 cm. To convert cm to meters, divide by 100.

5.2 TIME CONVERSION AND CAPACITY CONVERSION

1. Answer: D
Explanation: 0.004 L = 4 ml
60 ml - 4 ml = 56 ml
56 ml ÷ 4 ml = 14 days
15 days after the first day, so in 15 days

2. Answer: B
Explanation: There are 1,000 mL in 1 L
The empty space is $42 × 1,000 × \frac{2}{3} = 28,000$

3. Answer: x = 10 minutes and y = 6 hours
Explanation:
130 minutes = 2 hours 10 minutes, then
8 hours = y + 2 hours → y = 6 hours
x = 10 minutes

4. Answer: 408
Explanation: 425 feet is equivalent to (425×12)=5,100 inches. Divide 5100 by 25 to find the shoelaces produced in an hour. There are 204 shoelaces produced each hour, and 408 (204×2) shoelaces produced in 2 hours.

5. Answer: 2
Explanation: Convert 40 gallons to quarts by multiplying by 4. Then, divide by 80.

6. Answer: D
Explanation: 1 week 6 days = (7+6) =13 days
14 days –13 days 1 day
Emily stayed at the hotel 1 day longer

7. Answer: C
Explanation:
There are 2 cups in every pint. 50 × 2 = 100

8. Answer: 32 glasses
Explanation: One-gallon equals 128 ounces: 128/4 = 32 glasses are needed.

9. Answer: B
Explanation: 1 pint = 2 cups
2.5 pints = 2.5 × 2 = 5 cups
Tea left in the teapot:
20 cups - 5 cups = 15 cups

10. Answer: A
Explanation:
3 hours 30 minutes = (3×60+30) minutes
210 minutes - 150 minutes = 60 minutes

11. Answer: 18,000 ml
Explanation: B – bucket, C – container
B + C = 20 L
2B = 3(6C) = 18C
Then B = 9C
9C + C = 20L
10C = 20 L
C = 2 L
B = 20 - 2 = 18 L
1 liter = 1000 millilitres
18 liters = 18,000 milliliters

12. Answer: A
Explanation:
5 years 6 months = 60 + 6 = 66 months
6 years 4 months = 72 + 4 = 76 months
Difference 76 – 66 = 10 months

13. Answer: 72
Explanation: 72 pints = 72 × 2 = 144 cups
16 fl oz = 2 cup
Total number of pushes: 144 cups ÷ 2 cup=72

14. Answer: D
Explanation:
Time from 16:50 till 18:15: 1 hours 25 minutes
= (1×60+25) minutes = 85 minutes

15. Answer: B
Explanation: 1 quart = 2 pints
1 pint = 2 cups
4 quarts = 4 × 2 = 8 pints = 8 × 2 = 16 cups
Drinks: $\frac{1}{2}$ × 16 = 8 cups
Left: 16 cups – 8 cups = 8 cups

16. Answer: 0.35 L
Explanation: 1 cm³ = $\frac{1}{1000}$ L
350 cm³ = $\frac{350}{1000}$ = 0.35 L

17. Answer: A
Explanation: 4 years = 4 × 12 = 48 months
118 – 48 months = 70 months
70 months = 60 + 10 months =
5 years 10 months

18. Answer: B
Explanation: 1 pint = 2 cups
Total: 6 × 4 = 24 pints = 24 × 2 = 48 cups

19. Answer: 3 hours 20 minutes

Explanation: 1 hr = 60 min
$\frac{10}{3}$ hours = $3\frac{1}{3}$ hours= 3 hours $\frac{1}{3}$ ×60 minutes =
3 hours 20 minutes

20. Answer: 6 gallons
Explanation: 1 quart =$\frac{1}{4}$ gallon
Total: 12 × 2 = 24 quarts = 24 ÷ 4 = 6 gallons

1. Answer: 1
Explanation: Order data: 1, 1, 1, 1, 2, 2, 2, 2, 3, 3, 4, 4, 4, 5, 5, 5, 5, 5, 6, 6, 6, 7, 7
The minimum value is 1.

2. Answer: 8
Explanation: Order data: 1, 1, 1, 2, 2, 2, 3, 4, 4, 5, 5, 5, 5, 6, 6, 6, 7, 7, 8, 8, 8, 8
The maximum value is 8.

3. Answer: 6
Explanation: Create a line plot.

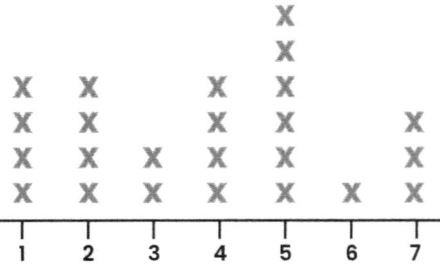

4. Answer: 3
Explanation: Create a line plot.

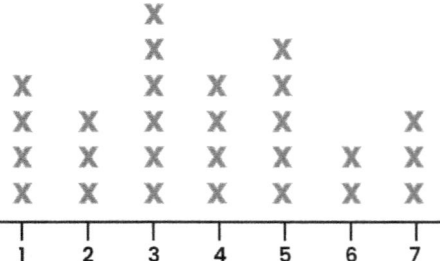

5. Answer: 27
Explanation: Create a line plot.

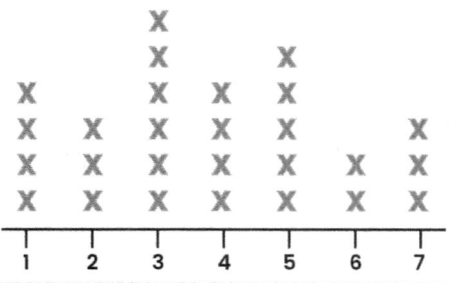

6. Answer: 4
Explanation: Create a line plot.

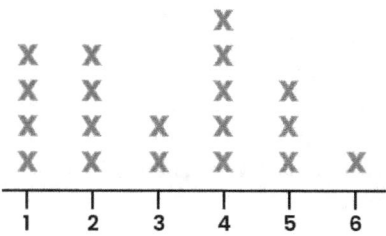

7. Answer: 12
Explanation: Order data:
6, 6, 6, 6, 6, 6, 6, 7, 7, 7, 7, 7, 7, 7, 8, 8, 8, 8, 8, 9, 9, 9, 9, 9, 10, 10, 10, 10, 10, 11, 12, 12, 12, 12
The maximum value is 12.

8. Answer: 1
Explanation: Order data: 0, 0, 0, 0, 0, 0, 1, 2, 2, 2, 2, 3, 3, 3, 4, 4, 4
Create a line plot.

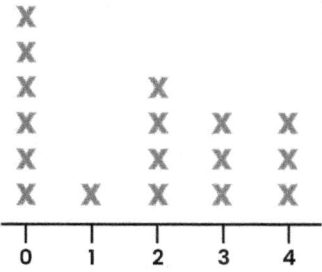

9. Answer: A
Explanation: The total cost of items with a price of $10: $10 × 4 = $40
The total cost of items with a price of $20: $20 × 3 = $60

10. Answer: D
Explanation: $5×2+$10×4=10+40=$50

11. Answer: 3 and 6
Explanation: Create a line plot.

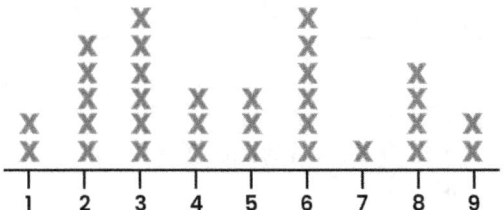

12. Answer: C
Explanation: Create a line plot.

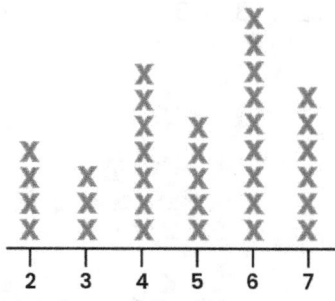

Count the number of Xs: 34

13. Answer: 7
Explanation: Order data: 2, 2, 2, 2, 2, 3, 3, 3, 3, 3, 3, 3, 3, 4, 4, 4, 4, 4, 4, 4, 4, 4, 5, 5, 5, 5, 5, 6, 6, 6, 6, 6, 6, 7, 7.
The maximum value is 7.

14. Answer: 6
Explanation: Order data: 6, 6, 6, 6, 6, 7, 7, 7, 7, 7, 7, 7, 8, 8, 8, 8, 8, 8, 8, 8, 8, 8, 9, 9, 9, 9, 9, 9, 9, 10, 10, 10, 10, 10, 10, 10
The minimum value is 6.

15. Answer: 19
Explanation: Order data: 6, 6, 6, 6, 6, 6, 7, 7, 8, 8, 8, 9, 10, 10, 11, 11, 11, 12, 12
Create a line plot.

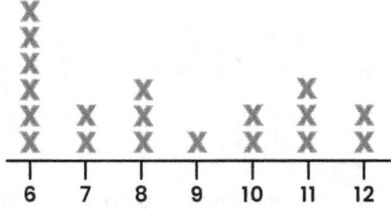

Count the number of Xs: 19

309

16. Answer: 31
Explanation: Order data: 0, 0, 1, 1, 1, 1, 1, 1, 1, 2, 2, 2, 2, 2, 2, 2, 2, 3, 3, 3, 3, 3, 3, 3, 3, 4, 4, 4, 4, 4
Create a line plot.

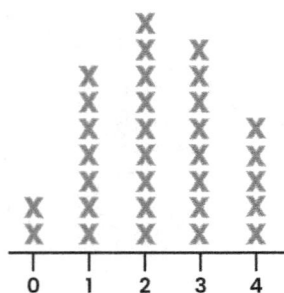

Count the number of Xs: 31

17. Answer: D
Explanation: Order data: 0, 0, 0, 0, 0, 1, 1, 2, 2, 2, 2, 2, 3, 3, 3, 3, 3, 3, 3
The highest number of cars for each household on the street is 3.

18. Answer: 1
Explanation: Order data: 1, 1, 1, 1, 1, 1, 2, 2, 2, 2, 3, 3, 3, 3, 4, 4, 4, 5, 5
The lowest number of goals of a handball player is 1.

19. Answer: 12
Explanation: Order data: 6, 6, 6, 6, 6, 6, 7, 7, 8, 8, 8, 9, 10, 10, 11, 11, 11, 12, 12
The highest score of a football player is 12 points.

20. Answer: A
Explanation: Goats with a weight of 40 kg:
40 × 5 = 200 kg
Goats with a weight of 50 kg: 50 × 4 = 200 kg.

5.4 INTERPRET GRAPHS

1. Answer: Categorical
Explanation: Graph shows the values of categories.

2. Answer: Refer the explanation
Explanation:

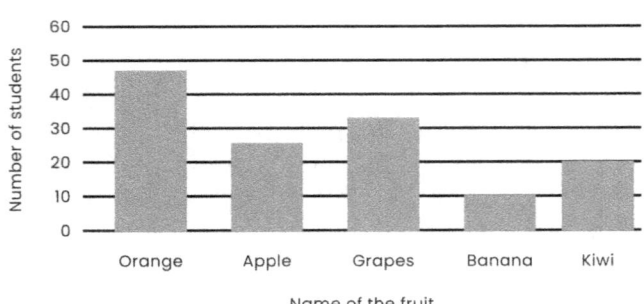

3. Answer: A
Explanation: There are 9 values (numbers) in the data set.

4. Answer: A
Explanation: Total 4 data points of 12 and 14 years old

5. Answer: C
Explanation: Subtract 16 – 5 = 11

6. Answer: B
Explanation: There are 4 insects that are $\frac{1}{4}$ inch long. Add $\frac{1}{4}$ four times or multiply $\frac{1}{4}$ and 4.

7. Answer:
Explanation: Order data set: 2, 2, 2, 3, 3, 3, 3, 3, 4, 4, 4, 4, 4, 5, 5, 5, 6, 6
Table:

Value	2	3	4	5	6
Frequency	3	5	5	3	2

Look for the frequency number of the value 2 in the table. It is 3.
Look for the frequency number of the value 3 in the table. It is 5.

Frequency number shows how many Xs should be above values 3 and 5.

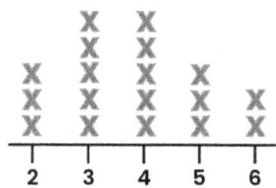

8. Answer: Categorical
Explanation: The pie chart shows the favorite flavors of ice cream (categorical).

9. Answer: D
Explanation: Add the values of bars:
2 + 6 + 4 + 2 + 5 = 19

10. Answer: A
Explanation: There are 6 students with 0 pets.

11. Answer: D
Explanation: Color with the greatest percentage is: Orange

12. Answer: A
Explanation: There are 6 students with 0 siblings.

13. Answer: C
Explanation: The month of April has the most visitors to the planetarium.

14. Answer: C
Explanation:
18 + 24 + 12 + 30 + 24 + 10 ÷ 6 = 19.7

15. Answer: D
Explanation: The least amount of temperature change is between February and March, and between May and June: 10°C.

16. Answer: A
Explanation: There is one student with 4 pets.

17. Answer:

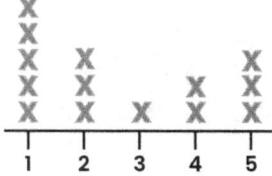

Explanation: Look for the frequency number of the value 2 in the table. It is 3.

18. Answer: A
Explanation: Add 2 + 6 = 8

19. Answer: A and C
Explanation: The numbers with the greatest percentage are: 4 and 6

20. Answer: There are 19 values or data points on this line plot. The temperature that occurred the most is 98 degrees Fahrenheit
Explanation: Students may describe the line plot by evaluating the number of data points and what the data points represent.

5.5 CHAPTER REVIEW

1. Answer: A
Explanation: There are 16 ounces in 1 pound, which means there are (16 × 6) or 96 ounces in 6 pounds. Divide 96 by 12=8.

2. Answer: C
Explanation: There are 16 ounces in 1 pound, which means there are (16×5) or 80 ounces in 5 pounds. Divide 80 by 5.1 and divide 80 by 5.5. The two answers are 15.7 and 14.6. The closest choice is 15.

3. Answer: D
Explanation: There are 16 ounces in 1 pound, which means there are (16 × 8) or 128 ounces in 8 pounds. Divide 128 by 8=16.

4. Answer: B
Explanation: There are no data points on $1\frac{1}{4}$ or 2 inches.

5. Answer: 5
Explanation: Even though there are 7 values to include on the line plot, two of the values $(\frac{1}{2}$ and $\frac{1}{4})$ repeat themselves.

6. Answer: B
Explanation: Apple A
Pear P
Peach p
$2A + 3P = 2,200$
$3A + 2p = 2,500$
$2P + 3p = 800$
Add;
$5A + 5P + 5p = 5,500$
Divide by 5 :
$A + P + p = 1100$ grams.

7. Answer: A
Explanation: 10 quarts = 10 × 2 = 20 pints = 20×2 = 40 cups = 40×8 = 320 fl oz = 16×20 fl oz

8. Answer: D
Explanation: 1 ton = 2000 pounds
 2.6 tons =2.6 × 2,000 pounds = 5,200 pounds

9. Answer: B
Explanation: 1 kg = $\frac{1}{1000}$ tons
Total: 14,000 kg = $\frac{14000}{1000}$ tons = 14 tons

10. Answer: D
Explanation: 1 mm = $\frac{1}{10}$ cm
Length of the necklace: 36 ×12 mm=432 mm
= $\frac{432}{10}$ cm = 43.2 cm

11. Answer: C
Explanation: 2.5 km=2,500 m
 2,500 m−700 m−760 m=2,500 m−1,460 m=1,040 m

12. Answer: D
Explanation: 1 gallon = 4 quarts
10 gallons = 10×4 = 40 quarts
40 ÷ 2.5 = 16 jars

13. Answer: C
Explanation: Two episodes: 2×40 minutes = 80 minutes = 1 hour 20 minutes
Total: 1 hour 40 minutes + 1 hour 20 minutes = 2 hours 60 minutes = 3 hours

14. Answer: A
Explanation: Empty: 3.5 pounds
Full: 8 pounds
Difference: 8 - 3.5 = 4.516 = 72 ounces

15. Answer: B
Explanation: 1 cup −180 minutes
1 cup −3 hours
24 ÷ 3 = 8 , then
8 cups = $\frac{8}{2}$ pints = 4 pints

16. Answer: The difference in weight is 0.75 ounce
Explanation: Subtract the least value from the greatest value. $6\frac{7}{8} - 6\frac{1}{8}$ = 0.75 oz

17. Answers: B
Explanation:
20 quarts = 20 × 2 = 40 pints = 40 × 2 = 80 cups = 80 × 8 = 640 fl oz = 16 × 40 fl oz

18. Answer: There were between 0 and $\frac{6}{8}$ quarts of orange juice consumed. Most students consumed $\frac{4}{8}$ quarts of juice. No students consumed $\frac{3}{8}$ or $\frac{5}{8}$ quarts of juice.
Explanation: Answers may vary. Students may observe the total number of data points and how it represents the number of students included in the data set, the greatest amount of juice consumed, the least amount of juice consumed, and the number of students who consume fractional amounts of juice.

19. Answer: A
Explanation: There are 10 data points in the line plot.

20. Answer:

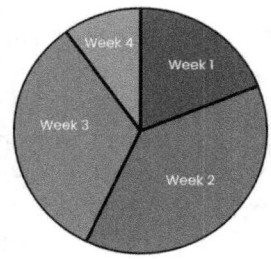

Explanation: A pie chart is a graphical representation technique that displays data in a circular-shaped graph. Pie charts are divided into sections to represent values of different sizes.

6. MEASUREMENT: VOLUMES

6.1 COUNTING AND MULTIPLICATION FOR CUBES

1. Answer: A
Explanation: 6 cubes

2. Answer: B
Explanation: 20 cubes

3. Answer: C
Explanation: Volume of the prism:
12 × 2 = 24 cubic inches

4. Answer: Prism A: 6×1 = 6; Prism B: 10×1 = 10
Explanation: Therefore, prism B has more volume than prism A.

5. Answer: 50 cubic units.
Explanation: Volume of the prism:
25 × 2 = 50 cubic inches

6. Answer: A
Explanation: Volume of the washing machine: 4 × 4 = 16 cubic feet

7. Answer: B
Explanation: Volume of the wardrobe:
4 × 7 = 28 cubic feet

8. Answer: C
Explanation: Number of visible cubes: 10
Number of invisible cubes: 38
Volume of the red prism 12×4 or 10+38=48 cubic units

9. Answer: 28 cubic units.
Explanation: Volume of the prism: 14×2=28 cubic inches

10. Answer: B
Explanation: 4 × 4 = 16

11. Answer: D
Explanation: 1 × 10 = 10

12. Answer: A
Explanation: 3 × 4

13. Answer: B
Explanation: Volume of the prism: 2 × 8 = 16

14. Answer: Prism A: 1×6 = 6; Prism B: 1×4 = 4
Explanation: Therefore, prism A has more volume than prism B.

15. Answer: Prism A: 1×10 = 10;
Prism B: 4×3 = 12
Explanation: Therefore, prism B has more volume than prism A.

16. Answer: There are 4 layers with 10 cubes in each layer. The volume of the prism is 40 cubic units.

17. Answer: A
Explanation: Volume of the prism: 1 × 20 = 20

18. Answer: B
Explanation: 4 × 12 = 48 cubic units

19. Answer: A
Explanation: 5 × 2 = 10 cubic units

20. Answer: C
Explanation: 20 cubes

6.2 VOLUME OF SOLIDS

1.Answer: B.
Explanation: The smaller rectangular prism has a volume of 18 cubes. Since the volume of both prisms is 66 cubic units, the volume of the second prism is (66-18) or 48 cubic units.

2. Answer: B
Explanation:
The smaller rectangular prism has a volume of 36 cubes. Since the volume of both prisms is 108 cubic units, the volume of the second prism is (108-36) or 72 cubic units.

3. Answer: A
Explanation: The volume can be determined by multiplying the number of cubes in the base of the box by the height of the box.

4.Answer: A.
Explanation: By multiplying the 3 dimensions of this box (25 16 3), it can be determined that the volume is 1200 cubic units.

5.Answer: C.
Explanation: The volume can be determined by multiplying the number of cubes in the base of the box by the height of the box.

6. Answer: C.
Explanation: The total volume of the box is 600 cubic centimeters. To determine the number of cubes on the bottom layer, divide the volume by the height. Dividing 600 by 20 is 30. There are 30 cubes in the bottom of the box.

7. Answer: A.
Explanation: The box is filled with ½ inch cubes. The length of the box is 12 cubes (6 × 2), the width of the box is 4 cubes (22), and the height of the box is 8 cubes (4 × 2). The number of cubes that will fill the box is (124 × 8) or 384 cubes.

8.Answer: B.
Explanation: The large crate has a volume of 64 cubic feet (44 × 4). Each small box has a volume of 0.512 cubic feet (0.80.80.8) Dividing 64 by 0.512 gives the number of small boxes that fit in each large box (64 0.512 = 125). Then, 600 125 = 4.8 large boxes. Round 4.8 up to 5. It will take 5 large boxes, but the last box will not be full.

9. Answer: C.
The volume of each prism: Prism A – 40 cubic inches, Prism B – 20 cubic inches, Prism C – 60 cubic inches, Prism D – 48 cubic inches.

10. Answer: B.
The volume of each prism: Prism A – 40 cubic inches, Prism B – 20 cubic inches, Prism C – 60 cubic inches, Prism D – 48 cubic inches.

11. Answer: D.
Explanation:

The solid consists of yellow and red prism.
The volume of the yellow prism is 6 cubic units.
The volume of the red prism is 4 cubic units.
The volume of the solid is 6+4=10 cubic units.

12. Answer: C.

Explanation:
The solid consists of green and red prism.
The volume of the green prism is 8 cubic units.
The volume of the red prism is 10 cubic units.
V = 8 + 10 cubic units

13. Answer: A.
Explanation:

The solid consists of green and maroon prism.
The volume of the green prism is 12 cubic units.
The volume of the maroon prism is 8 cubic units.

14. Answer: Prism B has greater volume.
Explanation:
Prism A

The solid consists of a green and red prism.
The volume of the green prism is 2 cubic units.
The volume of the red prism is 4 cubic units.
 2+4=6 cubic units.

Prism B

The solid consists of a green and red prism.
The volume of the green prism is 6 cubic units.
The volume of the red prism is 4 cubic units.
6 + 4 = 10 cubic units.
15 + 20 = 35 cubic units.

15. Answer: 15+20=35 cubic units.
Explanation:

The solid consists of a green and red prism.
The volume of the green prism is 15 cubic units.
The volume of the red prism is 20 cubic units.
15+20=35 cubic units.

16. Answer: A.
Explanation:
The large crate has a volume of 8 cubic feet (22 × 2). Each small box has a volume of 0.064 cubic feet (0.40.40.4) Dividing 8 by 0.064 gives the number of small boxes that fit in each large box
(8 0.064 = 125). Then, 1000 125 = 8 large boxes.

17. Answer: 48 cubic inches.
Explanation:
Count the number of cubes:6.
The volume of a cube is 2×2×2=8 cubic inches.
The volume of a solid is 6×8=48

18. Answer: A
Explanation:
Count the number of cubes: 17
The volume of a cube is 3×3×3=27 cubic inches.
The volume of a solid is 17×27=459 cubic inches.

19. Answer: A
Explanation:
Count the number of cubes: 8
The volume of a cube is 5×5×5=125 cubic inches.
The volume of a solid is 8×125=1000 cubic inches.

20. Answer: 18 cubic units

Explanation:
The solid consists of a green and red prism.
The volume of the green prism is 12 cubic units.
The volume of the red prism is 6 cubic units.
12+6=18 cubic units

6.3 WORD PROBLEMS USING FORMULAS

1. Answer: A.
Explanation: Use formula $V = Bh$
$V = Bh = 14×6 = 84$

2. Answer: B.
Explanation: Use formula $V = Bh$
$V = Bh = 20×5 = 100$

3. Answer: C.
Explanation: Use formula $V = lwh$
$V = lwh = 4×8×3 = 96$

4. Answer: V=24 cubic units.
Explanation: Use formula $V = lwh$
$V = lwh = 4×3×2 = 24$

5. Answer: A.
Explanation: Use formula $V = Bh$
$V = Bh → h = \frac{V}{B} = \frac{160}{20} = 8$ cubic units

6. Answer: B.
Explanation: Use formula $V = Bh$
$V = Bh → B = \frac{V}{h} = \frac{280}{14} = 20$ cubic units

7. Answer: D.
Explanation: Use formula $V = Bh$
$V = Bh = 20×6 = 120$ in³

8. Answer: A.
Explanation: Use formula $V = Bh$
$V = Bh → B = \frac{V}{h} = \frac{560}{20} = 28$ cubic units

9. Answer: B.
Explanation: Use formula $V = Bh$
$V = Bh → h = \frac{V}{B} = \frac{440}{11} = 40$ cubic units

10. Answer: B.
Explanation: Use formula $V=lwh$. The volume of a new prism is $V_1 = l_1w_1h_1$. Compare the dimensions of the new prism with the dimensions of the old prism.
$l_1 = 3l$
$w_1 = 3w$
$h_1 = h$
Express the volume of the new prism, V1 in terms of the volume of the old prism, V.
$V_1 = l_1w_1h_1 = 3l.3w.h = 9(lwh) = 9V$
So, the volume of the prism is increased 9 times.

11. Answer: B.
Explanation: Use formula $V = Bh$
$V = Bh = 20×11 = 220$

12. Answer: C.
Explanation: Use formula $V = Bh$
$V = Bh = 55×22 = 1210$

13. Answer: C.
Explanation: Use formula $V = Bh$
$V = Bh → h = \frac{V}{B} = \frac{560}{40} = 14$ cubic units

14. Answer: D.
Explanation: Use formula $V = Bh$
$V = Bh → h = \frac{V}{B} = \frac{450}{30} = 15$ cubic units

15.Answer: A.
Explanation: Use formula $V = lwh$
$V = lwh = 12×24×6 = 1728$

16. Answer: V = 20 cubic units.
Explanation: Use formula $V = lwh$
$V = lwh = 2 \times 2 \times 5 = 20$

17. Answer: C.
Explanation: Use formula $V = Bh$
$V = Bh \rightarrow B = \frac{V}{h} = \frac{465}{15} = 31$ cubic units

18. Answer: B.
Explanation: Use formula $V = lwh$
$V = lwh = 10 \times 15 \times 5 = 750$

19. Answer: B.
Explanation: Use formula $V = Bh$
$V = Bh \rightarrow B = \frac{V}{h} = \frac{560}{14} = 40$ cubic units

20. Answer: B.
Explanation: Use formula $V = lwh$. The volume of a new prism is $V_1 = l_1 w_1 h_1$. Compare the dimensions of the new prism with the dimensions of the old prism.
$l_1 = l$
$w_1 = w$
$h_1 = 3h$
Express the volume of the new prism, V1 in terms of the volume of the old prism, V .
$V_1 = l_1 w_1 h_1 = w(h + 2) = l.3w.3h = 9(lwh) = 9V$
So, the volume of the prism is increased 9 times.

6.4 CHAPTER REVIEW

1.Answer: C.
Explanation: 8 cubes

2. Answer: A.
Explanation: Volume of the prism: $16 \times 2 = 32$ cubic inches

3. Answer: 48 cubic units.
Explanation: Volume of the prism : $24 \times 2 = 48$ cubic inches

4. Answer: C.
Explanation: $3 \times 4 = 12$

5. Answer: A.
Explanation: Volume of the Prism: $2 \times 24 = 48$

6. Answer: B.
Explanation: 16 cubes

7. Answer: A.
Explanation: The smaller rectangular prism has a volume of 8 cubes. Since the volume of both prisms is 44 cubic units, the volume of the second prism is (44–8) or 36 cubic units.

8. Answer: A.
Explanation: The volume can be determined by multiplying the number of cubes in the base of the box by the height of the box.
$56 \times 40 = 2240$.

9. Answer: 864 cubic inches.
Explanation: 864 cubic inches
Count the number of cubes:4
The volume of a cube is $6 \times 6 \times 6 = 216$ cubic inches.
The volume of a solid is $4 \times 216 = 864$ cubic inches.

10. Answer: A
Explanation: Count the number of cubes: 5
The volume of a cube is $4 \times 4 \times 4 = 64$ cubic inches.
The volume of a solid is $5 \times 64 = 320$ cubic inches.

11. Answer: B.
Explanation: Use formula $V = Bh$
$V = Bh = 15 \times 6 = 90$

12. Answer: C.
Explanation: Use formula $V = lwh$
$V = lwh = 7 \times 14 \times 5 = 490$

13.Answer: C.
Explanation: Use formula $V = Bh$
$V = Bh \rightarrow h = \frac{V}{B} = \frac{250}{25} = 10$ cubic units

14. Answer: D.
Explanation: Use formula V = Bh
$V = Bh \rightarrow B = \frac{V}{h} = \frac{480}{16}$ = 30 cubic units

15. Answer: C.
Explanation: Use formula V = lwh. The volume of a new prism is $V_1 = l_1 w_1 h_1$. Compare the dimensions of the new prism with the dimensions of the old prism.
$l_1 = 4l$
$w_1 = 4w$
$h_1 = h$
Express the volume of the new prism, V1 in terms of the volume of the old prism, V.
$V_1 = l_1 w_1 h_1 = 4l. 4w. h = 16(lwh) = 16V$
So, the volume of the prism is increased 16 times.

16. Answer: A.
Explanation: Use formula V = Bh
$V = Bh \rightarrow h = \frac{V}{B} = \frac{550}{10}$ = 55 cubic units

17. Answer: C.
Explanation: Use formula V = Bh
$V = Bh = 30 \times 16 = 480$

18. Answer: B.
Explanation: Use formula V = lwh
$V = lwh = 10 \times 30 \times 7 = 2100$

19. Answer: A.
Explanation: Use formula V = Bh
$V = Bh \rightarrow B = \frac{V}{h} = \frac{300}{15}$ = 20 cubic units

20. Answer: B.
Explanation: Use formula V = Bh
$V = Bh = 8 \times 4 = 32.$

7. GEOMETRIC MEASUREMENT

7.1 PROPERTIES OF SIDES, ANGLES, AND SYMMETRY

1. Answer: B
Explanation: Perimeter of the square = 4a
The length of the side of the square is 12 cm.
$4 \times 12 = 48$ cm

2. Answer: D
Explanation: Perimeter of the square 4a = 72
Per side = $\frac{72}{4} \Rightarrow 18$

3. Answer: A
Explanation: The rhombus has 4 sides.
Perimeter

4. Answer: C
Explanation: Longest side = 19 cm
Shortest side = 11 cm
Perimeter = 2(Longest Side + Shortest Side) = 2(19+11) = 2(30) = 60

5. Answer: A
Explanation: Perimeter = 92 in
4 (sides) = 92in $\Rightarrow$ side $\frac{92}{4}$ = 23 in

6. Answer: D
Explanation: Longest side = 20 cm
Perimeter = 2 (Longest Side +Shortest Side), therefore,
58 = 2(20+Shortest Side)
20 + Shortest side = 29
Shortest side = 29 - 20 = 9 cm

7. Answer: B
Explanation: Shortest side = 8 cm
Perimeter = 2 (Longest Side +Shortest Side), therefore
48 = 2(8+Longest Side)
8 + Longest side = 24
Longest side = 24 - 8 = 16 cm

8. Answer: C
Explanation: Perimeter of isosceles trapezoid =Shorter Base + Longer Base + 2 Legs
Therefore,
68 = 17 + 25 + 2 Legs
2 Legs = 68 - 17 - 25 = 26
Leg = 13 in

9. Answer: A
Explanation: Length = 24 cm
Width = 16cm
Area = 24 × 16 = 384 cm²

10. Answer: D
Explanation: Area = LengthWidth
30 = Length × 6
Length = $\frac{30}{6}$ = 5 in

11. Answer: B
Explanation: m∠R = m∠S = 40°

12. Answer: A
Explanation: m∠V + m∠S = 180°
m∠V = 180° - 110° = 70°

13. Answer: A
Explanation: The opposite angles are equal in a rhombus.

14. Answer: C
Explanation: Measure of third angle =
180° - 60° - 75° = 45°

15. Answer: B
Explanation: Measure of two remaining equal angles = 360° - 2(90°) = 180°
Measure of one of these angles = $\frac{180}{2}$ = 90°

16. Answer: D
Explanation: Measure of third angle =
180° - 2(75°) = 30°

17. Answer: A
Explanation:
m∠A + m∠B + m∠C + m∠D = 360°
m∠B = 360° - 100° - 115° - 65° = 80°.

18. Answer: C
Explanation:

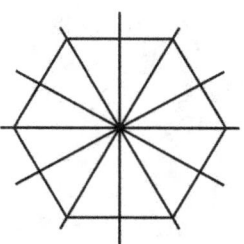

19. Answer: B
Explanation: A trapezoid has no lines of symmetry.

20. Answer: A
Explanation: A kite has one line of symmetry.

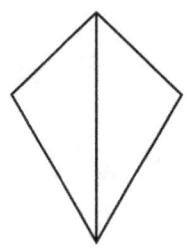

> **7.2 AREA OF RECTANGLES, SQUARES, RHOMBUSES, AND TRAPEZOIDS**

1. Answer: B
Explanation: Area = 5² = 25 sq. units

2. Answer: C
Explanation: Area of rectangle = length×width
Area = 4 × 7 = 28 sq. units

3. Answer: A
Explanation: Area = 8² = 64 cm²

4. Answer: C
Explanation: Area of rectangle = length×width
Area = 11 × 9 = 99 cm²

5. Answer: D
Explanation: 75 mm = 7.5 cm
Area = 7.5 × 4 = 30 cm²

6. Answer: A
Explanation: A. Area = 14×12 = 168 cm²
B. Area = 17×3 = 51 cm²
C. Area = 7×15 = 105 cm²
D. Area = 21×6 = 126 cm²

7. Answer: C
Explanation: A. Area = 24×32 = 768 cm²
B. Area = 27×33 =891 cm²
C. Area = 31×21 = 651 cm²
D. Area = 29×29 = 841 cm²

8. Answer: B
Explanation: Area = 9×5 = 45 m²

9. Answer: D
Explanation: Area = 55² = 3,025 cm²

10. Answer: A
Explanation: Area = 8×14 = 112 ft²

11. Answer: B
Explanation: Area = $\frac{1}{2}$×6×9 = 27 cm²

12. Answer: D
Explanation: Area = 12×10 = 120 cm²

13. Answer: C
Explanation: Area = 6×4 = 24 cm²

14. Answer: D
Explanation: Area = 10×9 = 90 cm²

15. Answer: A
Explanation:
Area = $\frac{(9+5)}{2}$×2 = $\frac{14}{2}$ ×2 = 7×2 = 14 cm²

16. Answer: C
Explanation:
Area = $\frac{(16+8)}{2}$ ×5 = $\frac{24}{2}$ ×5 = 12×5 = 60 cm²
Area = $\frac{(11+11)}{2}$ ×3 = $\frac{22}{2}$ ×3 = 11×3 = 33 cm²
Area = $\frac{(11+11)}{2}$ ×9 = $\frac{24}{2}$ ×9 = 12×9 = 108 cm²
Area = $\frac{(15+13)}{2}$ ×4 = $\frac{28}{2}$ ×4 = 14×4 = 56 cm²

17. Answer: A
Explanation: Area = 16×8 = 128 cm²
Area = $\frac{1}{2}$×24×14 = 168 cm²
Area = 17×13 = 221 cm²
Area = $\frac{1}{2}$×20×18 = 180 cm²

18. Answer: B
Explanation:
Area = $\frac{(60+120)}{2}$ ×30 = $\frac{180}{2}$ ×30= 90×30 = 2,700 cm²

19. Answer: D
Explanation: Area = 50×85 = 4,250 cm²

20. Answer: C
Explanation: Area = $\frac{(30+36)}{2}$ ×13 = $\frac{66}{2}$ ×13 = 33×13 = 429 cm²

7.3 THE PERIMETER OF RECTANGLES, SQUARES, RHOMBUSES, AND TRAPEZOIDS

1. Answer: A
Explanation: Perimeter of square = 4a
Perimeter = 4×8 = 32 units

2. Answer: C
Explanation: Perimeter of square = 4a
Perimeter = 4×11 = 44 units

3. Answer: A
Explanation: Perimeter of rectangle = 2(l+w)
Perimeter = 2(6+8) = 28 cm

4. Answer: B
Explanation: Perimeter of square = 4a
A. Perimeter = 4×3 = 12 cm
B. Perimeter = 4×4 = 16 cm
C. Perimeter = 4×5 = 20 cm
D. Perimeter = 4×6 = 24 cm

5. Answer: A
Explanation: Perimeter of rectangle = 2(l+w)
A. Perimeter = 2(5+3) = 16 cm
B. Perimeter = 2(8+7) = 30 cm
C. Perimeter = 2(12+13) = 50 cm
D. Perimeter = 2(9+3) = 24 cm

6. Answer: D
Explanation: Perimeter of square = 4a
A. Perimeter =4×21=84 cm
B. Perimeter =4×19=76 cm
C. Perimeter =4×12=48 cm
D. Perimeter =4×23=92 cm

7. Answer: B
Explanation: Perimeter of rectangle = 2(l+w)
Perimeter = 2(12+7) = 2(19) = 38 m

8. Answer: C
Explanation: Perimeter of rectangle = 2(l+w)
Perimeter = 2(100+80) = 2(180) = 360 cm
= 3.6 m

9. Answer: A
Explanation:
Width = $\frac{perimeter}{4}$ –Length=$\frac{52}{2}$-18 =26-18= 8 cm

10. Answer: D
Explanation: P_{square} = 80 cm => $Side_{square}$ = $\frac{80}{4}$
= 20 cm
$Length_{rectangle}$ = 20 cm
$Width_{rectangle}$ = $\frac{Area}{Width}$ = $\frac{160}{20}$ = 8 cm

11. Answer: C
Explanation: Perimeter of rhombus = 4a
Perimeter = 4×7.5 = 30 cm

12. Answer: B
Explanation:
Perimeter of the trapezoid = a + b + c + d
Perimeter = 6 + 8 + 6 + 13 = 33 cm

13. Answer: A
Explanation: Perimeter of rhombus = 4a
Perimeter = 4×4.7 = 18.8 m

14. Answer: C
Explanation:
Perimeter of the trapezoid = a + b + c + d
Perimeter = 14 + 12 + 10 + 8 = 44 cm

15. Answer: D
Explanation:
Perimeter of the trapezoid = a + b + c + d
Perimeter = 4.6 + 7 + 8.4 + 9 = 29 cm

16. Answer: B
Explanation:
Perimeter of the trapezoid = a + b + c + d
A. Perimeter = 31 + 27 + 24 + 21 = 103 cm
B. Perimeter = 35 + 33 + 30 + 27 = 125 cm
C. Perimeter = 30 + 26 + 21 + 18 = 95 cm
D. Perimeter = 32 + 28 + 22 + 15 = 97 cm

17. Answer: C
Explanation: Perimeter of rhombus = 4a
A. Perimeter = 4×27 = 108 cm
B. Perimeter = 4×21 = 84 cm
C. Perimeter = 4×14 = 56 cm
D. Perimeter = 4×19 = 76 cm

18. Answer: D
Explanation:
Perimeter of the trapezoid = a + b + c + d
Perimeter = 24 + 26 + 28 + 28 = 106 ft

19. Answer: A
Explanation: Perimeter of rhombus = 4a
Perimeter = 4 × 1.8 = 7.2 m

20. Answer: B
Explanation: Perimeter of rhombus = 4a
Perimeter = 4 × 99 = 396 mm = 3.96 cm.

7.4 COORDINATE PLANE AND GRAPH POINTS

1. Answer: C
Explanation: To find the x-coordinate of a point, count the horizontal units from the origin to the point.

2. Answer: A
Explanation: To find the y-coordinate of a point, count the vertical units from the origin to the point. If the point is below the x-axis, the value is negative.

3. Answer: D
Explanation: An ordered pair (x, y) describes the location of a point on the coordinate plane. The first number is called the x-coordinate, which is the number of horizontal units to the left (-) or right (+) of the origin, and the second number is called the y-coordinate, which is the number of vertical units up (+) or down (-) from the origin.

4. Answer: B
Explanation: An ordered pair (x, y) describes the location of a point on the coordinate plane. The first number is called the x-coordinate, which is the number of horizontal units to the left (-) or right (+) of the origin, and the second number is called the y-coordinate, which is the number of vertical units up (+) or down (-) from the origin.

5. Answer: A
Explanation: An ordered pair (x, y) describes the location of a point on the coordinate plane. The first number is called the x-coordinate, which is the number of horizontal units to the left (-) or right (+) of the origin, and the second number is called the y-coordinate, which is the number of vertical units up (+) or down (-) from the origin.

6. Answer: (-2, 4)
Explanation: An ordered pair (x, y) describes the location of a point on the coordinate plane. The first number is called the x-coordinate and the second number is called the y- coordinate. Point A is -2 units to the left of the origin and 4 units upward from the origin.

7. Answer: (-4, 0)
Explanation: An ordered pair (x, y) describes the location of a point on the coordinate plane. The first number is called the x-coordinate and the second number is called the y- coordinate. Point Z is -4 units to the left of the origin and 0 units upward from the origin.

8. Answer: (-2, -1)
Explanation: An ordered pair (x, y) describes the location of a point on the coordinate plane. The first number is called the x-coordinate and the second number is called the y- coordinate. Point T is -2 units to the left of the origin and -1 unit downward from the origin.

9. Answer: (3, 6)
Explanation: An ordered pair (x, y) describes the location of a point on the coordinate plane. The first number is called the x-coordinate and the second number is called the y-coordinate. Point F is 3 units to the right of the origin and 6 units upward from the origin.

10. Answer: (-6, 5)
Explanation: An ordered pair (x, y) describes the location of a point on the coordinate plane. The first number is called the x-coordinate and the second number is called the y-coordinate. Point K is -6 units to the left of the origin and 5 units upward from the origin.

11. Answer: A
Explanation: To find the x-coordinate of a point, count the horizontal units from the origin to the point.

12. Answer: C
Explanation: An ordered pair (x, y) describes the location of a point on the coordinate plane. The first number is called the x-coordinate, which is the number of horizontal units to the left (−) or right (+) of the origin, and the second number is called the y-coordinate, which is the number of vertical units up (+) or down (−) from the origin.

13. Answer: B
Explanation: An ordered pair (x, y) describes the location of a point on the coordinate plane. The first number is called the x-coordinate, which is the number of horizontal units to the left (−) or right (+) of the origin, and the second number is called the y-coordinate, which is the number of vertical units up (+) or down (−) from the origin.

14. Answer: D
Explanation: An ordered pair (x, y) describes the location of a point on the coordinate plane. The first number is called the x-coordinate, which is the number of horizontal units to the left (−) or right (+) of the origin, and the second number is called the y-coordinate, which is the number of vertical units up (+) or down (−) from the origin.

15. Answer: A
Explanation: An ordered pair (x, y) describes the location of a point on the coordinate plane. The first number is called the x-coordinate, which is the number of horizontal units to the left (−) or right (+) of the origin, and the second number is called the y-coordinate, which is the number of vertical units up (+) or down (−) from the origin.

16. Answer: C
Explanation: An ordered pair (x, y) describes the location of a point on the coordinate plane. The first number is called the x-coordinate, which is the number of horizontal units to the left (−) or right (+) of the origin, and the second number is called the y-coordinate, which is the number of vertical units up (+) or down (−) from the origin.

17. Answer: B
Explanation: An ordered pair (x, y) describes the location of a point on the coordinate plane. The first number is called the x-coordinate, which is the number of horizontal units to the left (−) or right (+) of the origin, and the second number is called the y-coordinate, which is the number of vertical units up (+) or down (−) from the origin.

18. Answer: D
Explanation: An ordered pair (x, y) describes the location of a point on the coordinate plane. The first number is called the x-coordinate, which is the number of horizontal units to the left (−) or right (+) of the origin, and the second number is called the y-coordinate, which is the number of vertical units up (+) or down (−) from the origin.

19. Answer: C
Explanation: An ordered pair (x, y) describes the location of a point on the coordinate plane. The first number is called the x-coordinate, which is the number of horizontal units to the left (−) or right (+) of the origin, and the second number is called the y-coordinate, which is the number of vertical units up (+) or down (−) from the origin.

20. Answer: B
Explanation: An ordered pair (x, y) describes the location of a point on the coordinate plane. The first number is called the x-coordinate, which is the number of horizontal units to the left (–) or right (+) of the origin, and the second number is called the y-coordinate, which is the number of vertical units up (+) or down (–) from the origin.

7.5 CHAPTER REVIEW

1. Answer: C
Explanation: Shortest side =4 cm
Perimeter = 2 (Longest Side +Shortest Side), therefore
20 = 2(4+Longest Side)
8 + 2 Longest side = 20
Longest side(2L) = 20 – 8 = 12 cm, L = 6 cm

2. Answer: D
Explanation: Area of rectangle = LengthWidth
80 = 10 × Width
Width = $\frac{80}{10}$ = 8 in

3. Answer: B
Explanation: Total angle of triangle = 180°
Measure of third angle = 180° – 50° – 55°=75°

4. Answer: A
Explanation:

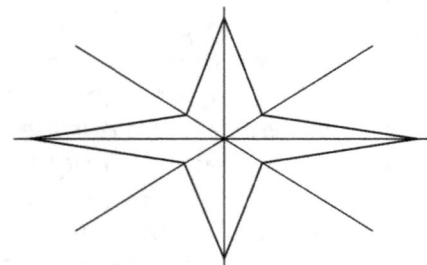

5. Answer: D
Explanation: Area of square = a^2
Area = 10^2 = 100 sq.units.

6. Answer: B
Explanation:
Area of rectangle = length×width
Area = 12 × 5 = 60 sq. units

7. Answer: C
Explanation:
Area of rectangle = length×width
Area = 15 × 11 = 165 cm²

8. Answer: A
Explanation: Area = 17 × 21 = 357 cm²

9. Answer: C
Explanation:
Area of trapezoid = $\frac{a+b}{2}$ × h
Area = $\frac{(6+8)}{2}$ ×5 = $\frac{14}{2}$×5 = 7×5 = 35 cm²
Area = $\frac{(10+6)}{2}$×3 = $\frac{16}{2}$×3 = 8×3 = 24 cm²
Area = $\frac{(4+2)}{2}$ ×6 = $\frac{6}{2}$×6 = 3×6 = 18 cm²
Area = $\frac{(7+9)}{2}$ ×4 = $\frac{16}{2}$×4 = 8×4 = 32 cm²

10. Answer: B
Explanation: Perimeter of square = 4a
Perimeter = 4 × 31 = 124 cm

11. Answer: D
Explanation: Perimeter of rectangle = 2(l+w)
Perimeter =2(100+65) = 2(165) = 330 cm

12. Answer: C
Explanation: Perimeter of rhombus = 4a
Perimeter = 4 × 8.5 = 34 m

13. Answer: A
Explanation: Perimeter of the trapezoid
= a + b + c + d
Perimeter = 8 + 14 + 12 + 11 = 45 cm

14. Answer: D
Explanation: Perimeter of rhombus = 4a
A. Perimeter = 4 × 29 = 116cm
B. Perimeter = 4 × 31 = 124 cm
C. Perimeter = 4 × 24 = 96 cm
D. Perimeter = 4 × 39 = 156 cm

15. Answer:

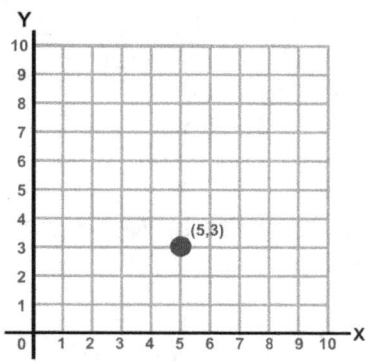

Explanation: (5, 3). To find the x-location, from the origin move 5 units to the right. To find the y-location, move 3 units up from the x-axis.

16. Answer: B
Explanation: An ordered pair (x, y) describes the location of a point on the coordinate plane. The x-coordinate is 3 units to the right of the origin. The y- coordinate is -2 units down from the x-axis.

17. Answer: B
Explanation: A regular heptagon has 7 sides.

18. Answer: C
Explanation: Width of the rectangle = x cm
Length of the rectangle x + 4 cm
Perimeter of the rectangle = 2(x+x+4) = 2(2x+4) = 4x+8 = 4(x+2) cm
Perimeter of the rectangle = Perimeter of the rhombus, then 4(x+2) = 4(Side)
Side of the rhombus = x + 2 cm
Therefore, the width of the rectangle is 2 cm smaller than the side of the rhombus.

19. Answer: 80 cm and 384 cm²
Explanation: Area of the square = Side², then
Side² = 256 Side = 16
Width of the rectangle = 16 cm
Length of the rectangle = 16 + 8 = 24 cm
Perimeter of the rectangle = 2(16+24) = 240 = 80 cm
Area of the rectangle = 16 × 24 = 384 cm²

20. Answer: A
Explanation: Smaller base = x in

Height = x in

Greater base = 2x in

Area of the trapezoid = $\frac{x+2x}{2} \times x = \frac{3}{2} . x . x = \frac{3}{2}x^2$ in²

Therefore,

$\frac{3}{2}x^2 = 96$

$x^2 = \frac{2}{3}(96) = \frac{192}{3} = 64$

x = 8 in

COMPREHENSIVE ASSESSMENT – I

1. Answer: A
Explanation: To equal 21, the expression must include 3 × 7. The number 56 divided by 8 equals 7, so 3 + 5 must be performed first. Then 3 × 7 = 21.

2. Answer: D
Explanation: Expression for Tim buys five paperbacks = 6 × 2.75
Expression for Tara buys two paperbacks = 3 × 6
Tara receives = 40 - [(6 × 2.75) + (3 × 6)] = 40 - [16.5 + 18] = 40 - 34.5 = $5.5.

3. Answer: C
Explanation: Given k + 8 × 6 = 250
k + 48 = 250
k = 250 - 48 = 202

4. Answer: No
Explanation: Answers must include a reasonable explanation such as, "No, the expression would need parenthesis around 632 +92 to show eight times the sum. As written, it shows 8 times 632 + 92.

5. Answer: A
Explanation: John has 70 yards of ribbon. He wants to use 4-yard ribbon pieces to wrap 5 boxes = 4 × 5 and 6 - yard ribbon pieces to wrap 7 boxes = 6 × 7 Therefore, the amount of ribbon John has left after wrapping = 70 – 4 × 5 + (6×7).

6. Answer: B
Explanation:
Given expression is {7000_55200_120_250}
{7000 – 55(200 –120) – 250}
[7000–55×(80)] – 250
[7000–4400]–250
2600–250
2350

7. Answer: D
Explanation:
Total number of raffle tickets = 5700
Number of players = 1900
Number of tickets per player = 5700 ÷ 1900=3

8. Answer: A
Explanation: Total hours Edwin trained football athletes = 55+75+156 = 286
Each athlete trains for 22 hours each
286 ÷ 22 = 13.

9. Answer: C
Explanation: Maria ran 12.9 minutes
Mercy ran 8 times as long = 12.9 × 8 = 103.2 minutes
The combined total would be 12.9 + 103.2 = 116.1 minutes

10. Answer: B
Explanation: Multiply 120, 8, 3 in any order. 120 times 3 is 360; 360 times 8 is 2880.

11. Answer: B
Explanation: The decimal place was moved 2 places to the left. Thus, to retain the original value, multiply by 100. The given expression (49.2 × 10,000) is 492,000.

12. Answer: D
Explanation: The decimal place was moved 3 places to the left. Thus, to retain the original value, multiply by 1,000:
520.95 × 1,000 = 520,950.

13. Answer: A
Explanation: The 9 in the hundredth-place rounds the 5 up.

14. Answer: A
Explanation: Given 0.998_0.762
Multiply both sides by 1000 to get 998 and 762, which is >.

15. Answer: A and C
Explanation: Given option
A. 6.48 + 9.17 = 15.65
B. 4.12 + 9.22 = 13.32 ≠ 15.65
C. 6.18 + 9.47 = 15.65
D. 5.22 + 7.17 = 13.29 ≠ 15.55

16. Answer: A
Explanation: 7.50 – 6.72 = 0.78
7.50 = 6.72 + 0.78
8.28 = 7.50 + 0.78
9.06 = 8.28 + 0.78
9.84 = 9.06 + 0.78

17. Answer: A
Explanation: 15.27 × 323.18 ≈ 15 × 320 = 4,800
7.025 × 283.5 ≈ 7 × 280 = 1,960
Therefore, 15.27 × 323.18 > 7.025 × 283.5

18. Answer: C
Explanation: First round 5.20 to 5 and multiply by 25. 25 times 5 is 125.

19. Answer: 20.85.2=4
Explanation: 20._____≈20
20 ÷ 4 = 5,then the divisor is 5.2 and the dividend is 5.2 × 4 = 20.8
Therefore, 20.85.2 = 4

20. Answer: C
Explanation: 42 - 8.4 = 33.6
33.6 - 8.4 = 25.2
25.2 - 8.4 = 16.8
16.8 - 8.4 = 8.4
8.4 - 8.4 = 0

21. Answer: 532.279
Explanation: Five hundred thirty-two is 532 and two hundred seventy-nine thousandths is **.279**. The decimal place is where the word "and" is when the number is properly written with words.

22. Answer: C
Explanation:

A. Riya – Ninety-five and eight hundredths =95.08

B. Tim – $95\frac{8}{100}$ = 95.08

C. Angel – Ninety-five and eight tenths≠95.08

D. Jack – $90+5+\frac{8}{100}$ =95.08

23. Answer: 1
Explanation: $\frac{1}{8}+\frac{1}{4}-\frac{5}{16}=\frac{2+4-5}{16}=\frac{1}{16}$

24. Answer: B
Explanation: To solve for x, subtract $\frac{9}{6}$ from both sides of the equation:

$\frac{5}{3}-\frac{9}{6}=\frac{10-9}{6}=\frac{1}{6}$

25. Answer: B
Explanation: When multiplying fractions, multiply the numerators and multiply the denominators.

$\frac{7}{4}\times\frac{8}{5}=\frac{7\times8}{4\times5}=\frac{56}{20}=\frac{14}{5}$

26. Answer: C
Explanation: Multiply: $56\times\frac{1}{7}$= 8

27. Answer: Incorrect
Explanation: $\frac{3}{8}\times\frac{5}{7}=\frac{15}{56}\rightarrow(1)$

$\frac{3}{5}\times\frac{8}{7}=\frac{24}{23}\rightarrow(2)$

$(1)\neq(2)$

28. Answer: B
Explanation: Cleaned rooms: $\frac{15}{18}$
Listened to the music: $\frac{15}{18}\times\frac{3}{5}=\frac{3}{6}=\frac{1}{2}$ hour
With headphones: $\frac{1}{2}\times\frac{1}{2}=\frac{1}{4}$ hour

29. Answer: C
Explanation: The volume can be determined by multiplying the number of cubes in the base of the box by the height of the box.
30 x 25 = 750 cubes

30. Answer: A
Explanation: The box is filled with ½ inch cubes. The length of the box is 14 cubes (7 × 2), the height of the box is 5 cubes (52), and the width of the box is 3 cubes (3 × 2). The number of cubes that will fill the box is (14 × 10 × 6) or 840 cubes.

31. Answer: C
Explanation: Longest side = 23 cm
Shortest side = 13 cm
Perimeter = 2 Longest Side + Shortest Side = 2 (23+13) = 2(36) = 72

32. Answer: C
Explanation: Perimeter of isosceles trapezoid =Shorter Base + Longer Base +2 Legs
Therefore,
72 = 19 + 35 + 2 Legs
2 Legs = 72 - 19 - 35 = 18
Leg = 9 in

33. Answer: C
Explanation: A. Area = 13 × 11 = 143 cm²
B. Area = 17 × 3 = 51 cm²
C. Area = 17 × 15 = 255 cm²
D. Area = 23 × 8 = 184 cm²

34. Answer: A
Explanation:
Area = $\frac{(12+8)}{2}\times3=\frac{20}{2}\times3=10\times3=30$ cm²

35. Answer: C

Explanation: Width = $\frac{perimeter}{4}$ − Length = $\frac{72}{2}$−28 = 36 − 28 = 8 cm

36. Answer: D

Explanation:

P_{square} = 92 cm => $Side_{square}$ = $\frac{92}{4}$ = 23 cm

$Length_{rectangle}$ = 23 cm

$Width_{rectangle}$ = $\frac{Area}{Width}$ = $\frac{207}{23}$ = 9 cm

37. Answer: A
Explanation: Width of the rectangle = x cm
Length of the rectangle x + 8 cm
Perimeter of the rectangle
= 2(x+x+8) = 2(2x+8) = 4x + 16 = 4(x+4) cm
Perimeter of the rectangle = Perimeter of the rhombus, then 4(x+4) = 4(Side)
Side of the rhombus = x + 4 cm
Therefore, the width of the rectangle is 4 cm smaller than the side of the rhombus.

38. Answer: 78 cm and 360 cm²
Explanation: Area of the square =Side2, then
Side2 = 225 ⇒ Side = 15
Width of the rectangle = 15 cm
Length of the rectangle = 15 + 9 = 24 cm
Perimeter of the rectangle = 2(15+24) = 2(39)
= 78 cm
Area of the rectangle = 15 × 24 = 360 cm²

39. Answer: B
Explanation:
Use formula V = Bh
V = Bh→B = $\frac{V}{h}$ = $\frac{330}{15}$ = 22 cubic units

40. Answer: B
Explanation: Use formula V = lwh. The volume of a new prism is V_1 = $l_1w_1h_1$. Compare the dimensions of the new prism with the dimensions of the old prism.
l_1 = 2l
w_1 = 2w
h_1 = h

Express the volume of the new prism, V1 in terms of the volume of the old prism, V.
V_1 = $l_1w_1h_1$ = 2l . 2w . h = 4(lwh) = 4V
So, the volume of the prism is increases 4 times.

41. Answer: C
Explanation: Use formula V = lwh
V = lwh = 13 × 22 × 9 = 2574

42. Answer: D
10 cubes

43. Answer: A
Explanation: Total amount Melissa paid =
8 + 10 + 8 = 26
Melissa paid with $58
Expression = 58 − 8 + 10 + 8 = 58 − 26 = 32$

44. Answer: A
Explanation: The decimal place was moved 2 places to the left. Thus, to retain the original value, multiply by 100. The given expression (332.2 × 100) is 33220.

45. Answer: True
Explanation: The table follows the pattern of x is always 8 less than y.

COMPREHENSIVE ASSESSMENT – II

1. Answer: C
Explanation: If he subtracts 5 from 20 first, the expression will equal 40, so he should place the parentheses around 20 − 5
30 × 20 ÷ (20 − 5) = 600 ÷ 15 = 40

2. Answer: B
Explanation: Number of floors = 8
Number of shops on each floor = 35
Number of shops being used = 280
Number of shops vacant =
(8×35) − 230 = 280 − 230 = 50 empty shops.

3. Answer: D
Explanation: The expression 7 × (3216 + 175) means 7 times more than the sum of 3216 and 175. When an expression includes a number times a parenthesis that includes a + or a – , it means the number times a sum or a difference.

4. Answer: A
Explanation: The rule for x is add 5 to find the next x, and the rule for y is add 10 to find the next y. The next ordered pair is (15+5, 30+10) = (20, 40).

5. Answer: D
Explanation: Yes
Side A = 35 cm
Side B = 35 – 10 cm
Side C = (35–10) + 8 cm
Perimeter of the triangle:
{35 + (35–10) + (35 – 10 + 8)} =
{35 + 25 + 33} = 93.

6. Answer: B
Explanation:
Angel buys 7 pizzas for 12 dollars = 12
She also buys 5 french fries for 3 dollars each = 5 × 3 and 6 Pepsi sodas for 3 dollars each = 6 × 3 Expression of how much Angel spends on pizzas, french fries and Pepsi = 12 + 5 × 3 + 6 × 3

7. Answer: A
Explanation: Total number of minutes = 5,60
Number of children = 80
Number of minutes per child = 5,60 ÷ 80 = 7

8. Answer: 9,848
Explanation: Given Mary baked 8 dozen cookies day 1
She increased her baking by 30 times on day 2: 8 × 30 = 240. She increased the baking from day 2 by 40 times for day 3:
240 × 40 = 9,600
Total cookies: 8 + 240 + 9,600 = 9,848.

9. Answer: Yes
Explanation:
Number of glue sticks per box : 50
Number of scissors per box: 42
Mr. Peter plan to purchase 100 boxes of each.
Total number of glue sticks = 50×100 = 5000
Total number of scissors = 42×100 = 4200
Number of students at the school - 4000
They have enough glue sticks and scissors for the students.

10. Answer: A
Explanation: Multiply 7 × 75 and 5 × 75 and then add the answers to get 525 + 375 = 900

11. Answer: B
Explanation: The decimal moves over four places to the right.

12. Answer: Agree
Explanation: Given $600 ÷ [10^2 × 3] = 600$
[100×3] = 600 ÷ 300 = 2
Therefore, Jerry got the correct answer.

13. Answer: B
Explanation: Comparing all students, James ran the most miles. (Hundredth place is 9 which is the highest value compared to the others).

14. Answer: D
Explanation: 10 is less than 32, therefore 8.10 is the possible weight of the second chicken.

15. Answer: 5.85 and 4.25
Explanation:
Sum – difference = 10.10 – 1.60 = 8.5
Two equal parts = 8.5
One of these parts = 4.25
1st decimal = 4.25
2nd decimal = 4.25 + 1.60 = 5.85.

16. Answer: D
Explanation: Width cm = 21.75 cm
Length cm = 21.75 + 8.82 = 30.57 cm
Perimeter cm = 2(l+w) = 2(30.57+21.75) = 2(52.32) = 104.64 cm.

17. Answer: A
Explanation: $(3.8x - 0.8) = 52.7 \times 0.9$
$3.8x - 0.8 = 47.43$
$3.8x = 47.43 + 0.8$
$3.8x = 48.23$
$x = 12.69$

18. Answer: A

Explanation: Area $= \frac{21+9}{2} \times 5 = \frac{30}{2} \times 5 =$
$15 \times 5 = 75$ cm²

19. Answer: B
Explanation: $97.2 - 24.3 = 72.9$
$72.9 - 24.3 = 48.6$
$48.6 - 24.3 = 24.3$
$24.3 - 24.3 = 0$

20. Answer: 25.53 and 9.70
Explanation:
If $b = 0.38a$, then $a - 0.38a = 15.83$
$(1 - 0.38)\, a = 15.83$
$0.62a = 15.83$
$a = 15.83 \div 0.62$
$a = 25.53$
$b = 0.38 \times 30.44 = 9.70$

21. Answer: >
Explanation: Left side: Seven hundred thirty-nine and three hundred seventy-four thousandths = 739.374
Right side: Seven hundred thirty-nine and two hundred fifty-five thousandths = 739.255
Therefore: 739.374 > 739.255

22. Answer: C
Explanation: 808.82 can be expressed:
$800 + 8 + \frac{8}{10} + \frac{2}{100}$

23. Answer: B
Explanation: The whole number portion of the mixed number is changed from
$5\frac{1}{2} + 2 = \frac{7}{2} \rightarrow \frac{11}{2} + 2 = \frac{11+4}{2} = \frac{15}{2} \neq \frac{7}{2}$.

24. Answer: D
Explanation: Scheduled time: $2\frac{2}{8} - 1\frac{1}{2} =$
$(2-1) + \left(\frac{2}{8} + \frac{1}{2}\right) = 1 + \frac{6}{8} = 1\frac{3}{4}$.

25. Answer: B
Explanation: To simplify $\frac{1}{5} \div 11$ you must find the reciprocal of 11 and multiply
$\frac{1}{5} \times \frac{1}{11} = \frac{1}{55}$

26. Answer: A
Explanation: Multiply: $3\frac{1}{2} \times 4\frac{1}{2} = \frac{7}{2} \times \frac{9}{2} = \frac{63}{4} = 15\frac{3}{4}$

27. Answer: $\frac{1}{7}$
Explanation: Mark: $\frac{5}{10}$ of a mile
Peter: $\frac{5}{7} \times \frac{5}{10} = \frac{5}{14}$ of a mile
Jessy: $\frac{3}{7} \times \frac{5}{10} = \frac{3}{14}$ of a mile
Peter walked the furthest with Mark:
$\frac{5}{14} - \frac{3}{14} = \frac{5-3}{14} = \frac{2}{14} = \frac{1}{7}$ of a mile

28. Answer: B
Explanation: Multiply: $\frac{7}{10} \times \frac{1}{8} = \frac{7}{80}$

29. Answer: B
Explanation: Shortest side = 12 in
Perimeter = 2 (Longest Side + Shortest Side), therefore
52 = 2 (12 + Longest Side)
12 + Longest side = 26
Longest side = 26 − 12 = 14 in

30. Answer: D
Explanation: Measure of third angle
$= 180° - 2(85°) = 10°$

31. Answer: D
Explanation: 95 mm = 9.5 cm
Area = 9.5 × 6 = 57 cm²

32. Answer: (4,-1)
Explanation: An ordered pair (x, y) describes the location of a point on the coordinate plane. The first number is called the x-coordinate and the second number is called the y-coordinate. Point A is 4 units to the right of the origin and -1 units downward from the origin.

33. Answer: D
Explanation: A. Area = 25 × 35 = 875 cm²
B. Area = 23 × 38 = 874 cm²
C. Area = 33 × 25 = 825 cm²
D. Area = 23 × 23 = 529 cm²

34. Answer: A
Explanation: Area = 18 × 10 = 180 cm²
Area = $\frac{1}{2}$ × 28 × 18 = 252 cm²
Area = 15 × 17 = 255 cm²
Area = $\frac{1}{2}$ × 26 × 22 = 286 cm²

35. Answer: B
Explanation: Perimeter of square = 4a
Perimeter = 4 × 5 = 20 units

36. Answer: D
Explanation:
Width = $\frac{\text{perimeter}}{4}$ – Length = $\frac{68}{2}$ – 22 = 34 – 22 = 12 cm

37. Answer: 24 cubic units
Volume of the prism : 12×2 = 24 cubic inches

38. Answer: A
Explanation: An ordered pair (x, y) describes the location of a point on the coordinate plane. The first number is called the x-coordinate, which is the number of horizontal units to the left (–) or right (+) of the origin, and the second number is called the y-coordinate, which is the number of vertical units up (+) or down (–) from the origin.

39. Answer: B
Explanation: The large box has a volume of 27 cubic feet (3×3×3). Each small box has a volume of 0.125 cubic feet (0.5×0.5×0.5) Dividing 27 by 0.125 gives the number of small boxes that fit in each large box (27 ÷ 0.125 = 216) Then, 700 ÷ 216 = 3.2 large boxes. Round 3.2 up to 4. It will take 4 large boxes, but the last box will not be full.

40. Answer: A
Explanation: Use formula V = Bh
V = Bh→h = $\frac{V}{B}$ = $\frac{195}{15}$ = 13 cubic units

41. Answer: B
Volume of the Prism: 7 × 4 = 28

42. Answer: B
Explanation:
The left expression is simplified as follows:
18 + [35 ÷ (6+1)] = 18 + [35÷7] = 18 + 5 = 23
The right expression is simplified as follows:
9 + (5×14) – 8 = 9 + 70 – 8 = 71
The missing symbol is <.

43. Answer: C
Explanation:
Four of the members have a motorbike and a car each = 4 × 2
Another member has only a car = 2 × 1
Total number of vehicles
4 × 2 + 2 × 1 = 8 + 2 = 10

44. Answer: A
Explanation: Given expression is
200 ÷ [5 × (6+8+6)]} + 30
{200 ÷ [5 × (20)]} + 30
{200 ÷ [100]} + 30
2 + 30
32

45. Answer: D
Explanation: Total hours Robert trained athletes = 75 + 85 + 220 = 380
Each player trains for 20 hours each
380 ÷ 20 = 19.